# TRENCH

*A Christian Guide to the Culture War*

Written by Mark Fairley

# Other Titles.

## Stay Free
*Why Society Can't Survive Without God*

## The War On Truth
*How A Generation Abandoned Reality*

## The Restless Church
*Rediscovering New Testament Christianity*

## The Coming Summer
*Exploring The Signs of Jesus' Return*

## The Secret of Joy
*Ten Biblical Antidotes for Depression & Anxiety*

## Revelation
*The Fuel Project Guide*

## The Reason For Pain
*Why God Allows Suffering*

## thefuelproject.org

*Visit our website for a complete list of books and video series.*

# Quote.

"We will speak the truth in love, growing in every way more and more like Christ, who is the head of his body, the church."

Ephesians 4:15

# Contents.

INTRODUCTION

## SECTION ONE | VIRTUE SETS

1. The Two Virtues
2. Two Caricatures
3. The Violent Monster
4. The Simple Softie
5. The Cross
6. Biases
7. Head v Heart
8. Equality v Inequality
9. Competition v Cooperation
10. Individualism v Collectivism
11. Anchors and Fires
12. Men and Women
13. Disconnected

## SECTION TWO | THE AGES

1. Three Ages
2. From Darkness to Light
3. Faltering Modernity
4. Heartless
5. The Love Revolution
6. Brainless
7. Immoral

## SECTION THREE | THE LEFT TRENCH

1. The Story So Far
2. Brainless
3. Anti-Knowledge
4. Tyranny
5. Collectivism
6. Globalism
7. Inevitable Globalism
8. No Religion
9. Ice Cream
10. No Country
11. No Possessions
12. Hypocrats
13. China
14. The Present Is Female
15. The War Continues
16. Toxic Femininity
17. Safetyism
18. The Fear Economy
19. Immorality
20. The Paradox of Evil
21. Polarisation

## CONCLUSION

# Introduction.

(How The "Trench Theory" Came To Be)

In 2017, I wrote a book called *"The War on Truth"*, in which I introduced the concept of *"Hard Virtues"* and *"Soft Virtues"* as a means of explaining the state of Western civilisation, and of predicting its future. The book was, as with all Fuel Project titles, turned into a video series that was released in weekly instalments on YouTube, and then made available for digital download on the website. From that moment on, whenever someone asked for my favourite Fuel Project series to-date, or the best place to start with this ministry, I would always say that one.

## A Long Journey.

It had been a long time in the making and it really started when, as a teenager, I noticed that if someone stated their opinion on one topical issue, you could then curiously but quite accurately predict their position on a whole range of other, seemingly unconnected issues. For example, I noticed that if someone stated they were a feminist, they'd also almost certainly be an advocate for gun control, socialism, gay marriage, green politics, and were possibly a vegetarian or vegan.

"Why?", I wondered. *"What's the connecting thread here? What have guns got to do with female emancipation? And what has veganism got to do with your preferred economic model?"* To me it made as much sense as saying, *"if someone's favourite colour is blue, their favourite sport will be badminton, and they're guaranteed to enjoy eating noodles."* In other words, there seemed to be no obvious connection at all.

However, if in the course of life you discovered that everyone you met whose favourite colour was blue also happened to be a badminton-addicted noodle enthusiast, you'd begin to think there was indeed something to be uncovered. And that's what intrigued me about this whole subject. Although it wasn't immediately obvious, some link clearly did exist. And I would often find myself wondering about it over the years. Because of course, the reverse holds true as well. If you discover someone is strongly in *favour* of unrestricted gun ownership, you can then accurately predict they'll have a preference for capitalism, traditional family values, and will probably enjoy a good steak.

With the passing of the years, I felt I was beginning to connect the dots and developed a theory around a concept of *"Hard Virtues"* and *"Soft Virtues"*. I've never given it a name before, but I guess I would now call it *"Trench Theory"* in honour of this book. It was something that made sense to me at least, and by 2014, I felt confident enough to share my ideas publicly for the first time.

Actually, that's not entirely true. I didn't feel confident at all. This is how the story goes. In 2014, The Fuel Project had only been in existence for three years, and with no previous experience of live teaching, I was invited to Canada to do some speaking engagements. Up until that year, I'd always rejected such invitations, partly because I had too much work to be getting on with in terms of new books and videos, partly because I didn't feel live teaching was my calling, but mainly to be perfectly honest, because I was afraid of it. One day I may explain where that fear was rooted. However, all I'll say here is that I was getting so many of these invitations that I was beginning to examine myself. What if God *was* calling me down that route? What if he wanted me to make live teaching a part of The Fuel Project ministry? And what if it was really only fear that was stopping me from accepting the offers?

Throughout the preceding year in 2013, I'd made a book and video series called *"The Restless Church"* that encouraged people to step outside of their comfort zones and to act in faith. I felt it was hypocritical of me to tell others to bravely push past their fears if God was calling me to speak to live audiences and the main reason I was refusing was because I wasn't willing to push past my own. I decided therefore to make a promise to God that if he wanted me to make live teaching a part of The Fuel Project ministry, I'd be prepared to follow him wherever he led. Indeed, at the beginning of 2014, I made a resolution–a pact with God. I told him that throughout the coming year, I would start accepting these invitations and that I would face my greatest fears if he called me to. Therefore, when Canada came calling that year, I literally couldn't turn it down.

For the two weeks I spent in Ontario, it felt like jumping into the deep end without knowing how to swim. It was a far more packed schedule than I'd anticipated–often I was lined up to do several events on the same day, at community centres, churches or homes. I rushed from one place to the next, feeling constantly out of my depth, entirely unprepared, using every spare moment I could to try to put cohesive sessions together. I remember one particularly horrifying day when I'd been scheduled to do a morning event for recovering addicts at a community centre in Ottawa. Having finished, and while having lunch with the program director, he asked me what I had planned for the afternoon. I had nothing! I didn't even know I'd been booked for the afternoon. Lunch had to be immediately cut short so I could rush off and put some teaching together in the car. The fact is I just didn't have enough content yet for two solid weeks of teaching, and like people who jump into the deep end might, I was struggling to keep my head above the water.

Now this feeling probably peaked when, towards the end of my time in Canada, I was asked by the ministry that was hosting me to lead a morning study with their team. I think it lasted around an hour or two and I simply had nothing to give them. Most of them had already heard the content I'd been using throughout my time there–and they already knew about the books and videos I'd been releasing online–so I needed to think of something fresh. And it was then that I reached for this roughly sketched idea about *"Hard Virtues"* and *"Soft Virtues."* This concept that had been intriguing me and evolving over many years.

I know that if asked, those present would be kind enough to say otherwise, but to me that morning felt like a stumbling shambles. I'm pretty sure it didn't make any sense and I'm equally sure it wasn't really what the ministry director was hoping for. I think he wanted something along the lines of a morning devotional–something to bring encouragement to the team perhaps—and yet here I was incoherently talking about feminism, guns, politics and all kinds of other things.

However, I have to say I wasn't overly discouraged afterwards. Even though its first public airing had not exactly been a roaring success, I came away from that study more convinced than ever that there was something important here—something urgent even—and if I could only better understand it myself first, it could bring so much clarity. I once heard it said that *"If you can't explain something to a six-year old, you don't really understand it yourself."*[1] That was me in 2014 with the Trench Theory. Forget about six-year olds though...I couldn't even explain it to a room of adults yet!

But I would one day. One day I would understand this thing well enough to teach. It would just take time. For the next few years, I felt a bubbling excitement about this project. It distilled in my mind and as the months passed, more elements of it fell into place. As it took on clarity and form, the more far-reaching and important it seemed to be. In time, I realised that this concept of *"Hard Virtues"* and *"Soft Virtues"* not only explained the connection between feminism, economic preferences, attitudes towards guns and meat, but it made sense of so much more besides. World history. Human behaviour. The times in which we live. As they've been called, "The Culture Wars." Perhaps it could even provide a framework by which to understand the future.

The scientific method says that when you produce an hypothesis like this, the next step is to try to falsify it—find its flaws and weaknesses. Only if it can't be disproved, do you hold the theory as being true. Well, not only could I not disprove

*Trench Theory*, but every time I tried, the stronger it seemed to get and the more it seemed to explain.

By 2017 then—three years after I'd first aired it to a small group in Canada—I finally felt ready to present it to the world. That was the book and subsequent video series that became *"The War on Truth"*.

## Five Reasons To Revisit The Trench Theory.

I was happy with how *"The War on Truth"* turned out. As I mentioned at the beginning, whenever anyone thereafter asked me which Fuel Project series to watch first, I would always say that one. However, as I write this book, we are now in 2022, and that means five years have passed since its release. And in those five years, five things have happened to make me want to revisit the concept.

Firstly, it's five more years in which I've been able to evolve and understand the *Trench Theory* in my own head. That should hopefully mean I can now explain it even more clearly than before. I'll possibly never be able to reach a six-year old with this, but if it makes clearer sense to the adults reading this book, that will do me just fine!

Secondly, I'm revisiting this concept because I just have far more to say about it. So much has happened since 2017. We've had the Black Lives Matter movement, Brexit, Covid-19, the economic fallout of that, a surge of authoritarianism, an intensification of the culture wars, transgender controversies, the encroaching cashless society, the rise of China, the Great Reset, the Climate Agenda, and more. These things alone make this subject worth revisiting. We need a Christian perspective on what's happening in our Age and we need the church to be clear about what's unfolding. I believe to that end, the *Trench Theory* is a tool that will help immensely. Indeed, I anticipate that in the future I'll be talking about these topical issues a great deal, and I want to establish *Trench Theory* in people's minds so that I can refer to it in short-hand in the years to come.

Thirdly, I feel like in hindsight I could have been bolder in *"The War on Truth."* There were things that the *Trench Theory* could have predicted would happen in our generation, and I wish I'd said it at the time because they are now coming to pass, but which I held back from saying in 2017. For example, applying the *Trench Theory* to this Age would have told us that people would start denying basic truths like two plus two equalling four. In 2017, that seemed too far-fetched. Surely people wouldn't really ever deny basic mathematics? I felt I'd have undermined my whole argument if I predicted something so absurd and it didn't come true. And yet, in the past couple of years, it's started happening. In spite of my doubts, the *Trench Theory* has held true and people have started denying that two plus two equals four. This time around then, I've determined to be bolder in trusting its outcomes. At the very least, I will make the case for what the *Trench Theory* predicts and leave you to make up your own mind about whether it could feasibly happen.

Fourthly, I think honestly *"The War on Truth"* just didn't reach as many people as I wanted it to, or felt it should. I can't tell you how many times I've watched world events unfolding in recent years, witnessed the confused responses and the despair of people around me and thought, *"Please watch 'The War on Truth.' It will explain everything! I promise it will!"* I almost have a sense of desperation for people to understand the *Trench Theory* and I feel like if I can just get this message to more people–Christians especially–it will bring much needed clarity in the middle of a very difficult time in world history. I guess I keep thinking, *"But why haven't enough people watched it already? Maybe I need to explain it more clearly? Or present it in a more accessible way than before? What can I do to amplify this message?"* I don't know, but I just have this unrelenting sense of urgency to give it another go.

And that leads to the fifth and final reason to dive into the *Trench Theory* again. After this book has been released, as is the routine with all Fuel Project books, I will start presenting it as a video series and releasing it on YouTube. And quite simply, I feel I can present it better today than I could in 2017. Indeed, I'm going all out with this project. If you've been following the YouTube channel in recent times, you'll be aware that until now, I've made Fuel Project videos in a small loft space in my one-bedroom home. The small size has limited what I've been able to do in terms of presentation, so to give this new series every possible chance of reaching a wider audience, I've decided to sell my house and looking for somewhere with a larger room. My hope is that with a better space to create, I can elevate the content. I'm also hoping to invest in better equipment to furnish the new studio and besides that, after spending my days writing this book, I'm using the evenings to learn Adobe After Effects, with the intention that I'll be able to animate and add better visuals. In short, I am putting everything I have into making this project the best that I'm capable of. All my time, energy, investment, thoughts, and prayers are currently fixed on one solitary goal—to get this piece of content to as many eyes and ears as I can...because I believe so much in the importance of this message. Whether I'm right to believe so passionately in this message is something that will only the passing of time can reveal. Nevertheless, I want to know for the sake of my own conscience that I gave it my best shot.

We're nearly ready to get started then, but before we do, I will warn you that the first section of this book is almost identical to the beginning of *"The War on Truth."* If you have read that book or watched the series, it's going to feel very familiar at first. I hope you don't feel short changed by that. However, from that familiar foundation, we will then begin following new threads, and cover a much wider range of topics.

My hope is that by the time you close the final page, it will feel like you've put on a pair of glasses. What I mean is, I hope that where the world once seemed fuzzy, indistinct and confusing, it will make sense. I hope that where you may have been worried about the unfolding events of our time, this book will bring a sense of peace and calm. And ultimately, as with everything I do for The Fuel Project, I hope this book grows your faith in God, His Son, His Spirit, and His Word. Remember as you read this book, *"Do not be afraid or discouraged, for the Lord will personally go ahead of [us]. He will be with [us]; he will neither fail or abandon [us]."* (Deuteronomy 31:8) May this book lead to resolve and action within the church.

Without any further ado then, let's just get right into it. Here is your Christian guide to the culture war and the Postmodern Age. Welcome to *"Trench"*.

God bless
Mark Fairley

# Section One.
## VIRTUE SETS

# 1

# The Two Virtues.

Broadly speaking, there are two distinct types of virtue. For the purposes of this book, I'm going to call them *"The Hard Virtues"* and *"The Soft Virtues"*. I think we can understand both better by considering the life of a police officer.

## The Police Officer At Work.

First, let's consider the police officer at work. *All About Careers* summarises the job description by saying, *"In a nutshell, police officers maintain law and order, protect the general public, investigate crimes and prevent criminal activity. If you become a police officer, your career will be all about crime prevention, prosecution and punishment."*[1] Perhaps a more succinct way of describing the job is to say that the police exist to uphold and enforce the cause of *Justice*. They bring murderers, rapists, thieves, drug-dealers, money launderers, terrorists, and so forth to account so that the general public are protected from their harms.

This is all very good. But let's think about what that looks like in practice. What does it mean to uphold and enforce *Justice*? Honestly, it can be uncomfortable to think about. Sometimes enforcing *Justice* means chasing uncooperative criminals and wrestling them to the floor. Sometimes it means barging into homes to catch them red-handed. Sometimes it means beating violent offenders into submission with batons. Sometimes it means immobilising them with tasers, or dispersing warring crowds with water-cannon. Sometimes it means forcibly handcuffing criminals at the wrists and banishing them to austere, barred jail cells. As a last resort, if someone is posing an immediate and mortal threat to innocent life, sometimes enforcing *Justice* even means drawing a gun and shooting perpetrators dead.

This was the case in December 2019 for an Islamic terrorist called Usman Khan. Khan had been jailed in 2012 for plotting an attack on the London Stock Exchange, but was released half-way through his 16-year sentence. Not long after his release, he resurfaced in Fishmonger's Hall near London Bridge in England, seemingly equipped with a suicide vest and a knife. He was rampaging around the area indiscriminately stabbing members of the public. Khan managed to kill two, seriously injure three, and was fighting with some brave civilians when the Metropolitan Police arrived on the scene. Realising that Khan posed a deadly threat to these people, as well as innocent bystanders; that he was not responding to verbal commands to desist; and that he appeared to be reaching for the trigger on his suicide vest, they were left with no option but to fire their weapons and shoot Khan dead.

Now there are several adjectives that could describe the police response that day. We could say it was shocking. Violent. Fierce. Terrifying. Sad. All those words would be applicable. Perhaps onlookers would have had to turn away as the shots were fired because it was so brutal. But after all was said and done, we would have to rest on the conclusion that what the police had done that day was ultimately...*good*.

It was *good* that Usman Khan–this unrepentant madman–had been stopped in his tracks. It was *good* that he'd been thwarted in his murderous rampage. It was *good* that he been blocked from taking more innocent lives. The police officers had carried out their duty well. They had fulfilled their job description to uphold the cause of *Justice*. They had extinguished evil, and protected the innocent. Violent and uncomfortable though it was, they had done what was right.

This is why *Justice* can be considered a *"Hard Virtue"*. Because although it's undoubtedly good, and certainly necessary, its implementation is often shocking, violent, terrifying, and uncompromising. According to Dictionary.com, to be "just" means:

1. *To be guided by truth, reason, justice and fairness.*
2. *That which is done according to principle; equitable; proper.*
3. *That which is right; rightful; lawful*
4. *That which is in keeping with truth or fact; true; correct.*[2]

All these words that are connected to *Justice–Truth, Fact, Reason, Fairness, Righteousness, Lawfulness*–can also be considered part of the *"Hard Virtue"* set. To deal in any of these is to deal in uncompromising and decisive ways. If you deal in *Truth*, you're dealing in what's right and wrong. If you're dealing in *Fact*, you're dealing in what is, and what isn't. If you're dealing in *Righteousness*, you're dealing in what's moral and what's immoral. But we'll explain more about that later.

## The Police Officer At Home.

First, let's get acquainted with *"The Soft Virtues"*. We can perhaps best understand them by considering the same police officer when he finishes his shift, takes off his uniform, and returns home to his wife and family. After all, would we expect to see him at home, behaving in the same way he'd behaved at work? Would he be as unyielding and hard with his family as he'd been with criminals and terrorists? Probably not. I mean, certainly not if he's a *good* man. In the home context, we would expect to see him exhibiting a rather different set of virtues.

We might see the man showing *Love* for his wife when he comes through the front door by giving her hugs and kisses. We'd perhaps see him wrestling with his kids on the floor, but with *Gentleness*, withholding his true strength so they can clamber over him and pin him to the floor. He may show *Grace* and *Forgiveness* when a flailing foot accidentally strikes him on the face. Perhaps he'd show *Kindness* and *Compassion* if he accidentally hurt them. Perhaps later that evening, we might see him teaching his children to read their bedtime story and showing *Patience* when they're not getting the words right. And these would be *"The Soft Virtues"*. They perhaps need less explaining. *Love, Forgiveness, Grace, Mercy, Patience, Humility,* and *Kindness*. These virtues are good—every bit as good as *"The Hard Virtues"*–but they obviously look very different in action.

## Goodness Is Hard and Soft.

This is what we need to understand, then. Indeed, this is the foundation for the whole book. The goodness that exists within our police officer manifests itself in two very different ways throughout the course of his life. Sometimes the good within him expresses itself in *Hard* ways, and sometimes it expresses itself in *Soft* ways. Sometimes his goodness is fierce and sometimes it's gentle. Sometimes it's violent and sometimes it's compassionate. Sometimes it's uncompromising and sometimes it's patient. But it's the *same* goodness at work in both circumstances.

The police officer demonstrates the *"Hard Virtues"* at work because that is good–upholding *Justice*, punishing evil and establishing *Truth*. That's good. And the same police officer demonstrates the *"Soft Virtues"* at home because that is good too–showing *Love, Grace, Patience* and *Compassion* to his family. It's the same core good that is driving his behaviour in both contexts.

| Soft | Hard |
|---|---|
| Love | Justice |
| Grace | Righteousness |
| Mercy | Truth |
| Forgiveness | Fact |
| Patience | Reason |
| Kindness | Lawfulness |
| Gentleness | |
| Compassion | |

To emphasise how important both kinds of virtue are, let's imagine a scenario where the police officer tries to navigate life using only *one* set.

For example, let's imagine a police officer who uses only *The Soft Virtues*. He goes to work and he comes across a thief but he refuses to tackle him because he wants to be *"Compassionate"*. He sees a money launderer but he turns a blind eye because he wants to demonstrate *"Kindness"*. Imagine he lets a criminal go unpunished because he doesn't think it would be *"Loving"* of him to put him in a cold, barred jail cell. Or let's bring it into real life—imagine the officer who shot Usman Khan on London Bridge decided to let him continue his rampage because he wanted to be *"Gentle"* or *"Patient"* with the terrorist.

What would we think of that officer who refuses to employ the *Hard Virtues* at any time? Probably, at best, we'd think him incompetent, cowardly and completely unfit for his job. At worst, we would suspect he was corrupt—an accomplice of evil. Whatever we thought of him, we wouldn't think of him as a *good* man. We wouldn't hold him in high esteem at all. Because while there is a time for *Soft Virtues*, there's a time to break out the *Hard* edge too. There's a time for *Justice*. And if he refuses to do what's necessary, he can't call himself good.

On the other hand, imagine a scenario where the police officer tries to navigate life using only *The Hard Virtues* and never the *Soft*. Let's imagine he returns home from his shift and he doesn't show any *Love* for his wife and gives no hugs or kisses. When his children try to play wrestling games with him, he doesn't withhold his strength but beats them with no *Mercy*. When one child accidentally whacks him with a flailing arm on the nose, imagine he shows no *Forgiveness* but instead whacks them back equally hard. When a child is struggling to read their bedtime story, imagine he has no *Patience* so he launches into a furious tirade. Imagine his house is entirely without *Compassion* so his wife and kids are terrified of him.

What would we think of the man who refuses to demonstrate the *Soft Virtues* at any time? Probably at best, we'd think he was a cold-hearted monster who was completely unfit to be a husband or father. We'd feel sorry for his family. At worst, we'd be calling the police or social services to rescue them from him. Whatever we thought of him, we wouldn't think of him as a *good* man. We wouldn't hold him in high esteem at all. Because while there is a time for *Hard Virtues*, there must be a time for the *Soft* too. And if he never demonstrates them, he simply cannot call himself good.

From these examples then, we can see that it's not wise to jettison either virtue set entirely. We need both held in balance. If we try to utilise only one set without the other, what begins as a virtue can actually turn into a vice. All *Soft* and no

*Hard* leads to evil; all *Hard* and no *Soft* does likewise. Being a good person means expressing both, in the right context, and in the right measure.

| Soft | Hard |
|---|---|
| Love | Justice |
| Grace | Righteousness |
| Mercy | Truth |
| Forgiveness | Fact |
| Patience | Reason |
| Kindness | Lawfulness |
| Gentleness | |
| Compassion | |

*NB: I'll post this visual at regular intervals and we'll keep developing it as we progress through the chapters.*

# 2
# Two Caricatures.

Imagine an alien came to earth without any concept of police officers at all and he sees our man at work, running around the city; raiding homes; beating people with batons; tasering them; blasting them with water-cannon; cuffing them; throwing them into barred cages, and then shooting people dead on the street. It's possible the alien might see our man in that context alone and form a rather one-dimensional caricature in his mind. He might think, *"Wow, what a violent maniac this guy is! What an evil monster!"*

Conversely, if the alien came to earth and peered in through the officer's window while he was at home one evening, he might come up with another caricature from the other direction. He might see him being pinned by little humans a quarter of his size and think he was extraordinarily weak. He might see him dressing up in silly outfits to entertain his children or reading their books at bedtime and think he was not very smart: *"Wow, what a simple softie this guy is! What a weakling!"*

Whichever side the alien witnesses first, it's possible he could quickly form a one-dimensional caricature in his mind of what the officer is like, and he may have a great deal of difficulty believing that another side could possibly exist within the same person. *"Are you honestly trying to tell me that the guy who I saw beating people in the street and shooting them dead is the same one who lets small people pin him to the ground and reads children's stories? That can't be!"* But, of course, the alien would only be confused because he doesn't understand the fullness of a human character yet. We who understand the situation know the truth–the officer is neither a violent monster *or* a simple softie. Those are both misunderstandings based on shallow understanding and limited knowledge. And while there would be an element of truth in each caricature, neither would give a balanced or complete portrayal of the man.

## Caricatures.

It's difficult not to create one dimensional images of people when you only have limited knowledge. I remember watching boxing when I was younger and finding it difficult to believe these people weren't kept in cages. I'd see them going into battle, mouthing abuse at one another, teeth clenched, muscles flexed, sweat dripping, veins popping, barely able to contain their aggression. I'd see them pounding their opponent into a state of incapacitated unconsciousness and I'd think, *"Wow, what a violent monster. Surely they're a danger to society?"* It was difficult for me to witness that level of aggression and square it with the idea that once the bout is over, they will shake hands, embrace, compliment one another on a good fight, step out of the ring, go home to their wives and kids, and be compassionate and gentle. And yet, in reality, that's largely what happens.

Therefore, we must be careful not to caricature people in our minds based upon limited knowledge. Just as we would hope

Trench

nobody would caricature us. After all, if we are good, we will all regularly manifest both the *Hard* and *Soft Virtues* too.

If you're a soldier, you'll have to fight and kill terrorists on one hand, but then distribute aid and food to innocent victims on the other. If you're a teacher, you'll dish out strict punishments in the classroom to a pupil who cheats, but then lavish praise on the same child when he works hard to improve his behaviour. If you're a CEO of a company, you'll fire an employee for laziness on the one hand, but then reward another with a bonus for doing a fine job. If you're a personal trainer, you'll drill clients with punishing circuits, but then encourage them when they reach targets. If you're a judge, you'll send criminals to prison to pay for crimes and then happily pardon the innocent who are falsely accused. If you're a parent, you'll discipline your children when they misbehave and then show gentleness and love when they need it too. If people only ever saw one expression of your goodness in isolation, their limited knowledge could lead them to caricature you as either a violent monster or a timid softie too. Neither would be accurate portrayals. And therefore, again, we must be careful not to make this mistake with others.

## God.

We must be even more careful not to make this mistake with God. And the problem is that it's easier to do with God. You see, God isn't just good as we are—he is *absolutely* good. His goodness is perfect. Therefore, when he expresses his goodness through the *Hard Virtues*, they are perfectly *Hard*. Likewise, when he expresses his goodness through the *Soft Virtues*, they are perfectly *Soft*. It's these absolute, more extreme expressions of good, that make him easier to caricature.

For example, we humans believe in *Hard Justice* so we punish criminals. God's *Justice* however, is perfect, which means he not only punishes evil but he obliterates it entirely, wiping it from the face of the earth. And while a human police officer may look rather frightening as he enforces *Justice* in a community, a perfect God would look utterly terrifying. Similarly, we humans believe in *Righteousness* and so believe in moral behaviour. God's sense of *Righteousness* however, is perfect, and therefore he demands not just moral behaviour like we would, but complete moral perfection.

At the same time, we humans believe in *Soft Love* so we try to give it to others where we can. God's *Love* however, is perfect, which means he not only *Loves* like we do, but he *Loves* beyond measure. We humans believe in *Compassion, Grace* and *Mercy* so we try to practice those things in daily life too. God's *Compassion, Grace* and *Mercy* however, is absolute, so he lavishes it upon people beyond reason.

In other words, a perfect God is harder at times than we are, and he's softer at times than we are. His *Justice* is more unyielding than ours, but his *Love* is more extravagant than ours. His *Righteousness* is more ferocious than ours, but his *Mercy* is more lavish than ours. And again, it's the extremities of his perfection that make God easier to mischaracterise–either as a violent monster if your knowledge of him is limited to his *Hard Virtues*, or as a timid softie if your knowledge of him is limited to his *Soft Virtues*.

This is indeed, exactly what tends to happen. Without question, the most common way people misunderstand God's character, is by viewing his *Hard Virtues* or *Soft Virtues* in isolation, and then with that shallow understanding, they create an imbalanced conclusion about what he is like. Having seen one side of his character, they find it difficult to grasp that another aspect could possibly exist within the same Person. *"Are you honestly trying to tell me that the God who wiped out the world in a terrifying flood is the same one who is seen hanging weak and naked from a cross? That can't be!"*

Sometimes people mischaracterise him deliberately—it's easier to dismiss a God who has been caricatured. Others genuinely misunderstand him. But whether it's purposeful or not, you will tend to find that most people who have a shallow understanding of the Bible have done this to some extent.

Take Richard Dawkins' view of God for example. As one of the most prominent fathers of New Atheism, he sees God as nothing more than a violent monster. He once described God as, *"...arguably the most unpleasant character in all fiction: jealous and proud of it; a petty, unjust, unforgiving control-freak; a vindictive, bloodthirsty ethnic cleanser; a misogynistic, homophobic, racist, infanticidal, genocidal, filicidal, pestilential, megalomaniacal, sadomasochistic, capriciously malevolent bully."*[1] The Portuguese Nobel Laureate, Jose Saramango, said something similar. He called God *"cruel, spiteful, vengeful, jealous and unbearable."*[2]

Where could Dawkins and Saramango be getting such a monstrous image from? Well, they would argue they're getting it from the Bible. They would point to Old Testament stories in particular, where God destroys cities, sends plagues and floods, and calls for the destruction of idols. It's these events that cause him to shout, *"What a bully! What an evil monster!"*

On the other hand, there are people like Douglas Adams, the writer who penned *"Hitchhiker's Guide To The Galaxy"*. He once said that Jesus was *"nailed to a tree for saying how great it would be if people were nice to each other for a change."*[3] Honestly, that's all he thought Jesus came to say: *"Be nice to each other...won't you please?"* Adams' view of Jesus is that he was a sort of hippie who went around calling for nothing other than peace and love.

Now why Adams thought Jesus would be crucified for merely saying "be nice to each other" is anyone's guess, and the fact that he *was* crucified should hint that he did have slightly more hard-edged, controversial, and uncompromising things to say. But let's not get ahead of ourselves here. All we need to establish here is that two different people—Dawkins and Adams—were (presumably) reading the same Bible and yet came up with polar opposite views of what God was like. Both thought they had a true grip on his character. But in reality, both were dealing in one dimensional caricatures based on limited understanding. Let's fix that.

Trench

## Soft

Love
Grace
Mercy
Forgiveness
Patience
Kindness
Gentleness
Compassion

## Hard

Justice
Righteousness
Truth
Fact
Reason
Lawfulness

# 3
# The Violent Monster.

Is God just a violent monster? Richard Dawkins thought so. And he, like many other atheists, would point to several Bible stories to support his claim. The earliest of these would likely be Noah's Flood.

## Noah.

The Bible tells us that in the distant past, God once wiped out the known world with a flood. He said, *"I will wipe this human race I have created from the face of the earth. Yes, and I will destroy every living thing—all the people, the large animals, the small animals that scurry along the ground, and even the birds of the sky. I am sorry I ever made them." (Genesis 6:7)* It's at this point that Dawkins (and Saramango) would close the Bible, dust their hands and say, "well there you go. *Killing men, women and children. He's a monster."*

But hang on a second. What if, like the good police officer, God was enforcing some *Hard Justice* here? What if he was rooting out and extinguishing evil? We already know and accept that such things sometimes look violent, shocking and unyielding. And that's exactly what God was doing. The Bible tells us in the preceding verses, "The LORD observed the extent of human wickedness on the earth, and he saw that everything they thought or imagined was consistently and totally evil."

*(Genesis 6:5)* The planet was in a mess. Humanity had descended into unfettered evil. There was violence, murder, rape, deceit, theft, corruption, and depravity. Nothing short of a hell on earth. And of course, because God is good, he had to take decisive action. He had to enforce *Justice*.

Now really think about this. Was God wrong? Should he have let the evil go unchecked forever? Earlier in this book, we noted that if the police officer who shot Usman Khan had let him continue his rampage in the name of *"Kindness"* and *"Gentleness"*, we would have regarded that officer as corrupt and an accomplice to evil. Certainly, we wouldn't have thought of him as a good man. Well, couldn't the same accusation have been thrown at God if he had watched evil overtaking the world and didn't step in either? Wouldn't God have been corrupt and an accomplice to evil if he refused to break out the *Hard* edge and refused to uphold *Justice*? Though it's difficult and terrifying to witness police officers eliminating terrorists on the street, we know that ultimately it's good. Similarly, it may be terrifying to contemplate God eliminating evil on the earth, but that is good too. Deep down, we want this. We *should* want this. We want *Justice* to prevail.

Now you may reply, *"But didn't you say that for anyone to be considered good, they must demonstrate a regard for the Soft Virtues too? And that someone who operates only with one set is off balance? So where is God's Love here? Where's his Grace and Mercy for these people?"*

Well, read the story in more depth and you'll notice that even within this context of judgement, God does demonstrate the *Soft Virtues*. For example, you'll notice that although humanity was sliding into depravity, God didn't wipe them out immediately. Instead, he gave the people of the world a *Grace* period where they could repent and change their ways. He raised up a prophet called Noah to forewarn the people of the flood to come. The Bible specifies that it took up to 120 years for Noah to build the Ark, and that he was to warn the people continuously during that period. So for over a century, the people were given warning-after-warning of what was to come. They were urged to give up their evil ways before it was too late. They were told to repent. They were given *every* possible chance to escape and be saved. *Grace. Patience.* Undeserved *Love* for a wicked generation. It's all there.

And yet when the people didn't listen and persisted with their wickedness, after a hundred years, the *Grace* period elapsed, and God's judgement fell. It had to. Again, it's like the police officer on London Bridge. He called out to Usman Khan several times to desist and drop his weapon. He gave him that chance to do the right thing and live. But when Khan didn't heed the warnings and persisted with his evil intentions, the *Grace* period elapsed, the officer drew his weapon, and judgement fell.

You'll find that same pattern occurring consistently with God throughout the Bible. It's a pattern. He gives fair warning, offers a lengthy *Grace* period up front, but if the evil continues unabated, he eventually acts. You can call it shocking. Violent. Fierce. Terrifying. Sad. All those words would be applicable. But after all is said and done, the destruction of evil is ultimately...*good*. This is what *Justice* and *Righteousness* sometimes needs to look like.

And finally, it should also be remembered that through Noah's family and the animals on the Ark, God graciously gave humanity, and all living things, a second chance to thrive. He didn't have to do that; it wasn't even deserved. But he did it because of his *Kindness*. Both the *Hard* and *Soft Virtues* are present in this story.

## Sodom & Gomorrah.

Another story that atheists take umbrage with is the story of Sodom and Gomorrah in Genesis 18-19. Here, God orders the destruction of two whole cities, but again, if we read the passage, we discover it's to uphold the cause of *Justice*.

Sodom had become an evil midden. The Lord said, *"I have heard a great outcry from Sodom and Gomorrah, because their sin is so flagrant."* (Genesis 18:20) *"Flagrant"* means *"unhidden"* or *"brazen"*. People were no longer ashamed of their sin in those cities. They boasted about it. They took pride in it. They flaunted it in broad daylight. It was an unimaginably debased society that, like the earth in Noah's time, had drifted beyond a point of no return. Should God have let that evil continue forever? Of course not. *Justice* demands that there comes a day of reckoning.

The *Soft Virtues* are present in this story too though. Prior to the destruction, the Bible records a conversation between God and Abraham. God is contemplating what to do about Sodom when Abraham asks, *"Will you sweep away both the righteous and the wicked? Suppose you find fifty righteous people living there in the city—will you still sweep it away and not spare it for their sakes?...the LORD replied, "If I find fifty righteous people in Sodom, I will spare the entire city for their sake."* (Genesis 18:24,26) God is reluctant to destroy it. He wants to give the people every possible chance to be spared. And he knows that even if there are just fifty righteous people left in the city, there remains some hope for moral regeneration.

Abraham inquires further by whittling the hypothetical number down. *"Suppose there are forty righteous people in the city?"* Again, God replies *"I will not destroy it for the sake of forty."* Abraham keeps going. Thirty? Twenty? Ten? God replies, *"I will not destroy it for the sake of the ten."* (Genesis 18:29,32) It's clear that if there is even a modicum of good left in that city, God would be willing to stay his hand. And he won't stand for collateral damage either. No innocent people were to be harmed.

In the next chapter, God even sends two angels into the city to give the citizens a final chance to repent. However, not only did the Sodomites have no intention of listening to these angels, they even tried to rape them! The Bible says that Lot then preached to *"all the men of Sodom, young and old."* (Genesis 19:4) Just like in Noah's day, everyone is forewarned about what's to come multiple times. Everyone is given a chance to repent and escape the judgement. There's *Love, Grace* and *Mercy* here. But just like in Noah's time, not even ten will heed the warning. And so God reluctantly goes ahead with its annihilation. *Justice* is enacted. *Righteousness* is upheld. It's all terrifying, fierce and lamentable...but it's *good*.

If you read the story, you'll also notice that just like in Noah's time, God makes sure the righteous are spared. Lot and his family are given an escape route and a chance to start over.

Trench

## The Amalekites.

This is perhaps the story that people have most trouble with. And at first glance you can see why. God said to Saul, *"Now go and completely destroy the entire Amalekite nation—men, women, children, babies, cattle, sheep, goats, camels, and donkeys."* (1 Samuel 15:3) A God who explicitly orders the destruction of women, children and even babies surely *must* be evil. Surely God has gone too far this time?

Well, let's look at who the Amalekites were, lest we be tempted to imagine them as innocent, peace-loving farmers who were disposed to minding their own business.

They weren't. The Amalekites were the descendants of Esau, Jacob's brother. If you remember the story, Jacob received the blessing from his father, Isaac, that Esau felt should have been his. Jacob's descendants then went on to spawn the nation of Israel—God's special people—while Esau's descendants, the Amalekites, seethed with generational bitterness and jealousy.

And it showed. The Amalekites were renowned as a wicked and warring people—their very name actually translates as "war-like", "people of prey" and even "people who lick blood".[1] We know that this tribe practiced child sacrifice to their pagan gods, and we also know from the Bible that they persistently launched genocidal attacks on Israel.

The first record of these attacks came while Moses was leading the Israelites out of captivity in Egypt through the desert to the Promised Land. The Bible talks about the treatment they were subjected to: *"Never forget what the Amalekites did to you as you came from Egypt. They attacked you when you were exhausted and weary, and they struck down those who were straggling behind."* (Deuteronomy 25:17-19)

Not only did the Amalekites go after the Israelites when they were at their weakest in the wilderness, but they made a habit of targeting the ones who lagged at the back of the group. Who were the ones that lagged at the back? It was the elderly, the young, the sick, the women with babies and young children, the ones with livestock, and the exhausted. In other words, The Amalekites deliberately trailed the Israelites through the desert and preyed on the weakest, killing the women, children and babies. We're not talking about peace-loving villagers; we're talking about genocidal terrorists.

Now, after Israel had settled in the Promised Land, the Amalekites continued their campaign against Israel by forming alliances with surrounding nations. The Book of Judges reports, *"Soon afterward the armies of Midian, Amalek, and the people of the east formed an alliance against Israel and crossed the Jordan, camping in the valley of Jezreel."* (Judges 6:33)

This was their strategy: *"Whenever the Israelites planted their crops, marauders from Midian, Amalek, and the people of the east would attack Israel, camping in the land and destroying crops as far away as Gaza. They left the Israelites with nothing to eat, taking all the sheep, goats, cattle, and donkeys. These enemy hordes, coming with their livestock and tents, were as thick as locusts; they arrived on droves of camels too numerous to count. And they stayed until the land was stripped bare. So Israel was reduced to starvation by the*

*Midianites. Then the Israelites cried out to the LORD for help."*
(Judges 6:3-6)

While Israel was attempting to farm the land, the Amalekites, in alliance with the Midianites, were sending armies to thieve, murder, vandalise, terrorise, and strip the land bare. By destroying the crops, the plan was to starve the Israelites to death. And it was then that the Israelites called out to God for help.

Since Israel was the chosen nation through whom God intended to bring salvation to the world, and the nation through whom Jesus Christ would come, this was an offence to his sense of *Justice*. And so, because of their persistent wickedness, God eventually ordered that the Amalekites should receive a taste of their own medicine. Everything they had done to Israel would simply be visited back upon them. *Justice* would be done. It would be terrifying, fierce, sad, shocking...but ultimately *good*.

And again, even within this context, God's *Soft Virtues* are evident. The Bible tells us that God actually gave the Amalekites 400 years to turn away from their sin. *Four hundred years!* That was the length of time between the first Amalekite attacks on Israel as they came out of Egypt, and God finally issuing the order to wipe them out.

Just like with Noah and Lot, God sent warnings ahead of time through prophets too. There was a distinct tribe living within Amalekite society called the Kenites. They were innocent of the crimes so God sent messengers warning to them to leave the area so that they wouldn't be caught up in the coming judgement. The Bible says, *'Saul sent this warning to the Kenites: 'Move away from where the Amalekites live, or you will die with them. For you showed kindness to all the people of Israel when they came up from Egypt.' So the Kenites packed up and left.'* (1 Samuel 15:6).

Obviously, the Amalekites would have heard these warnings too, and certainly enquired about why the Kenites within their borders were suddenly packing up and leaving. But rather than heeding the warnings and repenting, they simply dug their heels in. That's when God's judgement eventually fell.

As the Bible says, *"the LORD is slow to anger and filled with unfailing love, forgiving every kind of sin and rebellion. But he does not excuse the guilty."* (Numbers 14:18) God is slow to break out the *Hard* edge, but when it comes, it comes. And that is *good*.

Now some might argue, *"Couldn't he have spared some?"* Well, as it turns out, no. Remember, God's *Justice* is more complete than ours. And time proved God's wisdom in this. You see, Saul was the man tasked with carrying out these orders and he actually let some of the Amalekites go free. This turned out to be a nearly fatal mistake because in the passing of time, it meant the Amalekites were able to repopulate. One of the Amalekite descendants—a powerful man called Haman—still burning with generational hatred for Israel, later tried to have all the Jews killed in a mass genocide in Persia. He would have achieved it too if not for Esther, who was strategically placed at "such a time as this" to save Israel. Indeed, if not for her dramatic intervention, the lineage that led to the coming of Jesus—the "branch of Jesse"—would have ended, salvation couldn't have come to the world, and the Bible may not have survived.

God knew what he was doing. Of course he did. It was regretful that the whole Amalekite tribe had to be eliminated. But their persistent hatred meant that even if just a few of them survived, they would re-populate, re-strengthen and would never stop trying to wipe out Israel. You can see something similar in Islamic society today–a bitter hatred for Israel is being passed down through the generations and is so hardwired into their culture, that they seem unlikely to ever stop trying to wipe their enemy from the map.[2]

## Nineveh.

You're probably picking up the pattern now, and it's repeated all throughout the Bible. God offers *Soft Grace* up front, he gives a chance for evil-doers to desist and repent. But if they don't, *Hard Justice* eventually falls. Terrifying. Fierce. Shocking. Sad. Good.

I'm just going to briefly highlight the Nineveh story here before we move on, because it has a slightly different outcome to the others. You see, the Bible reports that God was preparing to pour out his judgement on the city of Nineveh, and for the same reasons as always. God said, *"I have seen how wicked its people are."* (Jonah 1:2)

Conforming to the usual pattern, God didn't destroy Nineveh in a fit of uncontrolled rage, but rather he demonstrated *Patience* and *Grace* by sending the prophet Jonah into the city ahead of time to forewarn the people. He gave them a chance to repent and be saved.

And indeed, this is where the twist comes in. Because in this case, the people actually *did* listen to God's prophet and they *did* repent! So guess what? God had *Mercy* on them and didn't destroy the city. Timothy Keller makes an interesting observation about this. He says, *"There was no indication that the Ninevites became Jews or converted to full service of the God of Israel. Nothing like that happened, and yet God refrained from punishment, so predominant is his will to save rather than to punish."*[3]

Let's lay out the pattern that we get from God in all these Old Testament stories then:

1. God sees that wickedness is beginning to overwhelm a city, region or planet. God's *Justice* means the evil must be punished. *(Hard)*
2. Prior to the judgement, God patiently warns the people through prophets and exhorts them to repent. Everyone is given a *Grace* period to be saved. Sometimes this *Grace* period lasts for hundreds of years! *(Soft)*
3. Any innocent or repentant people are spared. *(Soft)*
4. The judgement eventually falls on the wicked. *(Hard)*
5. There is always a new beginning or renewed hope that comes out of the story. The innocent are given another chance to move forward in *Righteousness*. *(Soft)*

So you see, all these stories demonstrate a blend of God's *Hard* and *Soft Virtues*. God is holding in tension, *Justice* with *Mercy* and *Righteousness* with *Grace*. Is God's hardness harder than ours would have been at times? Yes, because he's perfectly good and we're not. Is God's softness softer than ours would have been at times? Yes, because he's perfectly good and we're not—I'm not sure I'd have been patient enough to give the Amalekites four hundred years of grace.

Regardless, God is far from a violent monster, as mischaracterised by Dawkins and Saramango. Yes, he must deal with evil, it's true. His goodness demands that he cannot excuse unrepentant wickedness forever. And we should be glad of that. But he is also *Patient*, and full of *Mercy* to anyone who turns from their evil ways.

| Soft | Hard |
|---|---|
| Love |  |
| Grace | Justice |
| Mercy | Righteousness |
| Forgiveness | Truth |
| Patience | Fact |
| Kindness | Reason |
| Gentleness | Lawfulness |
| Compassion |  |

# 4
# The Simple Softie.

Was Jesus Christ, as Douglas Adams suggests, really just *"nailed to a tree for saying how great it would be if people were nice to each other for a change"*? Was he basically just a hippie who advocated for nothing more challenging than *Peace* and *Love*?

Jesus undoubtedly spoke a lot about the *Soft Virtues* and they're evident throughout the gospels. The Bible records Jesus showing *Grace* to sinners, prostitutes, beggars and despised tax collectors. It tells of a time he forgave and rescued an adulterous woman from stoning by calling to the baying mob, *'let the one who has never sinned cast the first stone!' (John 8:7)* It records the Sermon on the Mount where Jesus said, *'Love your enemies! Pray for those who persecute you!' (Matthew 5:44)* It tells of how Jesus offered *Mercy* to the sick, the lame, the blind and the deaf. Jesus involved himself with the ones that were oppressed and marginalised. He gave dignity to women and showed *Compassion* to the weak. The Bible explains how Jesus let his teaching be interrupted by little children who wanted to come and sit by his side: *'Let the children come to me. Don't stop them!'* was his message. *'And he placed his hands on their heads and blessed them before they left.' (Matthew 19:14-15)*

Every year at Christmas, we are accustomed to thinking of Jesus as a *Gentle* baby—meek and mild, helpless in a manger. We hold that baby up as a symbol of peace on earth and goodwill to all men. It's an unthreatening picture of God that we perhaps feel most comfortable with. At the other end of his life on earth, we also remember how Jesus offered no resistance to Roman guards as they came to take him away for trial. We remember how he chastised Peter for drawing a sword to fight back. How he healed the ear of the Roman officer. And then we read how he suffered in silence as he was tortured, mocked, nailed to a cross and left to hang in the midday sun, looking about as weak and helpless as any man could. *"For God so loved the world that he gave his one and only begotten Son, so that whoever believes in him will not perish but have eternal life."* (John 3:16)

    The *Soft Virtues* are there, we love them, and they're good. Those who understand the overarching narrative of the Bible will know that it was especially necessary for Jesus to proclaim the *Soft Virtues* at that time. Not only was he counterbalancing the hard legalism of the Pharisees with his teaching, but the very reason he came was to offer *Forgiveness* through his death on the cross. *"God sent his Son into the world not to judge the world, but to save the world through him."* (John 3:17) Jesus had a very specific job to do.

## The Hard Edge of Christ.

However, even within the context of this salvation mission to *Love, Forgive* and rescue, we don't have to look very far to discover that Jesus demonstrated the *Hard Virtues* too. He demanded that *Truth, Righteousness* and *Justice* prevail.

    Take this example. The Bible says, *"The blind and the lame came to him in the Temple, and he healed them"* (Matthew 21:14) Now this is the Jesus that most recognise and have no problem with. Jesus is showing *Grace, Mercy* and *Kindness* to the sick. Very well. But if we rewind just two verses, we see a very different and much harder edge. Because when Jesus first arrived at the Temple that day, he had witnessed corrupt money-changers turning his Father's house into a "den of thieves". His sense of *Justice* was so incensed by this that he *"...entered the Temple and began to drive out all the people buying and selling animals for sacrifice. He knocked over the tables of the money changers and the chairs of those selling doves."* (Matthew 21:12)

You may be able to picture the scene here. Jesus, full of *Righteous* indignation starts shouting with anger and flipping tables in the air. The doves' wings whistle as they flap away in distress. The chairs are kicked over and clatter to the ground, while coins scatter noisily across the stone floor. In John's account of this event, he says Jesus even made a whip from some nearby rope and used it to drive the corrupt individuals outside!

The Bible doesn't tell us how many money-changers and dove-sellers there were in the Temple that day, or how many tables and chairs had been set up, but for one man to cause so much panic that it caused the whole group to flee outside, it's clear that this was, in that moment at least, no timid softie. Jesus must have been a fearsome sight.

Yes, it's true that Jesus also saved a woman caught in adultery from stoning, but after rescuing her he warned that he expected *Righteousness* going forward: *"Go and sin no more."* (John 8:11) That was his command.

Let's not forget that Jesus was never shy about confronting the Pharisees with some hard words either. *"You snakes! You brood of vipers! How will you escape the judgement*

Trench

*of hell?' 'You hypocrites!...you are like whitewashed tombs."* These are all words uttered by Jesus. He even called the Pharisees *'sons of hell.'* Not very *"Kind"* of him, is it?

In Luke 11, there's a report of Jesus being invited to a Pharisee's home for dinner. Now, even in our 21st Century Western culture, an offer of a meal in someone's home is generally seen as an act of warm friendship. In 1st Century Jewish culture, this was even more true. Remember when Jesus was seen eating with sinners, the Pharisees said, *"Why does [he] eat with such scum?"* (Matthew 9:11) Sharing food with someone signified friendship. So you can imagine that the Pharisee who extended the invitation to Jesus was basically saying something like, *"Look Jesus, we've had some clashes in the past but come to my house, let's eat together, discuss things, build bridges, find common ground and possibly even be friends."* It's likely the Pharisee was holding out an olive branch of sorts and reading between the lines, perhaps seeing his popularity with the crowds, he may even have hoped to make Jesus a part of their religious establishment.

Having been offered this generous hospitality, you may then expect to find Jesus being polite and gracious at the meal, doing everything possible to avoid saying anything that might offend his host. You might expect him to keep the conversation light.

But that's not what Jesus did. No. Jesus decided to use this dinner party to pick a fight. First of all, he didn't wash his hands before dinner because he knew it would provoke his host— the Pharisees placed a great deal of emphasis on outer cleanliness. Sure enough, Luke reports that *"His host was* amazed to see that he sat down to eat without first performing the hand-washing ceremony required by Jewish custom." (Luke 11:38) And you could say that from that point onwards things escalated pretty quickly. Before long, Jesus was openly calling those present "filthy," "greedy," "wicked," "foolish," and telling them great sorrow awaited them because of their sinful ways.

One of the other Pharisees present at the dinner was a little offended by this verbal assault and said to Jesus, "you have insulted us...in what you just said." (Luke 11:45) Not surprising, really. But did Jesus apologise and back down, realising that this wasn't very *"Gentle"* of him?

Not a bit of it. My goodness, no. He wants to teach these Pharisees a lesson about *Righteousness*. So he turns to the man who raised the objection and starts accusing him too, telling him that great sorrow awaited him because his type had crushed the people with "unbearable religious demands." Jesus can't stand the way these legalists have oppressed the Jewish people. Fuelled by *Righteous* indignation, he tells them that none of them can expect to enter the kingdom of God if they don't mend their ways.

One minute Jesus has been invited for a cosy meal with some potential new friends, and the next minute he has instigated a ruckus, condemning his hosts to hell in the process. Luke says that *"As Jesus was leaving, the teachers of religious law and the Pharisees became hostile."* (Luke 11:53) Jesus being willing to provoke hostility? Surely not the timid softie who only preached *Peace* and *Love*, and who only wanted people to be nice to each other?

Well, no, not that one. That one doesn't actually exist. That one is a one-dimensional caricature. The Jesus of the Bible on the other hand–the real Jesus–well, he had no problem at all in standing up for *Hard Truth, Righteousness* and *Justice* when the occasion demanded it. And indeed, if you actually read through Luke's Gospel and make note of how many times Jesus deliberately initiates confrontation with *Truth* claims, you might be surprised.

Don't forget this was also the Jesus who said things like, *"whoever does not believe will be condemned"* (Mark 16:16) and, *"I am the way, the truth and the life. No one can come to the Father except through me."* (John 14:6) Words don't get harder than this. Don't miss what Jesus is saying: *"Unless you accept The Hard Truth that I am your Lord and Saviour, your destination is hell."* Wow. Can't you be a little more 'nice', Jesus? Can't you be a little more *"Kind"*? No. When it comes to *Hard* matters of *Truth* and *Fact*, Jesus was ready to tell it straight.

Remember, Jesus isn't a perpetual baby in a manger. He grew up. And as we remember him offering no resistance on the cross, remember that he was, in that moment, only like the police officer who withholds his strength while his children clamber over him and pin him to the ground. On the cross, Jesus merely put away his strength for a moment, letting his children overpower him so that he could save them from their sins. In truth, Jesus isn't on the cross anymore. He is seated at his Father's right hand in glory preparing to judge the world. He was once a helpless, sacrificial Lamb, yes that is true, but don't get so comfortable with that image that you forget he is also *"the Lion of the tribe of Judah"* (Revelation 5:5). Jesus Christ, you see, is both the Lion *and* the Lamb. The God who hung on the tree to offer *Grace* to the world, is the same God who will one day judge the world in *Righteousness*.

## The Ferocious Second Coming.

It's important to remember this because some might say, *"a few hard words to the Pharisees from Jesus is hardly the same thing as annihilating whole tribes, cities and worlds, as we saw the God of the Old Testament do."* Perhaps not. But Revelation tells us that when Jesus comes again at the end of time, he is coming to destroy the wickedness on the earth, just as his Father had done in Old Testament times. Indeed, the image of Jesus when he returns to earth at the end of the age is so terrifying and fierce, that it makes the hairs on the back of your neck stand on end. If you think God wiping wickedness from the earth in Noah's day was scary, wait 'til you hear about what His Son will do: *"Then I saw heaven opened, and a white horse was standing there. Its rider was named Faithful and True, for he judges fairly and wages a righteous war. His eyes were like flames of fire, and on his head were many crowns. A name was written on him that no one understood except himself. He wore a robe dipped in blood, and his title was the Word of God. The armies of heaven, dressed in the finest of pure white linen, followed him on white horses. From his mouth came a sharp sword to strike down the nations. He will rule them with an iron rod. He will release the fierce wrath of God, the Almighty, like juice flowing from a winepress. On his robe at his thigh was written this title: King of all kings and Lord of all lords."* (Revelation 19:11-16)

Pause for a moment, re-read that passage and remember...this is Jesus being described here. This is the same Jesus who ate with sinners, forgave adulteresses, and had *Compassion* for the weak. But this is no one-dimensional simple softie. Here, he is a ferocious warrior in blood-stained robes who annihilates evil, who unleashes God's wrath, and who strikes down the nations.

At his first coming, Jesus was a "Lamb" simply because at that time, a Lamb is what the world needed him to be. When he comes again as a "Lion" however, the same will be true. We are today, a bit like those in Noah's Day and Lot's Day. In the same way they were given a long *Grace* period before judgement fell, the same is true for us. Our world is descending into sin and God is being patient with us and giving people time to repent. Peter writes, *'The Lord isn't really being slow about his promise [to return], as some people think. No, he is being patient for your sake. He does not want anyone to be destroyed, but wants everyone to repent.'* (2 Peter 3:9) But just like in Noah's Day and Lot's Day, if we don't repent, and the world keeps spiralling into wicked immorality, the *Hard* edge will eventually come and it will be Jesus administering it. It will be terrifying, fierce, shocking, sad...and *good*.

The ferocious "Lion" aspect of Jesus' character is famously embodied in Aslan–the Christ character in CS Lewis' Chronicles of Narnia. Mr Beaver describes him saying, *"Aslan is a lion–the Lion, the great Lion." "Ooh" said Susan. "I'd thought he was a man. Is he quite safe? I shall feel rather nervous about meeting a lion"..."Safe?" said Mr Beaver..."Who said anything about safe? 'Course he isn't safe. But he's good. He's the King, I tell you."¹* Jesus isn't safe. To evil-doers, he is the bringer of destruction and the destroyer of worlds. He's utterly terrifying.

But he's good. He's the King, I tell you.

## A Rounded Character.

Throughout these past two chapters then, I hope I have emphasised the consistency and multi-faceted, rounded nature of God's character. He's no one dimensional cartoon as Dawkins and Adams suggest. Or indeed, as anyone else may suggest. For this is quite a common accusation, that the God of the Old Testament seems so *Hard* and the Jesus of the New Testament seems so *Soft*. People do wonder if the two can possibly be the same. I hope I've demonstrated that the *Hard* and *Soft Virtues* are always held in tension within God's Person. At various times throughout history, it's true that we will see more of one virtue set than the other. Sometimes God will be *Hard* and sometimes he will be *Soft*. When he's *Hard*, he will be harder than we would be, and when he's *Soft*, he will be softer than we would be. But whatever side we see of him, it only depends on the context. God himself said, *"I am the Lord, and I do not change."* (Malachi 3:6) He is *Fierce* but *Compassionate*. *Terrifying* but *Kind*. *Just* but *Forgiving*. *Righteous* but *Merciful*. *Holy* but full of *Love*. And what does the cross, the central image of Christianity tell us, if not this very thing?

Trench

## Soft | ## Hard

| Soft | Hard |
|---|---|
| Love | Justice |
| Grace | Righteousness |
| Mercy | Truth |
| Forgiveness | Fact |
| Patience | Reason |
| Kindness | Lawfulness |
| Gentleness | |
| Compassion | |

# 5

# The Cross.

Here's a parable I often use to explain the tension between the *Hard* and *Soft Virtues*.

## A Parable.

"There were once two friends who grew up together. They lived in the same street, knew each other from their very earliest years and for as long as they could remember, they always did everything as a pair. When it was time to leave school, they even went to the same university and shared an apartment. One studied law and the other studied business.

It was only after graduation, that for the first time in their lives, they were forced to part ways, as their careers took them in different directions. The man who had studied law became a judge in his hometown, while the friend who had studied business took a job in a faraway city. Initially, they kept in touch with each other but as the years passed and the concerns of life took over, they lost contact completely.

Many years later, the businessman's life collapsed when he lost his job. His wife subsequently left him, taking their children with her, and this led him into a downward spiral of alcoholism and drug abuse. He wandered the country as a vagrant and before long, he was dabbling in serious crime to *fund his addictions. Finally, at his lowest ebb, he murdered an innocent person for money.*

*Now the police caught him and he was taken to stand trial in court. But when he entered the courtroom and looked up he was shocked to discover that this was no ordinary judge overseeing his case—it was his long, lost friend! As the memories flooded back of their innocent childhood days together, it was like he woke up from a stupor and suddenly saw himself for what he'd become. He'd never felt so ashamed. He stood in the dock now as nothing more than a wicked criminal, guilty of the worst kind of crime. He could barely lift his head to look his old friend, the judge, in the eye.*

*To add to the dramatic scene, the family of his victim were present in court that day, watching from the gallery above. They sat in anticipation, expecting that justice would be enacted and the criminal would be sentenced to the full extent of the law—which in this city, was the death penalty.*

*The judge, as you can imagine, now faced a huge dilemma. On the one hand, his friend was undoubtedly guilty. There were witnesses and he'd admitted it with his own lips. There was no doubt that if the judge was to act properly, he had to pass the sentence. Indeed, if he didn't convict this man of the crime, then justice wouldn't be done and he would be corrupt. A good judge, a righteous judge, has to make sure that wickedness is punished.*

*However, that didn't change the fact that the criminal in the dock <u>was</u> still his friend. He didn't want to condemn his friend to death because he loved him. He just couldn't bring* *himself to be the one that would, with the strike of a gavel, condemn him to death."*

Do you see the problem here? *Soft Love* dictates that the judge can't condemn his friend, yet *Hard Justice* demands that he *must*. What could he do? Both *Love* and *Justice* are undoubtedly virtues, and yet here they are, demanding contradictory outcomes to this case. Which one does he prioritise? To prioritise *Justice* would mean the execution of his friend. To prioritise *Love* would mean corruption.

Now this parable reveals why people often believe the two virtue sets are incompatible with each other, can't co-exist, and that one side must be prioritised above the other. Because whenever a moral dilemma presents itself like this, the *Hard* and *Soft Virtues* normally always demand completely opposing outcomes. And it's true that to break the deadlock, you often have to elevate one and diminish the other.

I guess the question is, is there a way that *both* the virtue sets be satisfied at the same time here? Remember, no-one can truly be called good until they demonstrate a respect for both sides. So is there a way for the good judge to administer *Hard Justice and Soft Love*, holding both sides in balance?

There is. And this is how he achieved it: Firstly, the judge passed the guilty verdict so that *Justice* was served. The full tariff of death was handed down to the criminal. By doing this, he satisfied *The Hard Virtues*. The victim's family could leave the courtroom satisfied that a life was going to be given to pay for the one taken.

But here's the twist. Instead of letting his friend suffer the punishment he deserved, the judge got up from his chair,

Trench

took off his robes, came down from his lofty position of power and came to speak to him. He said, *"Look, the law demands that a life be given for a life. Justice demands it. Therefore, I had to make the pronouncement. However, I can't let you take this punishment because you're my friend and I love you. Therefore, I'm going to hand myself over to the executioner to die in your place. With my death, justice will be satisfied. A life will be given for the life of the one you took. By dying in your place, by taking your punishment upon myself, the debt will be paid, and you can then go free. Now promise me that as you go free from here, you'll honour this gift, and that you'll never break the law again."* With that, the good judge left the room and to the astonishment of the court, handed himself over to be placed in handcuffs. He was led away voluntarily to be executed in the place of his guilty friend. The *Soft Virtues* have now been satisfied too.

Now you may be feel outraged at this story. I hope you do. The guilty scumbag walks free and the righteous, innocent judge dies in his place?! That's so unfair! It is. But remember, this is exactly what Jesus was doing when he went to the cross to die on *our* behalf. *We* are the guilty scumbag in this story. *We* are the sinner who deserves death. Every single one of us has lied, stolen, lusted, blasphemed and done immoral things throughout our lives. There's no point denying it, we know it's true. As the Bible says, *"Everyone has sinned; we all fall short of God's glorious standard." (Romans 3:23)*

Therefore, we are *all* deserving of *Justice*! And since God, in his perfect goodness, must destroy all evil and leave no trace, he must pass the guilty sentence on us and sentence us to death. He cannot simply give a divine shrug and excuse us of our sins, or he would be corrupt. The *Hard Virtues must* be satisfied. He *must* punish sin.

And yet that is only half the story. Because God is also perfectly *Loving, Kind, Merciful* and full of *Grace*. Therefore, having pronounced the punishment, he then came down from his lofty position to earth, to take that punishment upon himself. He came to die in our place, so that we can go free. *'There is no greater love than to lay down one's life for one's friends'* (John 15:13) Jesus said this. And that's exactly what he did. He laid down his life for us.

This is the genius of the cross then—that it satisfies the seemingly contradictory demands of both the *Hard* and *Soft Virtues* simultaneously. They are held in counter-balance with each other. Justice *and* Kindness. Holiness *and* Mercy. Righteousness *and* Grace. The cross of Christ symbolises the central ground where all virtue meets.

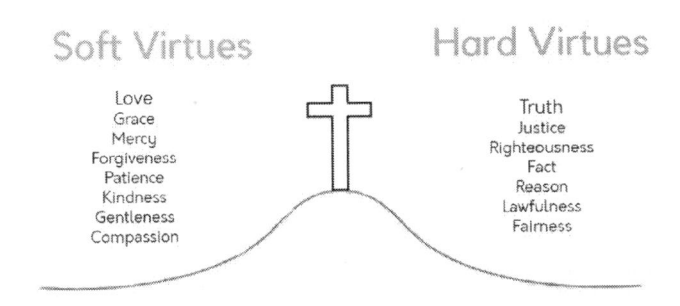

### Soft Virtues
Love
Grace
Mercy
Forgiveness
Patience
Kindness
Gentleness
Compassion

### Hard Virtues
Truth
Justice
Righteousness
Fact
Reason
Lawfulness
Fairness

Whenever we're faced with a moral dilemma in life then, it can help to picture this image. We can normally reach something approximating a good solution if we find room for both sets.

For example, if you're a parent whose child is misbehaving, how will you handle that situation? The *Soft Virtues* will suggest that you forgive and the *Hard Virtues* will demand that you punish. Which do you prioritise? Well, think of the cross and try to give place to both sets. Maybe you can offer *Grace* up front and give some warnings like God does. Maybe you can forgive the first time and give the child a chance to prove their misbehaviour was just an aberration. However, if the bad behaviour then continues and if they don't listen to your warnings, then perhaps you can bring out the *Hard* edge and punish them.

That's just one example. Sometimes we'll need to deploy one set, and sometimes the other. But remember, if we want to be good, over the course of our lives, we will need to retain a respect for both.

# 6

# Biases.

It's difficult for us to stay balanced with the virtue sets. Not only because the *Hard* and *Soft Virtues* so frequently seem to be in conflict with each other, demanding different outcomes to our moral dilemmas, and therefore making it difficult to know which side to prioritise, but also because we each have an internal bias that predisposes us to prefer one side over the other. Subconsciously, we all gravitate to *either* the *Soft or* the *Hard*. Rarely does a person like them both in equal measure.

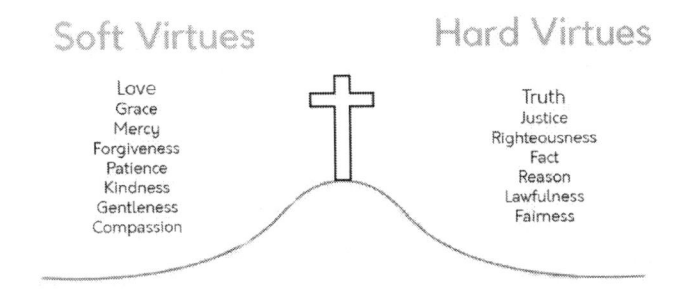

| Soft Virtues | Hard Virtues |
|---|---|
| Love | Truth |
| Grace | Justice |
| Mercy | Righteousness |
| Forgiveness | Fact |
| Patience | Reason |
| Kindness | Lawfulness |
| Gentleness | Fairness |
| Compassion | |

CS Lewis wrote, *"[The Devil] always sends errors into the world in pairs–pairs of opposites...He relies on your extra dislike of one to draw you gradually into the opposite one. But do not let us be fooled. We have to keep our eyes on the goal and go straight through between both errors. We have no other concern than that with either of them."*[1]

That's really an astute observation and it's certainly applicable here. People tend to have a natural affinity for *either* the *Soft* or the *Hard Virtues*. And because the two sets often seem to be in conflict with one another, we tend to develop an extra dislike for the set that appears to be opposing us. As time goes on, we can even become so entrenched in our own set that we develop a hatred for the opposing one.

## Liberals and Conservatives.

People who have a natural affinity for the *Soft Virtues* have traditionally become known as *Liberals*. I'm not sure the word is always appropriate but for the purposes of this book, we'll go with it. Liberals are often said to lean "left of centre", which is why I've put those virtues on the left side of the cross in our diagram:

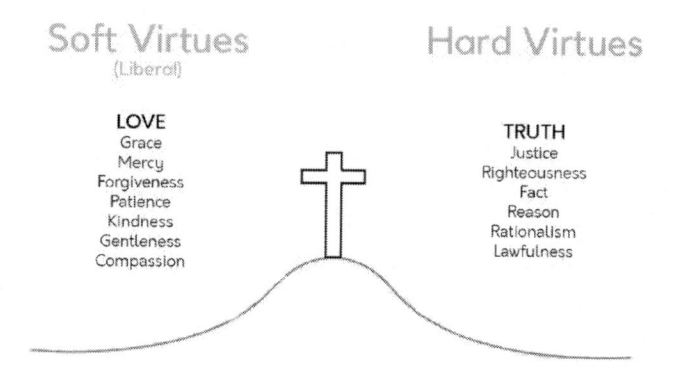

### Soft Virtues
(Liberal)

**LOVE**
Grace
Mercy
Forgiveness
Patience
Kindness
Gentleness
Compassion

### Hard Virtues

**TRUTH**
Justice
Righteousness
Fact
Reason
Rationalism
Lawfulness

If Liberals had to choose one value above all others, *Love* would be it. Therefore, I've now capitalised "*Love*" and placed it at the top of the *Soft* list. Indeed, to the Liberal, all other virtues are secondary. Wherever there's a conflict between *Love* and some other virtue, *Love* takes precedence. Always. And as the Liberal leans more deeply into the *Soft Virtues*, they tend to develop a dislike, or even a hatred, for the those seemingly contradictory values on the other side of the divide.

The same is true in reverse. People who have a natural affinity for the *Hard Virtues* have traditionally become known as *Conservatives*. They lean to the right of the cross and make "*Truth*" their ultimate value. Again, I've emphasised this by capitalising and placing "*Truth*" at the top of the *Hard* list:

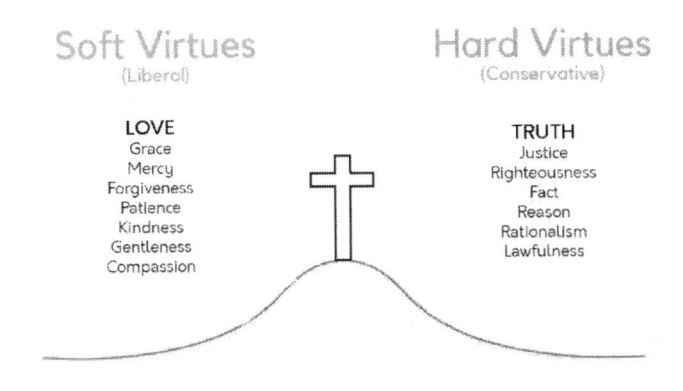

| Soft Virtues (Liberal) | Hard Virtues (Conservative) |
|---|---|
| **LOVE** | **TRUTH** |
| Grace | Justice |
| Mercy | Righteousness |
| Forgiveness | Fact |
| Patience | Reason |
| Kindness | Rationalism |
| Gentleness | Lawfulness |
| Compassion | |

If there's a conflict between *Truth* and any other virtue, then for the Conservative, *Truth* takes precedence. Always. And as the Conservative leans more deeply into the *Hard Virtues*, they tend to develop a dislike, or even a hatred, for those seemingly contradictory values on the other side of the divide.

## The Migration Dilemma.

Let's take a look at how this plays out in the real world by looking at the problem of illegal immigration. Around 2011, *The Arab Spring* occurred in the Middle-East. Citizens from various nations in that area became dissatisfied with the authoritarian regimes that governed them, and this gradually led to anti-establishment protests, uprisings and demonstrations. As the governments in these places reacted, there was violence in the following years, and hundreds of thousands of people decided to leave the region entirely. Primarily, they headed for the safety and freedom of Western civilisation.

The European Union largely encouraged them, and indeed welcomed the refugees with open arms. The German Chancellor Angela Merkel, in particular, who was then the most powerful figure in the EU, unilaterally decided to establish an open-door policy in 2015, promising homes, food and economic support to anyone who arrived on the doorstep. In 2015 then, 890,000 people arrived in Germany alone.[2]

Now, there's a law of economics which states that whatever you subsidise you will get more of. And once people across the world saw that there were financial benefits available for moving to Europe, it encouraged more to make the journey. Indeed, after the first wave of genuine refugees, there were soon economic migrants arriving on the doorstep—people from peaceful yet poor nations in Africa and Asia, where their lives were not threatened, but who had simply decided to move for the financial advantages.

The United Kingdom in particular seemed to hold a great appeal. Perhaps the internet has given people around the world an opportunity to peek into the lives of other nations, and whether it be the international ubiquity of the English language; the global reach of British music, television and sports; or the system of free education, homes, healthcare and even phones, many people seemed to zero in on Great Britain as their ultimate destination. Thus began an illegal immigration problem that has persisted ever since. A steady stream of people, primarily men of Middle-Eastern descent, began crossing the English Channel from France in inflatable dinghies and in 2021 alone, over 23,000 were successful.[3]

Now, Conservatives have always approached this problem through the lens of the *Hard Virtues*. They come at it with cold logic, fact, and reason. They ask, *"What is the Truth here? And what is the Just and Lawful response?"* In other words, how many of these people are truly refugees in need of help and how many are illegally coming to take free housing, education and healthcare? Can the British economy sustain tens of thousands of migrants putting a strain on the benefits system like this? Won't this destabilise our public finances and infrastructure? Don't we already have waiting lists for social housing amongst our own population? And don't we already have waiting lists for a healthcare service that's already under pressure? If they were truly refugees fleeing for safety, wouldn't they stay in the first safe country they set foot in? Well, haven't they passed through many safe European countries to arrive here and aren't they setting off from France? Isn't France safe? Why are they so desperate to cross the continent to reach the UK?

Indeed, why aren't they taking refuge in safe Middle Eastern countries which are much closer? Why Europe? If a law of economics states that whatever you subsidise, you'll get more of, isn't it true that if we subsidise these crossings, more will come and the problem will simply worsen? Therefore, isn't it true this isn't a viable long-term solution? How many people can we actually fit on this small island? Surely, not everyone who would like to come. People from Islamic cultures don't have a good track record of integration with Western values, so will this lead to social disruption? In the light of years of Islamic terrorist attacks, are we sure we're not welcoming future terrorists into our midst who will one day kill our citizens? Especially since the majority of the crossings are being made by young men. Aren't these immigrants being trafficked by illegal gangs who are profiting from this too? Doesn't *Justice* demand that we don't reward criminal behaviour? Isn't it true that some of the men arriving on our shores are lying about their age and pretending to be under eighteen because they know minors get preferential treatment? Should that deception be rewarded? Isn't it a kick in the teeth to migrants who try to enter the country legally and an encouragement to keep breaking the law? The Conservative primarily wants to know that *Justice* is being done, *Laws* are being observed, and *Truth* is being established. Indeed, in general, because of their innate regard for these values, Conservatives will generally always take the side of those who seek to uphold law and order. Police officers, soldiers and border guards for example, are heroic figures for a Conservative.

    The Liberal, however, is shocked by this attitude. They believe it's cold and heartless to even think about turning migrants away. Where's the warmth? Where's the *Love, Compassion* and humanity? These aren't just statistics; these are human beings with families and hopes and dreams. These people need our help, so let's give it to them!

The Liberal is leading with the *Soft Virtues*, you see. The *Truth* about who they are and why they're coming doesn't matter to the Liberal right now, if at all. The Liberal only sees human beings who need support. Neither does *Justice* particularly matter to the Liberal right now. That these immigrants are willing to break international laws, use trafficking gangs, and lie about their ages to reach our shores simply shows how desperate they are, and therefore proves how much they need our help! That's all the more reason to let them in! *Reason* isn't uppermost in the Liberal's mind here. Whether our economy and benefits system can cope with such a huge influx of migrants is something to be considered later, if at all. All that matters is that we find a way to lavish these poor souls with *Kindness*—money, food, shelter, clothing, and whatever else they may need. *Facts* aren't to be considered. So what if subsidising illegal immigration will mean we simply get more of it...let them come! All of them! Indeed, the Liberal not only advocates for an open door policy, but they would send boats to help people across the English Channel if they could—a ferry service. Unlike Conservatives who side with whoever is upholding the law, Liberals will side with whoever they believe to be oppressed.

## The Never-Ending Argument.

Do you see the problem here, then? The Conservatives are appealing to *Hard Truth* and *Justice* and conclude these immigrants mustn't be rewarded for criminality. The Liberals are appealing to *Soft Love* and *Compassion* and conclude these immigrants must be welcomed and cared for. It wouldn't be such a problem if both sides weren't rooting their argument in virtues...but they are. *Truth* and *Justice* are virtues no doubt, but so are *Love* and *Compassion*.

A difficult realisation then now dawns–that arguments between Conservatives and Liberals can never really end. Because as much as people in each camp like to paint the other side as being black-hearted villains or fools, it's not really the case. It's not that one side is drawing upon purely evil intentions while the other is all that's noble and good. We often think like that, but such tribalism is far too simplistic. Both Conservatives and Liberals are drawing upon essentially good virtues. It's just that they're drawing upon different *kinds* of good virtues. The Conservative prefers the *Hard* and Liberals prefer the *Soft*.

This explains why democracies always have debating chambers at their heart with Conservatives on one side and Liberals on the other. In the United Kingdom, the House of Commons has been a witness to arguments between these two sides for centuries. And it's why, after centuries of argument, neither side has ever managed to establish a complete supremacy of their ideas. Indeed, if you could distil all the centuries of debate into a simple concept it's that Conservatives have been shouting *"Truth!"* the whole time and Liberals have been shouting "*Love!*" And since both arguments have some merit to them, neither side can ever comprehensively win.

In recent times, the political landscape has become polarised, with each side becoming far more deeply entrenched in their ideology than ever. We'll explain more of why this has happened later. But remember, if we don't retain some respect for both types of virtue, and if we don't learn to blend and balance the two somehow, we will eventually find ourselves corrupt and doing evil. Remember our police officer from earlier–when he tried to live using only one set of virtues and ignored the other he ran into problems.

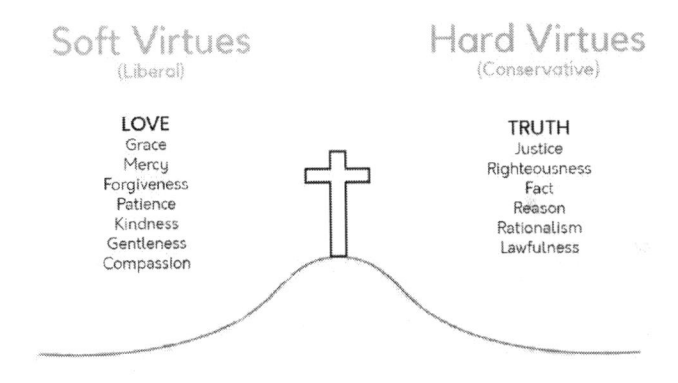

## Soft Virtues
(Liberal)

**LOVE**
Grace
Mercy
Forgiveness
Patience
Kindness
Gentleness
Compassion

## Hard Virtues
(Conservative)

**TRUTH**
Justice
Righteousness
Fact
Reason
Rationalism
Lawfulness

Remember too what CS Lewis said about this: *"[The Devil] always sends errors into the world in pairs–pairs of opposites...He relies on your extra dislike of one to draw you gradually into the opposite one. But do not let us be fooled. We have to keep our eyes on the goal and go straight through between both errors. We have no other concern than that with either of them."*

Because we've become so polarised, that's likely not what anyone in this generation wants to hear and I'll probably please nobody by saying it. You may even be tempted to close this book now. We generally want to hear that our own natural proclivity is pure and the side who oppose us are evil. I'm afraid it's just not true.

# 7
# Head v Heart.

As we continue building our understanding of Liberals and Conservatives, the next thing to notice about the virtues is that they are primarily processed through two different centres. The *Hard Virtues* favoured by Conservatives are processed through the head, while the *Soft Virtues* favoured by Liberals are processed through the heart.

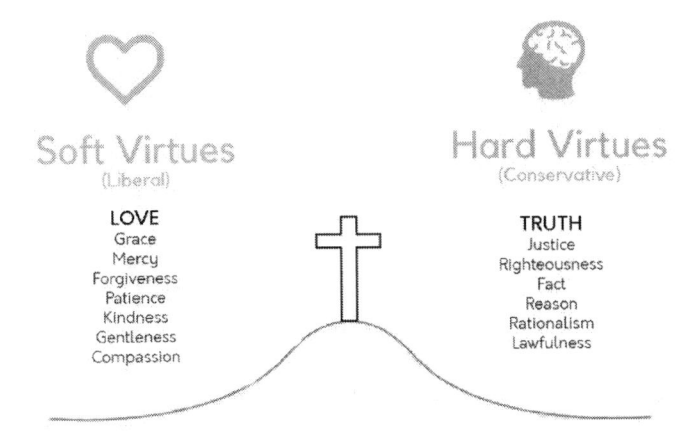

## Soft Virtues
(Liberal)

**LOVE**
Grace
Mercy
Forgiveness
Patience
Kindness
Gentleness
Compassion

## Hard Virtues
(Conservative)

**TRUTH**
Justice
Righteousness
Fact
Reason
Rationalism
Lawfulness

When Conservatives see illegal immigrants arriving on the shores of the United Kingdom, they lead with their head. They question and reason; they think in terms of statistics, economics, logic and rationale. They're driven by what they *know*.

When Liberals see illegal immigrants arriving on the shores of the United Kingdom, they lead with their heart. They feel sympathy and sadness for the plight of the suffering, and are motivated to offer help and compassion. They're driven by what they *feel*. If this means pouring out money, homes, food, clothing, or anything else, then so be it.

"*Now, hang on...*", says the Conservative to the Liberal. "*You're letting your emotions run away with you here and it's causing you to be irrational. Yes, they all look sad and tired. But where does the money come from to do all this? Where does the money come from to give them free houses and benefits? We already have a housing shortage in this country. We can't absorb everyone. And the NHS is already at breaking point. We shouldn't reward criminality either. It's criminal gangs that are profiting from human trafficking. If we subsidise this, we'll only exacerbate the problem, encourage more to come and reward crime. You're not thinking straight. You're being blinded by emotion. You're being irrational.*" They're operating from the head, you see.

"*How can you be so cold?!*", replies the Liberal. "*Are you even human? How can you be so heartless when you see these poor people desperate for entry? They need our help! Just give them help! Houses! Food! Shelter! They're human beings! You Conservatives are so cold-hearted and evil! The fact they're trying to enter illegally just shows how desperate they must be. And the fact they're using criminal gangs is a sign of their despair.*" They're operating from the heart, you see.

And so the argument rages on and takes a rather predictable form. Conservatives think Liberals are brainless; Liberals think Conservatives are heartless. And if the truth be told, as we've already seen, there's a danger that both stereotypes can become true. If there's a risk for the Conservative as they get deeply entrenched in the *Hard Virtues*, it is that they can begin to lack empathy for their fellow man. If there's a risk for the Liberal as they get deeply entrenched in the *Soft Virtues*, it's that they can begin to abandon reason and righteousness, and therefore do irrational and even corrupt things. The trick, as ever, is keeping a regard for both.

## My Own Leaning.

For the sake of transparency, I should lay my cards on the table and profess that my own natural leaning is towards the Right. Naturally, I'm a Conservative and I lead with my head. And if I'm perfectly honest, I've therefore felt this pull towards heartlessness.

When I see illegal immigration on the news, to be frank my first instinct isn't compassion, but indignation. It feels like an invasion to me to see tens of thousands of economic migrants landing on our shores, showing contempt for our borders and laws, and hoping to take from our tax-funded system without having contributed first. It's the same feeling I would have if someone broke into my house. I wouldn't feel compassion for them and think, *"aww, how desperate those poor criminals must have been to feel the need to come and take my things."* It would be an anger that they broke laws and felt entitled to take what wasn't theirs. It's especially infuriating for me when, as I've seen happen, migrants arrive and then complain that the free stuff they've been given isn't to their liking. I remember a news report where a local authority had run out of free houses, so they'd quite resourcefully converted shipping containers into homes with electricity, running water and furniture. The homes were basic but they were warm and dry—something genuine refugees would be glad of. However, recent arrivals were complaining they weren't luxurious enough. Others were complaining about being put into hotels too. My reaction was, *"we work hard to pay taxes to provide these free things for you. And you come here illegally and then complain the free things aren't nice enough? The entitlement. If they're not good enough, you can always leave?"* I haven't mentioned my concern that human traffickers are making millions by facilitating all this either, and that there is then less room for genuine refugees who are trying enter legally. It's unfair and it's not right. I feel it's legitimate to have a righteous indignation when laws are broken and criminality is rewarded.

However, on 24th November, 2021, it was reported that 27 people had drowned in the English Channel after their inflatable dinghy had proved unworthy of the voyage.[1] I'm going to be brutally honest here. Do you know what my first thought was upon hearing this news? *"Serves them right for trying to break in. Hopefully that will discourage others from trying."* At which point I had to catch myself. I had become so hardened to these people that I didn't have much compassion within me for them at all. That's dangerous. These are still human beings after all. While holding fast to *Truth* and *Righteousness* and while retaining indignation for criminal behaviour, there must also remain a part of me that remembers *Love* and *Mercy*. If I were to detach from these things entirely, I would become a monster. And therefore, I consciously had to recentre myself and remember to give the *Soft Virtues* their place. I remain opposed to the illegal crossings of course, but I do feel sympathy for those who died. I believe that's the balanced position to take.

On the other hand, it's easy to witness being Liberals being brainless on this issue and going too far in the other direction. In November, 2021, the British Government chartered a flight to deport 51 criminals to Jamaica–their country of birth. Amongst the cohort were convicted rapists, paedophiles, kidnappers and others guilty of assault. Combined, they had been handed prison sentences totalling 135 years. Others on the flight were immigration offenders who had no legal right to remain in the UK.[2] However, Liberals were so overwhelmed with compassion for these criminals that they protested outside the airport and tried to disrupt the flight from leaving. In the end, they were partially successful and most of the offenders were allowed to stay in Britain. Now just as I had to stop and reflect when I found little compassion in my heart for people drowning in the English Channel, the Left must stop and reflect when their singular pursuit of the *Soft Virtues* has led them to irrationally help rapists, paedophiles and kidnappers avoid justice. As we saw earlier with our police officer example, using only the *Soft Virtues* will eventually mean becoming a facilitator of evil.

Alexander Solzhenitsyn once said that *"the line separating good and evil passes not through states, nor between classes, nor between political parties–but right through every human heart–and through all human hearts. This line shifts. Inside us, it oscillates with the years. And even within hearts overwhelmed by evil, one small bridgehead of good is retained."*[3] In the context of this book, it slightly complicates things that he refers to the heart only. I would alter

Trench

it to say that the line between good and evil runs through both the heart *and* the mind, or more simply through the centre of every human being. And I would postulate that human beings don't generally become evil because they set out with the intention to be. Instead, humans usually become evil because the line within them shifts too far to one side or the other. In other words, they began pursuing either the *Soft* or *Hard Virtues* with such extreme fervour that at some point, they became detached from the other side.

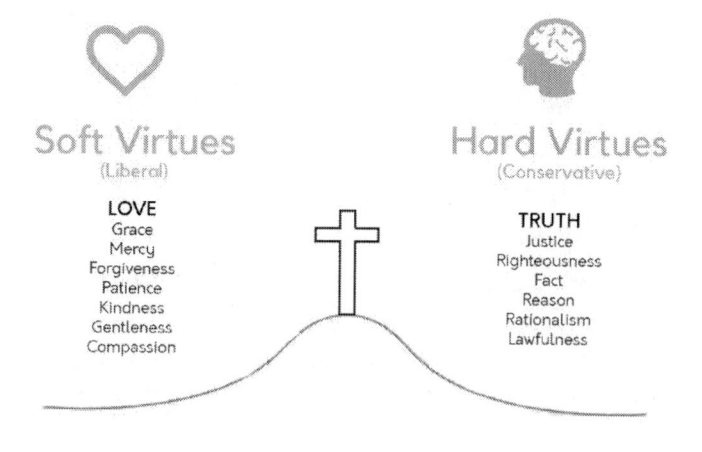

## Soft Virtues
(Liberal)

**LOVE**
Grace
Mercy
Forgiveness
Patience
Kindness
Gentleness
Compassion

## Hard Virtues
(Conservative)

**TRUTH**
Justice
Righteousness
Fact
Reason
Rationalism
Lawfulness

# 8
# Equality v Inequality.

Next, I want us to consider how Conservatives prioritising *Truth* and Liberals prioritising *Love* produces markedly different attitudes towards inequality.

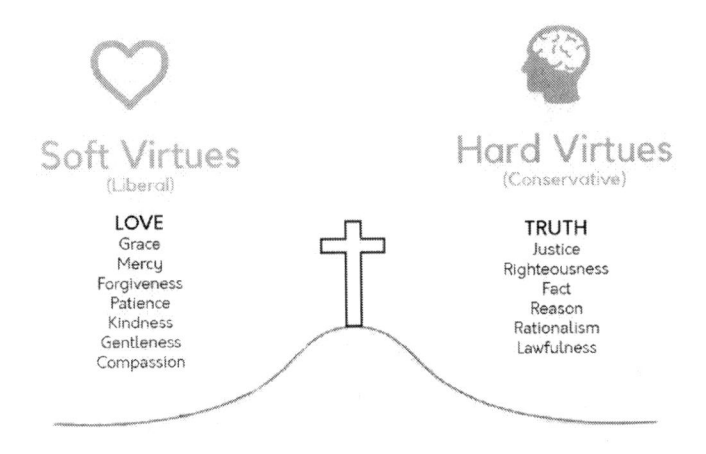

## Soft Virtues
(Liberal)

**LOVE**
Grace
Mercy
Forgiveness
Patience
Kindness
Gentleness
Compassion

## Hard Virtues
(Conservative)

**TRUTH**
Justice
Righteousness
Fact
Reason
Rationalism
Lawfulness

## Truth Excludes.

Let's start on the Conservative side by saying that whenever you deal in *Truth*, you are going to create inequality. It's unavoidable. Because *Truth* you see, by its very nature, is exclusive. Whenever you make a *Truth* statement—as soon as you assert that something thing is true—in that same moment, you exclude competing ideas as false. You create an inequality of ideas. To put it another way, when you say what something *is*, you automatically infer what *isn't*.

For example, if I make the *Truth* statement that grass is green, in that same moment I am excluding all other colours from being equally valid. By simply saying what colour the grass *is*, I'm automatically inferring what it's *not*. Because it is green, it's *not* blue, red, purple, pink, or indeed any other colour. No other colour is equal to green on this issue. Green is elevated as correct, therefore all others are discarded as false.

Now of course, when we speak *Truth* about the colour of grass, there's unlikely to be any argument. And I suppose, even if someone was adamant that grass was purple, the subject is so insignificant that it wouldn't cause much conflict–we could get along alright and remain friends. It's only grass, after all. However, let's imagine we were to deal in exclusive, un-equalising *Truths* about more significant things.

## The Party.

There's a Conservative man called Bob who's been invited by his boss to a party. Now, present within the room are people of all descriptions–including different political persuasions, ethnicities and religious backgrounds. Bob is talking to a mixed group of people when he decides to make a bold *Truth* claim: *"Illegal immigration is bad."*

As with all *Truth* claims, this statement is exclusive. By stating that illegal immigration is bad, Bob is discarding the idea that it's good. That's what truth claims do–they exclude contrary positions. They create an inequality of ideas. However, there may be people at the party who hold to the contrary position, and who now feel offended and upset by what Bob has said. There may even be an illegal immigrant present, or child of an illegal immigrant, who now feels unwelcome. And so, arguments about immigration will likely ensue and the host may be unhappy with Bob for disturbing the conviviality of the party. *"Why do you need to say such disruptive things, Bob? It doesn't matter whether illegal immigration is good or bad, just be nice and get along with everyone."*

Bob shrugs and decides to move the conversation onto religion instead. He makes another *Hard Truth* claim: *"Jesus is the only way to God."* He's done it again. By saying Jesus is the only way to God, he has again created an inequality of ideas. He's excluded Buddha, the Hindu gods, Allah, and all the rest. By stating what is true, he has inferred what is false. Now perhaps there are Muslims, Hindus, Buddhists or Atheists present who feel offended by being told their belief systems are unequal. Arguments probably ensue once more. Bob is possibly asked to get his coat and leave the party altogether. *"Why do you need to say such disruptive things, Bob? It doesn't matter whether Jesus or Buddha is the way. Just be nice and get along with everyone."*

Bob's boss is a Liberal, you see. His attitude is that because dealing in *Truth* causes division, we must never do so. Because in his mind, *Truth* isn't even the most important thing in life. *Love* is! It's not important that we establish who is right or wrong about these things. What's most important is that we all simply get along. He would agree with Anne Lamott who said, *"It's better to be kind than right."*[1]

Trench

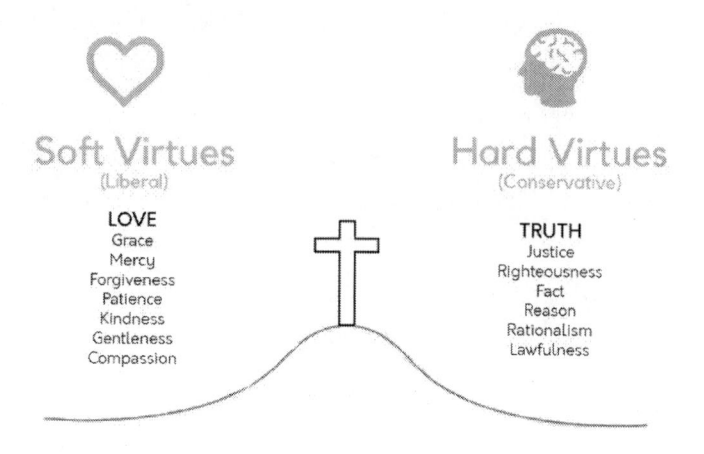

**Soft Virtues**
(Liberal)

LOVE
Grace
Mercy
Forgiveness
Patience
Kindness
Gentleness
Compassion

**Hard Virtues**
(Conservative)

TRUTH
Justice
Righteousness
Fact
Reason
Rationalism
Lawfulness

Do you see the problem here then? The Conservative wants to deal in *Truth* because that's what matters most to him, but though *Truth* is plainly a virtue, its very nature disturbs the *Love* in the room. It creates inequality and causes offence. Now the Conservative doesn't care so much about that—if it offends, it offends. But Liberals can't stomach this idea. They want *Love* to prevail. They want peace and unity. They just want everyone to get along and so would prefer to diminish *Truth's* importance. Indeed, the more extreme a Liberal becomes, the more they begin to hate this *Truth* that by its nature would un-equalise and dis-unify. *Truth* becomes an enemy of everything they hold dear. To them, we must therefore never claim things are absolutely true. "*Only the Sith deal in absolutes,*" as Obi-Wan Kenobi said to Anakin Skywalker in "Revenge of the Sith." The Liberal believes that to deal in hard facts is to deal in something essentially disruptive.[2]

## Good Inequality.

Now in the real world, though pursuing *Truth* is disruptive, it's necessary. Indeed, we generally call pursuing *Truth's* inequalities, "education." Education is simply the process of learning which ideas to elevate as right and which ones to therefore discard as wrong.

For example, once we learn it's absolutely true that human beings need water to survive, we elevate the idea of drinking it and we discard contrary positions that says it's not necessary. Once we learn it's absolutely true that two plus two equals four, we elevate that answer and discard contrary numbers from being equally correct. Once we learn we should capitalise the first letter of a new sentence when writing, we elevate that idea and discard contrary ones. Once we learn the Battle of Hastings was in 1066, we elevate that idea and discard other years. Once we learn it's absolutely true that gravity exists, we elevate the idea that we shouldn't jump off high bridges, and we discard contrary positions that say we can float or fly. Once we learn it's absolutely true that smoking causes disease, we elevate the idea that cigarettes are damaging and discard contrary positions that say they're not.

The pursuit of *Truth* is a persistent process of separating good ideas from bad ones–you could say a process of "un-equalising ideas"–so that we might grow in knowledge and wisdom...so that we might therefore make better choices...so that we might be healthier, happier and live longer. We're not used to thinking of words like "inequality" and "exclusion" in a positive sense these days but if what we're excluding is bad ideas, we're getting smarter. Which of course, for the Conservative who is centred in the mind, is very important indeed.

Now while Bob was at the party, he talked about illegal immigration and his boss told him to be quiet because it wasn't important. But isn't it quite important? Aren't some things worth the conflict of debate to establish the *Truth*? So that we can all grow in knowledge and wisdom and advance as a civilisation? I mean, the immigration issue has great consequences for the nation. It even has the potential to irrevocably change or collapse it entirely. Some things are worth the conflict that's necessary to establish *Truth*. Indeed, throughout history, a great many newly discovered truths have caused momentary disruption to society, and yet it was worth the debate.

Similarly at the party, Bob said Jesus was the only way to God. It caused offence so his boss told him to stop talking about it. But what if what Bob was saying is *true*? I mean, what if it's absolutely true? What if it's as true as needing water to survive? What if it's as true as gravity? What if the Buddhists, Muslims and Atheists really are on the way to hell because they reject Jesus' sacrifice for their sins? Surely it's better that Bob explains his reasons for believing in Jesus so everyone can debate the idea, thereafter have the necessary information to decide whether to elevate it as true or discard it as false? The Conservative would think so. Though it may momentarily cause some conflict in the room, that is after all how we grow in knowledge and wisdom. Pretending there is no absolute *Truth* at all, as the Liberal would suggest, just to keep some peace surely isn't advisable when eternities are at stake.

Either way, you can see the problem here. *Love* and *Truth* are both virtues but they're demanding contradictory things. *Love* wants equality but dealing in *Truth* means inequality. *Love* priorities peace but *Truth* means disruption. *Love* wants feelings to be preserved but *Truth* wants knowledge to grow. Which do you prioritise? The improvement of the head or the protection of the heart? For both Liberals and Conservatives, the answer to this question will be clear. They'll just so happen to be completely opposed.

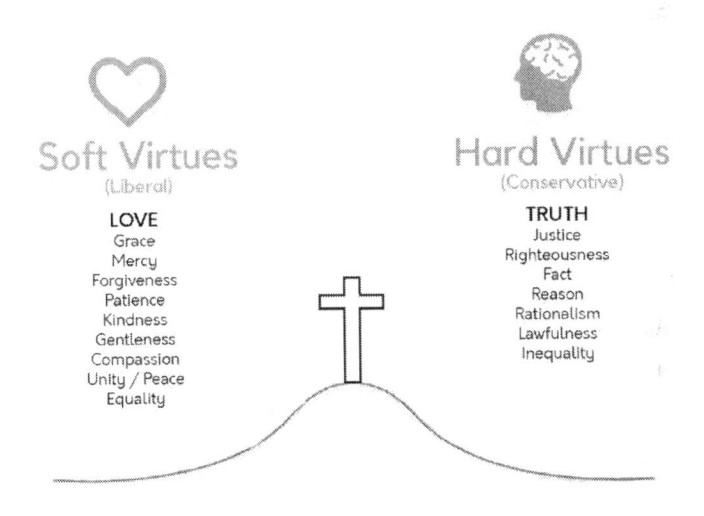

### Soft Virtues
(Liberal)

**LOVE**
Grace
Mercy
Forgiveness
Patience
Kindness
Gentleness
Compassion
Unity / Peace
Equality

### Hard Virtues
(Conservative)

**TRUTH**
Justice
Righteousness
Fact
Reason
Rationalism
Lawfulness
Inequality

NB: We introduced a few more values in this chapter so we can now update the diagram with "Unity", "Peace" and "Equality" on the Liberal side. We can also now add "Inequality" to the Hard side.

# 9
# Competition v Cooperation.

Very closely connected to the concept of inequality is the concept of competition. Conservatives like the inequality that competition creates, but Liberals don't. Liberals prefer co-operation. I'll add those to the graphic:

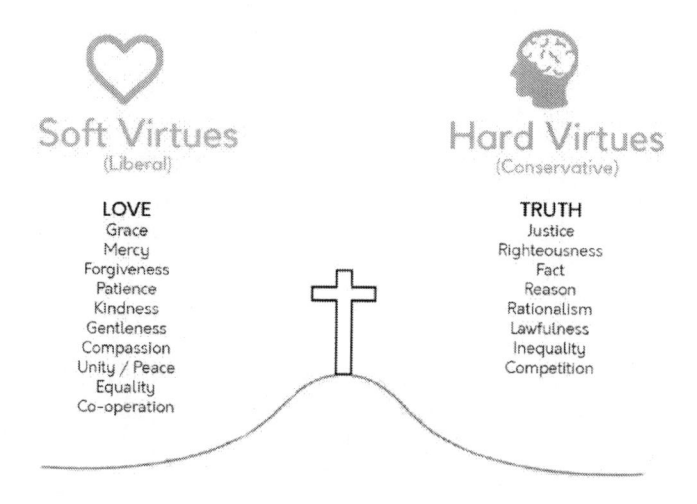

## Soft Virtues
(Liberal)

**LOVE**
Grace
Mercy
Forgiveness
Patience
Kindness
Gentleness
Compassion
Unity / Peace
Equality
Co-operation

## Hard Virtues
(Conservative)

**TRUTH**
Justice
Righteousness
Fact
Reason
Rationalism
Lawfulness
Inequality
Competition

## Liberals Against Competition.

If you think of a race, it's clear that although there are many competitors, only one can finish first and only three can make the podium. That means that the majority of runners in each competition are going to experience negative emotions at the finish line–disappointment, sadness, regret, frustration, and anger. The Liberal doesn't like this. It offends their values for two major reason.

Firstly, Liberals feel *Compassion* for the losers who don't get a medal and they empathise with their sadness. It hurts their heart when they see such despair.

Secondly, since they prioritise *Equality* and *Unity*, they don't like how competition elevates some to bask in glory, while discarding the rest. On a podium, this happens quite literally. The winners stand on different elevations to represent their respective positions, and are showered with honour, while the losers are excluded from the ceremony entirely.

*"This is not what life is all about,"* thinks the Liberal. *"Life shouldn't be about fighting to assert dominance over each other. Life shouldn't be about the conflict of creating winners and losers—some happy and some sad. Why can't everyone be a winner? Why can't everyone agree to be equal and share in the glory? Why can't everyone feel loved the same? That's what's important in life! Love! Peace! Harmony! Unity!"*

In recent years then, Liberal teachers have begun introducing the idea of participation medals at school sports days. The message they want to convey to pupils is that it doesn't matter whether they finished first or last—everyone is equally valued, everyone gets the same medal, and everyone gets the same amount of praise.

In more recent times, this has developed a step further and Liberal teachers have sought to remove competitive elements from sports days entirely. For example in 2019, the Irish Primary Physical Education Association (IPPEA) published a paper that encouraged schools to move away from competitive sports and play instead, *"co-operative games that emphasise participation by all."*[1] For the Liberal, co-operation is better than competition because it promotes the sense of *Unity* that they prize.

## Benefits of Competition.

It's not a bad thing to want *Unity* in life. I think we can understand the Liberal motivation here. However, the inequality that competition creates isn't a bad thing either. In fact, competition produces many benefits that it's impossible to gain in other ways.

Let's go back to the running race. Yes, in a field of competitors there will be winners and losers, and yes the winners will be momentarily happy and the losers will momentarily be sad. But after having experienced the pain of disappointment, isn't it clear that the losers will then be extra motivated to make sure they win the next time? And won't they therefore, work harder and be more disciplined in their training? And won't they seek to innovate and find new ways of elevating their performance? And doesn't that promote excellence, imagination and skill? Won't they unlock new levels of their potential that they didn't know existed? And won't they need to develop mental fortitude, resilience and courage to overcome the initial disappointment and try again? And aren't all these things *good*? I mean, hard work, discipline, innovation, skill, excellence, imagination, unlocking potential, mental fortitude, resilience and courage. Aren't these qualities very important not just for sport, but for life in general? It's unlikely the competitor gains these advantages any other way.

This is why schools and parents have traditionally always championed competitive sport as a vital part of a child's upbringing. It helps build vital qualities into their character, and this is never more true than when a child *loses*. It's through losing that we learn. It's through losing that we develop. Losing even builds self-awareness and humility as we are forced to honestly confront and tackle our weaknesses. For all these reasons and more, it's been said that pain is the *greatest* teacher and *best* motivator.[2]

The benefits of competition that build character in a child continue to produce positive effects in every aspect of adult life. In the business world, competition is the basis of strong economies that make life better for everyone. For example, think of a company that produces camera equipment, like Canon. There are a finite amount of customers who may be interested in buying cameras, and therefore a finite pot of money available in that market. Now because there are other camera companies like Nikon, Sony or Panasonic competing for that pot, they must each work hard and innovate to elevate themselves, making their product more attractive than the rest. In practice, this means devising new technologies and better features, improving quality of materials and workmanship, improving customer service, and finding ways to produce more efficiently so that prices can be kept low. As camera companies vie in these areas, customers benefit from a constant stream of better quality goods coming to market. And consequently, civilisation itself advances through these technological innovations.

Do some businesses, and therefore business owners, lose by the competition? Of course they do. Some companies will win the majority of market share and others will go bust. But as Abraham Lincoln said, *"That some should be rich, shows that others may become rich, and hence is encouragement to industry and enterprise."*[3] In other words, though you're a loser today, you can always come back and try again. If you're humble and honest about where you went wrong before; if you lose well and learn by your mistakes; if you then work hard, innovate, discipline yourself and pursue excellence, there's no reason why you can't be a winner tomorrow. It reminds me of the opening scene from *Indiana Jones and the Last Crusade* where a young Indiana is competing with an experienced adventurer to attain an important historical artefact. Indiana ultimately loses but the man tells him, *"you lost today, kid...but that doesn't mean you have to like it."* In other words, "don't give up. Use the pain of this loss as motivation to do better next time, and maybe you'll win."

This is what competition engenders within human beings—learning, humility, self-awareness, hard work, discipline, innovation, skill, excellence, imagination, unlocked potential, mental fortitude, resilience and courage. And therefore, as well-intentioned as Liberals may be with their focus on co-operation and participation trophies, a society devoid of competition will ultimately become a society devoid of very important qualities.

Once again, we see the dilemma though. Liberals prioritise one thing and Conservatives another. It's not that either of those things are bad in themselves—co-operation is good and competition is good. But they demand completely different outcomes. So which do you prioritise? What is more important? That we gain the benefits of competition and accept there will be sadness and despair for some along the way? Or that we live in peace and harmony but create a society devoid of resilience, innovation, humility, and other important character traits? Depending on what side of the divide you lean towards, the answers to these questions will be obvious. They'll also happen to be completely different.

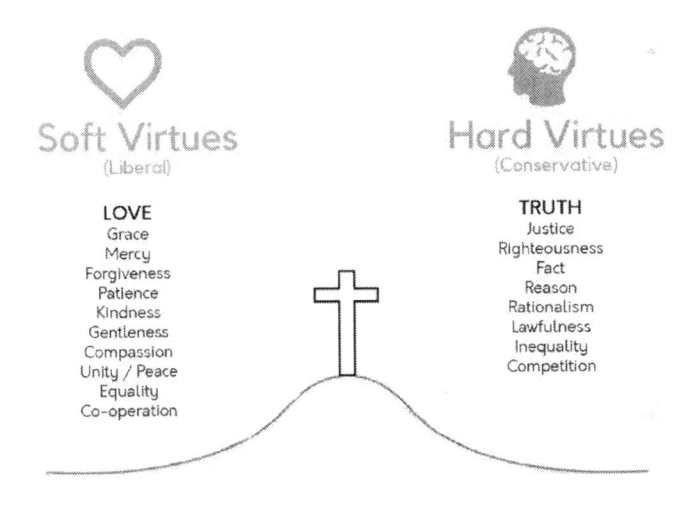

### Soft Virtues
(Liberal)

**LOVE**
Grace
Mercy
Forgiveness
Patience
Kindness
Gentleness
Compassion
Unity / Peace
Equality
Co-operation

### Hard Virtues
(Conservative)

**TRUTH**
Justice
Righteousness
Fact
Reason
Rationalism
Lawfulness
Inequality
Competition

NB: We added "co-operation" on the Liberal side and "competition" on the Conservative side.

# 10
# Individualism v Collectivism

From the Liberal prioritisation of *Love, Co-operation* and *Equality*, a political theory called *"Collectivism"* emerges. From the Conservative prioritisation of *Truth, Competition* and *Inequality*, an opposing political theory called *"Individualism"* comes to the fore. Let's add those terms:

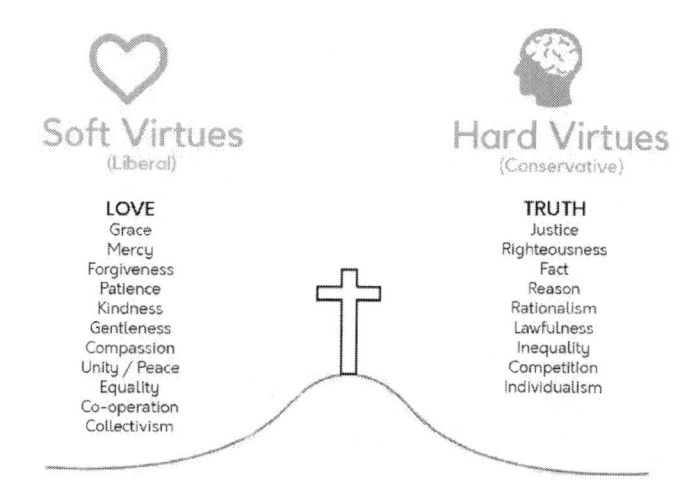

### Soft Virtues
(Liberal)

**LOVE**
Grace
Mercy
Forgiveness
Patience
Kindness
Gentleness
Compassion
Unity / Peace
Equality
Co-operation
Collectivism

### Hard Virtues
(Conservative)

**TRUTH**
Justice
Righteousness
Fact
Reason
Rationalism
Lawfulness
Inequality
Competition
Individualism

## The One and the Many.

Conservatives are essentially individualists. That is, they believe that each human being is unique and should therefore be dignified as such. In practice this means they believe each person should have the freedom to speak *Truth*, or even just their beliefs about *Truth*. Likewise, Conservatives believe people should have the ability to pursue their own goals in any way they choose, within the boundaries of the law, and as long as that doesn't infringe on someone else's individual liberty to do the same.

Now as we've already seen using the example of Bob at the party, speaking *Truth* freely inevitably leads to conflict. And as we've already established in the last chapter using the example of running races and companies, people pursuing their own goals will inevitably bring them into competition with others.

Conservatives don't mind the conflict that individualism creates because they see the advantages of it. By debating independent ideas, we're able to separate good ones from bad ones and therefore advance in knowledge and wisdom. Letting individuals speak their own mind gives room for individual genius to flourish and raises the chances of good ideas emerging in the first place. It helps the group see different perspectives too, so that wise solutions may be found to problems. Similarly, by competing with one another in various aspects of life, whether it be at school, on the sports field or in the business world, we encourage learning, humility, self-awareness, hard work, discipline, innovation, skill, excellence, imagination, unlocked potential, mental fortitude, resilience and courage. The Conservative believes the conflict of individualism is worth it.

Liberals, on the other hand, do not believe conflict is worth it. As we have already seen, Liberals prioritise *Love and Peace* so they are opposed to things that may disrupt harmony. In practice this means they are opposed to people speaking *Truth* freely, or even their independent beliefs about it. Likewise, Liberals are opposed to people pursuing their own goals in competition with others. Speaking and acting independently is going to lead to hurt feelings and inequality, perhaps selfish behaviours, and ultimately, that's going to disturb the *Unity* they prize so highly.

Liberal prioritisation of harmony makes them political collectivists. Liberals believe that we are not mere individuals but rather we are each a small piece of a larger idea called "society." They believe that if society is to function harmoniously, cohesion is of paramount importance. And this means preferring *Love* to *Truth*; *Equality* to *Inequality*; and *Co-operation* to *Competition*. They believe individual speech and goals should always be sacrificed for the peace of the whole. And indeed, any speech or behaviour that threatens to destabilise group cohesion must be discouraged and eliminated. This is why Bob's boss shut him down at the party and it's why Irish schools are trying to eliminate competitive sports. It's all done in the name of collective *Love*, *Equality* and *Unity*.

## Big and Small Government.

Now you may notice that the Individualist worldview requires very little by way of government. If people are to be left free to speak their minds and pursue their own personal goals, then it's up to individuals to form their own opinions, decide what their goals will be, and make their own plans on how to achieve them. The Individualist in fact, really only wants one thing from their government—to be left alone!

Okay, that's not entirely true, but it's not far off. At the extreme end of individualism you will find anarchists who want no government at all. But most individualists are better described as "libertarians." They simply want minimal government and minimal state interference. Indeed, they only really want the government to protect their fundamental right speak and live freely within the moral and just confines of the law. As the American Declaration of Independence put it, the government's job is to do little more than protect a citizen's inalienable rights of life, liberty and the pursuit of happiness.

On the other hand, you may notice that the Collectivist worldview requires big government. After all, if all the individuals in a society must be choreographed to work in unison for the greater good, there needs to be a grand choreographer of some kind. If we're all just cogs in a machine, what kind of machine is it? There must be some top-down power establishing what the collective goals of the society will be, and therefore what words and behaviours are acceptable in the shared pursuit. Such a government must have far-reaching, authoritarian powers to shut down any independent speech or activities that may disrupt the group. Therefore, whereas the far right would produce anarchism, the far left produces authoritarianism.

And indeed, it's for this reason that Liberals are far more trusting of authority than Conservatives. A study on individualism versus collectivism was conducted in 2013 by Rebecca Le Febvre and Volker Franke and they discovered that Liberals score much more highly than Conservatives in the trait of dependence.[1] It simply means that while Conservatives are more likely to take issues into their own hands and assume independent, personal responsibility for their life outcomes, Liberals are more likely to look to the government or some other respected authority for guidance and direction.

We saw this distinction in response to the Covid-19 outbreak. Conservatives didn't trust the government's response, were horrified that the government might attempt to take their liberty through lockdowns, and didn't trust the authorities in regard to the safety and efficacy of the vaccines. On the other hand, Liberals did trust the government's response, did look to the government for guidance and protection at all times, and did trust them regarding the safety and efficacy of the vaccines. Conservatives wanted to preserve their individual freedoms but Liberals wanted the government to eliminate individual freedoms for the greater good.

We won't say any more about this at the moment, because we'll be expanding on it later. But again, we can see the dilemma. Which do you prioritise? Individual freedoms or collective cohesion? Freedom is good. Unity is good too. But each one demands different outcomes, so which should take precedence? Your answer to that will depend on whether you're a Conservative or Liberal.

Individualism v Collectivism

**Soft Virtues**
(Liberal)

LOVE
Grace
Mercy
Forgiveness
Patience
Kindness
Gentleness
Compassion
Unity / Peace
Equality
Co-operation
Collectivism
Big Government
Authoritarianism

**Hard Virtues**
(Conservative)

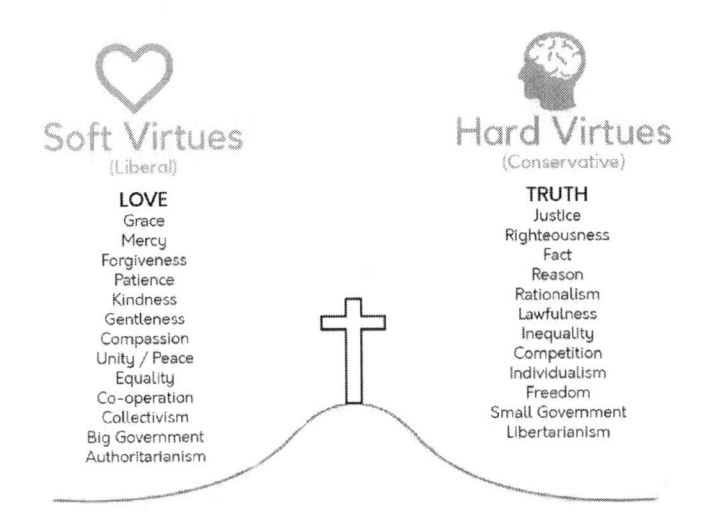

TRUTH
Justice
Righteousness
Fact
Reason
Rationalism
Lawfulness
Inequality
Competition
Individualism
Freedom
Small Government
Libertarianism

NB: We've now added "collectivism," "big government," and "authoritarianism" to the Liberal list of values, and we added "individualism," "freedom," "small government," and "libertarianism" to the Conservative side.

# 11
# Anchors v Fires.

The next point I want to make as we build our understanding of Conservatives and Liberals is that Conservatives are more stable. I'll represent it using a straight line on the *Hard* side and a wavy line on the *Soft* side.

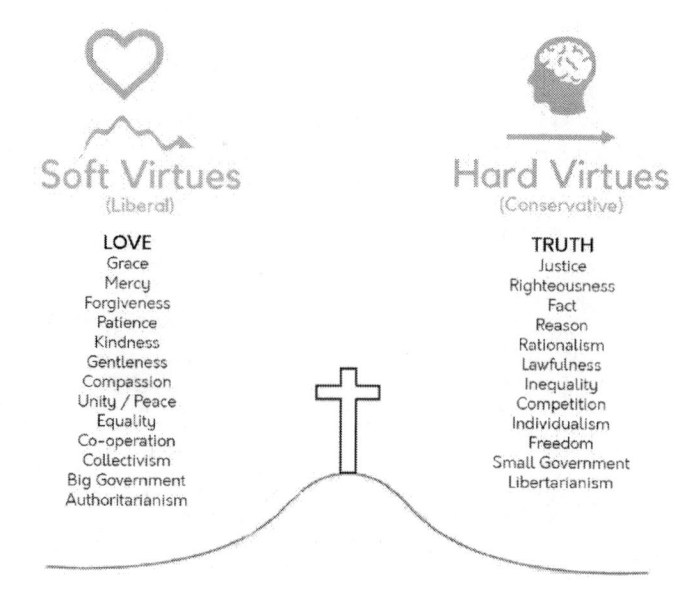

### Soft Virtues
(Liberal)

LOVE
Grace
Mercy
Forgiveness
Patience
Kindness
Gentleness
Compassion
Unity / Peace
Equality
Co-operation
Collectivism
Big Government
Authoritarianism

### Hard Virtues
(Conservative)

TRUTH
Justice
Righteousness
Fact
Reason
Rationalism
Lawfulness
Inequality
Competition
Individualism
Freedom
Small Government
Libertarianism

## The Stable Mind.

*Truth* is generally a very stable thing. To deal in it is to deal in something solid and dependable. Indeed, it's often completely unchanging. If the speed of light is 299,792,458 m/s today, then it will still be 299,792,458 m/s tomorrow. If the sun rose in the East today, you can bet it always has and always will. Murder is immoral, always has been immoral, and always will be immoral. These things are absolutely true and will never change.

Now other *Truths* called "Provisional Truths" do change over time...but mostly gradually. For example, as I write this book, it's true that the Queen of Great Britain is Elizabeth II. That will change one day of course, but at the time of writing it has not changed for over 70 years. As I write this book, it's true that the main road between Glasgow and Edinburgh is called the M8. That could change one day also, but in reality, it's most likely still going to be true next year, in five years, and in ten years. It's very rare that something is true one moment, false the next, and then true again a moment after.

Our understanding of *Truth* tends to evolve equally slowly too then. It takes a minimum twelve to thirteen years of schooling before we're considered to have acquired enough basic knowledge to be useful in the world, and much of it we will carry for the rest of our lives. For example, I learned that two plus two equals four when I was five years old. I still hold to that knowledge today, and will until the day I die. It's never going to change.

We adapt to provisional truths as we grow up and simply by continuing to live and assimilate new information, that can't help but gradually change our understanding of the world. But there's an emphasis on the word, "gradually." I mean, I may hold some different opinions now compared to what I held ten years ago. However, I'm quite certain I don't hold any different opinions now to what I held ten *seconds* ago! Indeed, if my beliefs about the nature of the world kept changing every ten seconds, that would likely indicate some kind of psychological disorder.

I hope you can see what I'm getting at here. If we once believe anything to be true, we tend to hold onto that belief indefinitely until some new piece of information presents itself that causes us to change our mind. And since that doesn't happen very often, to be centred in the mind and to make *Truth* your priority, is to deal in something very stable.

## The Unstable Heart.

The same can't be said for our feelings. What we feel from one moment to the next is far more volatile and tends to be subject to the whims of circumstance. As a Manchester United fan, I'm emotionally invested when I watch them play football—indeed, it could be described as being on an emotional rollercoaster. One moment, I'm feeling elated because I think they've scored a goal. The next second, I can be in the depths of despair because the goal has been ruled out for a foul. A moment later, I can be enraged with a call made by the referee. The next, I'm excited because they're on the attack. That can all happen within five minutes.

You know what it's like even if you're not a sports fan. You may be going about your day feeling happy, but then someone reminds you of a dentist's appointment you forgot about. Suddenly, you feel panic because you're late. Perhaps on the way to the surgery you begin to feel apprehension. You reach the waiting room on time however, and after the appointment feel relief. The world around us and our circumstances within it are constantly changing, and therefore our emotional responses are constantly altering too. Indeed, it's possible to feel the full gamut of emotions in a single day. Happiness, sadness, worry, stress, excitement, hope, anger, and all the rest. Perhaps I could simplify it by simply saying that what we *know* is far more stable than what we *feel*.

## Anchors.

Those who primarily lead with their heads then, tend to be more calm, consistent and stable in their behaviour. Those who are primarily led by their hearts will be more emotional, inconsistent and impulsive. As always, I don't mean to say that one is always good and the other is always bad—we've already established the pitfalls of being all head or all heart. We need something of both. And indeed, everyone does have something of both. But if you think of it as a sliding scale, Conservatives will be more weighted towards the head, and Liberals will be more weighted towards the heart.

Now it's because of the stability of the head that I sometimes think of it being an anchor. Grounding in *Truth* holds a person steady even as their emotions change violently and capriciously. Imagine, for example, a man is standing in a bar when another person brushes past him and accidentally spills his drink. The immediate emotional response is probably anger. Now if he is heart-centred, that emotion may overwhelm him and acting impulsively, he may start swinging his fists in blind rage.

The more head-centred this man is however, the more likely rationale will kick in and pull him back from an impulsive response. He'll assess the *Truth* that it was only an accident. The *Truth* is the stranger meant him no harm. The *Truth* is only a small amount has been spilled. The *Truth* is it's not a tragedy. The *Truth* is, if he starts fighting this guy, he may end up with injuries and a criminal record. The rational mind is able to quell the rush of boiling anger, keeping the man grounded and calm.

Whenever our moods are flying around in all directions, if we're beginning to feel out of control or even enslaved to those emotions, it helps to remind ourselves of what we *know*. If you're feeling anxious about something, speak *Truth* to yourself and remind yourself of what you know. If your faith is faltering, speak *Truth* to yourself and remind yourself of what you know. You will find that by speaking *Truth* to yourself in this way, you can often bring runaway emotions under control.[1]

## Fires.

On the other hand, I sometimes think of the heart as being a fire. By that I mean, without some emotion; without some feeling; life gets cold. Fire is sometimes unpredictable in its movements but it's warm. Indeed, sometimes the heart drives us to do impulsive things that don't make perfect sense to the rational mind, but which are ultimately good.

My favourite movie is *"It's A Wonderful Life,"* directed by Frank Capra and starring Jimmy Stewart. At several points in the story, the main character, George Bailey, is faced with a dilemma where he can do the logical thing, or do the irrationally loving thing. At the beginning of the movie for example, while still a child, his younger brother Harry falls through some frozen pond ice. Instead of thinking rationally about the danger to himself, George's love for his brother causes him to impulsively jump in to save him. He loses his hearing in one ear as a result, and could have lost his life.

When the Great Depression hits, George starts handing out money from his own personal savings to help the people of Bedford Falls get through it. It's not particularly rational and there's no guarantee he will have enough money, or that it will do much long term good—they don't yet know how big or long the Great Depression is going to be—but he loves these people enough to impulsively do whatever he can to help.

Near the end of the movie, his absent-minded Uncle Billy loses a large sum of money from the family company. If it's not recovered, someone will have to go to jail for suspected embezzlement. Even though in truth, Billy lost the money and should be the one to take the fall, George claims it was him so his uncle can remain free. It's not rational but it is loving.

Indeed, throughout the story George consistently makes choices that don't make sense to the rational mind. These choices threaten his opportunities, his livelihood, his financial security, and even his life. But by the final scene, because he has loved people so recklessly, his life is filled with warmth and happiness.

Think of marriage too. It's been said that if a couple sat down ahead of time and thought about the risks of it, nobody would ever do it! Marriage means a life of added complexity. It means spending the rest of your life putting someone else's needs before your own. It means self-sacrifice and relinquishing full autonomy over your life. From then on, you will spend days doing things you'd rather not be doing. You'll have more conflict, arguments and drama. There's a 33% chance it will end in divorce, and if it does the consequences will be ruinous.[2,3] If you thought about it rationally, it could anchor you into a state of paralysis.

But does that mean nobody should ever get married? Of course not. It could be the best thing you ever do! What would life be if every decision was made on cold rationale? Who would we be if we weren't moved by the heart from time-to-time? How much colder and empty would our lives be if we didn't occasionally do things that were completely, irrationally, insanely, self-sacrificially, this-doesn't-make-sense-but-I'm-going-to-do-it-anyway, loving?

## Migrant Crisis Revisited.

So we need something of the mind, and something of the heart too. Sometimes we need an anchor in life and sometimes we need a fire. But again, you can see how these two things might contradict one another and produce dilemmas? The heart tends to says one thing and the head says another. Think back to the migrant crisis example from earlier. The heart says let them in and the head says send them away. So which do we prioritise? The loving thing or the logical thing? The one you pick will largely depend on whether you're a Conservative or Liberal. But in *Truth*, it's best if we navigate life with something of both the head and the heart.

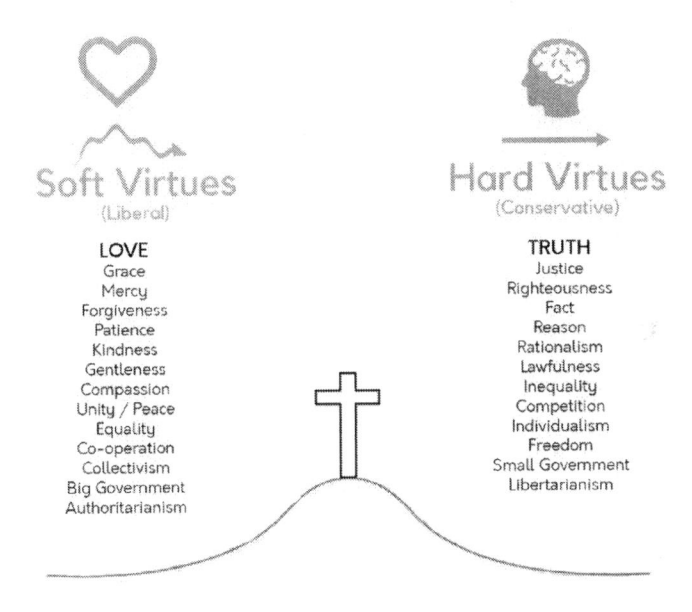

## Soft Virtues
(Liberal)

**LOVE**
Grace
Mercy
Forgiveness
Patience
Kindness
Gentleness
Compassion
Unity / Peace
Equality
Co-operation
Collectivism
Big Government
Authoritarianism

## Hard Virtues
(Conservative)

**TRUTH**
Justice
Righteousness
Fact
Reason
Rationalism
Lawfulness
Inequality
Competition
Individualism
Freedom
Small Government
Libertarianism

NB: The only thing we've added here is the wiggly line to represent emotion being unstable, and the straight line to represent truth being stable.

# 12
# Men and Women.

We now reach what I think is the first really controversial chapter of the book![1] The *Hard Virtues* are embodied by men while the *Soft Virtues* are embodied by women.

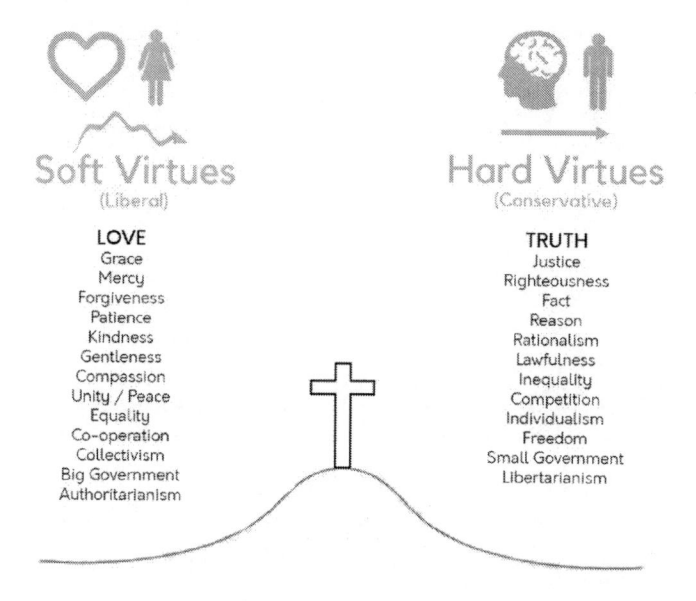

## Soft Virtues
(Liberal)

**LOVE**
Grace
Mercy
Forgiveness
Patience
Kindness
Gentleness
Compassion
Unity / Peace
Equality
Co-operation
Collectivism
Big Government
Authoritarianism

## Hard Virtues
(Conservative)

**TRUTH**
Justice
Righteousness
Fact
Reason
Rationalism
Lawfulness
Inequality
Competition
Individualism
Freedom
Small Government
Libertarianism

Please don't misunderstand me here—I'm not suggesting that all women are Liberals and all men are Conservatives. That would clearly not be true. What I'm saying is that the *Soft Virtues* are essentially feminine in their nature and can most visibly be seen in women, while the *Hard Virtues* are essentially masculine in nature and can most visibly be seen in men. Which is why, for example, Liberals of both sexes are far more likely to identify themselves as Feminists. It's also why Conservatives of both sexes are far more likely to believe in traditional family structures that place men in a place of leadership.

## Men The Head, Women The Heart.

I'll work my way down the two columns of our graphic from top-to-bottom in an attempt to explain this concept. And I'll start by saying that men tend to process the world primarily through their head, while women tend to process it primarily through their heart. Men are thinkers and women are feelers.

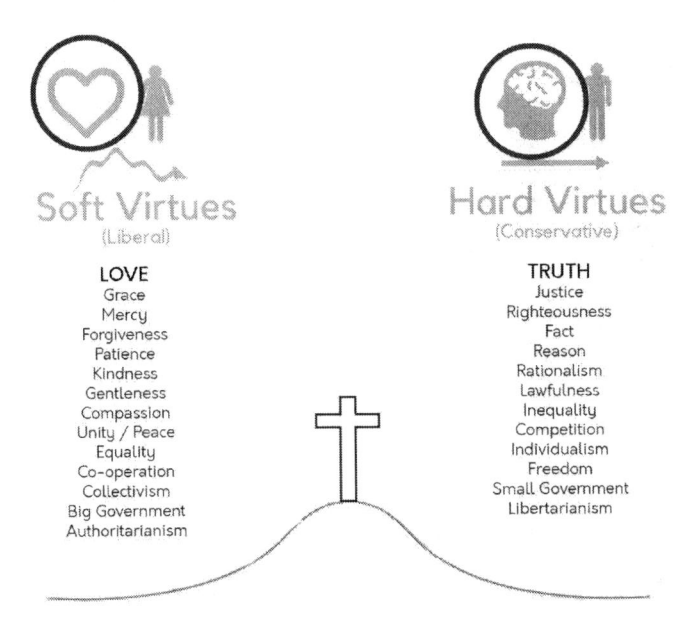

### Soft Virtues
(Liberal)

**LOVE**
Grace
Mercy
Forgiveness
Patience
Kindness
Gentleness
Compassion
Unity / Peace
Equality
Co-operation
Collectivism
Big Government
Authoritarianism

### Hard Virtues
(Conservative)

**TRUTH**
Justice
Righteousness
Fact
Reason
Rationalism
Lawfulness
Inequality
Competition
Individualism
Freedom
Small Government
Libertarianism

In practice, this fact means that men tend to be less emotional than women. They cry less for example, and they're less animated in showing excitement or enthusiasm. That's not to say they never cry or get excited at all, but they're on a more even emotional keel. Sometimes that makes their emotional state a harder read than women. If a man is happy or sad you might not know either way. They're better at speaking *Truth* to themselves to stay calm and if they're presented with a difficult problem, they're less likely to panic but instead refer to what they *know* in order to find solutions. Men are problem solvers in this respect.

Women, on the other hand, find it much harder to hide how they're feeling and are much more likely to let their emotions run away with them. If they're happy or sad, you tend to know about it, and those emotions can more readily overwhelm. In this way, you could say men are anchors and women are fires—men provide stability in life and women provide warmth.

## People and Things.

Being centred in the mind means that men tend to be more interested in concepts, technology, statistics and problem solving projects. Indeed, we can simplify by saying that men are often more interested in *things* than *people*. For this reason, men tend to gravitate towards STEM jobs i.e. Science, Technology, Engineering and Mathematics. In 2021, even after years of concerted efforts to make STEM jobs more attractive to women, men still made up 61% of those in physical sciences, 63% in mathematical sciences, 81% in computer sciences, and 81% in engineering sciences.[2]

Women however, being centred in the heart, are far more relational than men. They're more interested in *people* than *things*. While a man's mind is occupied by his new PC build or how he's going to construct a wall out the back and overcome the tricky slope, the woman is more likely thinking how her friend Olivia is doing since she had her baby. She's wondering if she should take a cake to Sarah, or phone Louise. She's concerned with communication and forming bonds with other humans. Indeed, women generally talk more...sometimes a lot more...than men! Men generally speak to communicate what they believe is important information, and once the information has been passed on in a reasonably ordered and direct way, they stop. Women talk to build relationships so it doesn't really matter what it's about, and they can meander and quickly get off-topic.

The female focus on people and the male focus on things means that women tend to have a much stronger support network of friends, and are more dependent on those relationships than men. It also means women are drawn more towards nurturing jobs like nursing and education. About 90% of nurses in the world are women, and about 76% of teachers are women.[3,4]

The female focus on people and the male focus on things can lead to crossed wires in romantic relationships. For example, when a woman pours out her heart to tell her husband about her problems, his instinct is that she's presenting him with a problem to solve. He's centred in the mind so he's processing it analytically and wants to find rational solutions. However, that's not really what the woman wants. She doesn't want the problem solved. She just wants him to listen. For her, sharing from the heart helps to form bonds and creates relational closeness.

Both women and men need to show patience with each other in this respect. Men need to show patience when the woman's focus on people causes her to talk at great lengths about what Olivia, Sarah and Louise are up to, even though he doesn't know them and has no interest, and wonders why his wife would think he would. Similarly, the woman needs to show patience when the man's focus on things causes him to obsesses about sports statistics, car engines and technological advancements, when she has no interest, and wonders why he thinks she would.

Being heart-centred makes women more empathetic and this helps build her relationships. I was watching a Manchester United podcast recently where two ex-players and one woman were interviewing Patrice Evra, the retired French international left-back who played at the club between 2006-2014. Evra was telling the story of his tough upbringing on the streets of Paris and how some days he was so hungry, he had to beg for food.

He then told the story of how proud he was when aged seventeen, his life changed forever after being chosen to play professionally for a club in Italy. He was given a clean room with a bed all to himself, and on it was laid out a brand new tracksuit and pair of fresh football boots. He said that despite all he went on to achieve as an adult, when he put on that tracksuit and pair of boots for the first time and looked himself in the mirror, it was the proudest moment of his life. He then went to eat a meal at the club with his teammates, and it was the first time in his life he'd ever been served food and seen a meal with two knives and forks on either side of the plate. I was struck that while the two men listened to this story respectfully, the female interviewer had tears streaming down her face. Simply because she could feel his emotions in a way the men couldn't. She could empathise.

This empathy is perhaps also the root of what many would call, "female intuition"–an ability to instinctively feel things about other people without fully understanding in her mind how.

## Predictable Men, Unpredictable Women.

This is where I really begin to get into trouble! Let's look at stability.

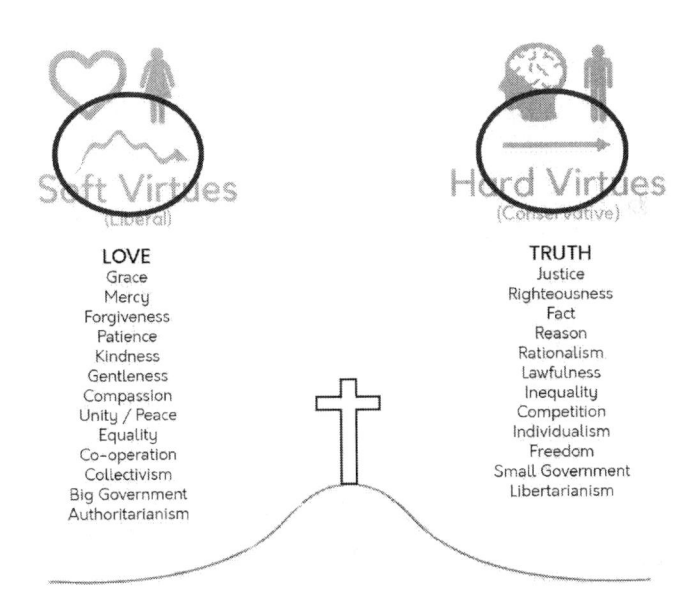

**Soft Virtues**
(Liberal)

**LOVE**
Grace
Mercy
Forgiveness
Patience
Kindness
Gentleness
Compassion
Unity / Peace
Equality
Co-operation
Collectivism
Big Government
Authoritarianism

**Hard Virtues**
(Conservative)

**TRUTH**
Justice
Righteousness
Fact
Reason
Rationalism
Lawfulness
Inequality
Competition
Individualism
Freedom
Small Government
Libertarianism

Because men primarily live from their head and they're on a more even keel, their behaviour tends to be more predictable and

Trench

consistent. When I was at university, I had a part-time job at Costco Wholesale working on the Front-End as a cashier.[5] There was a team of supervisors there who were in charge of the department and they were all female except for one. We used to joke about the stark differences. With the female "sups," you never quite knew which mood they were going to be in from day-to-day. Sometimes they were up and sometimes they were down. With the male "sup" however—Russell was his name—you got the exact same mood every time. That's not to say we liked him any more than the female "sups," but the contrast between them was just so noticeable.

Often women are quite aware that they're subject to fluctuating emotions and this perhaps plays a role in the fact they tend to trust their own judgement less. Women will second-guess their decisions more often, and it's even been noted that in speech, women tend to put question marks at the end of their sentences far more often than men. That's something to look out for if you haven't noticed it already. Even while making apparent statements of fact, women are prone to adding an upward inflection at the end that indicates they're looking for confirmation and affirmation from others.

It's sometimes even true that women don't know their own mind until someone tells it to them. I heard the story recently of how Mary Berry, the famous TV chef, got married. It was the 1960s and her boyfriend Paul, proposed. She wasn't sure about it and said "no." Paul persisted and asked again, but she was still in two minds and said, "no." Finally, Paul said, "look, I'm getting too old so this is the last time I'll ask. If you say no again, I'll have to walk away." Mary said yes to the third proposal and over fifty years later, they've had the happiest of marriages with many children and grandchildren. These stories are very common, especially from that era. Stories of how a man was single-minded in his pursuit of a woman who didn't yet know her own thoughts for certain, but could potentially be persuaded. And now decades later, they're still happily married.

You rarely hear these stories with the roles reversed though. Men are not as easily persuadable because they tend to have reasoned things out in their mind already and trust their judgement more. Which means they're more unyielding and you could even say stubborn once they've settled upon a course of action.

Remember how Le Febvre and Franke's 2013 study said that Liberals score more highly in the trait of dependence? Meaning those who centre on the *Soft Virtues* look for more guidance and leadership? And remember how Conservatives are more likely to act independently and take individual responsibility on their shoulders? Well, this is traditionally why women who embody the *Soft Virtues* have wanted strong male leadership from their husbands. Women are naturally more dependent and look for a man who can give a sense of stability and security—a man who knows what he's doing in life—who is clear-minded and decisive about the way forward. Women look for this in men because they don't always feel it in themselves, and good men generally want to provide this for women. They want to take that responsibility of leadership upon their shoulders. (It's always why feminists make a big deal of being independent and not needing men, because they don't like this norm.)

Of course, natural female empathy which can be a strength in many ways for forming relationships, also has a downside when it comes to leadership, in the sense that it makes them more susceptible to emotional manipulation. Once a man has decided upon a course of action, tears are unlikely to persuade him to change his mind. A woman finds it much harder to persist with her decision however, if she sees it's going to make people upset.

## Competitive Men, Co-operative Women.

Let's keep moving down the columns and talk about how the female emphasis on *Love* makes her prioritise co-operation, while the male emphasis on *Truth* makes him prioritise competition. For brevity, I'll just group the rest of the values together here and make some general observations.

Soft Virtues
(Liberal)

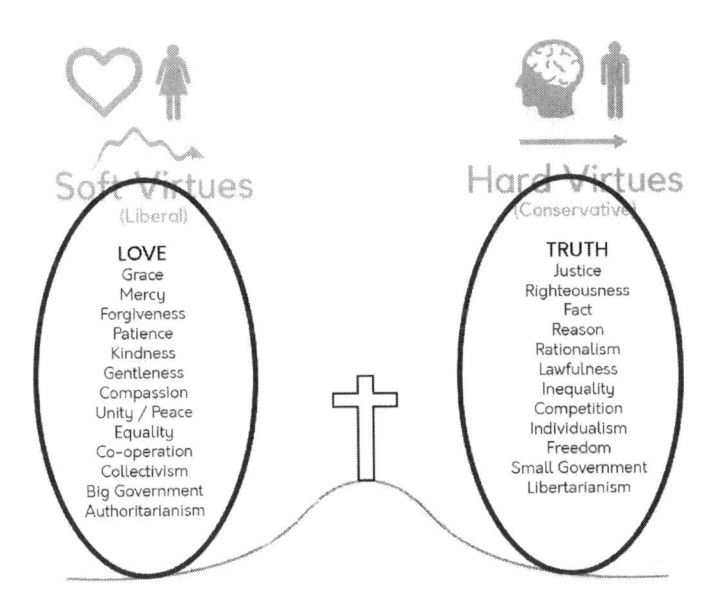

**LOVE**
Grace
Mercy
Forgiveness
Patience
Kindness
Gentleness
Compassion
Unity / Peace
Equality
Co-operation
Collectivism
Big Government
Authoritarianism

Hard Virtues
(Conservative)

**TRUTH**
Justice
Righteousness
Fact
Reason
Rationalism
Lawfulness
Inequality
Competition
Individualism
Freedom
Small Government
Libertarianism

When young boys are left alone to play games, they will tend to gravitate towards competitive ones with winners and losers, and clearly defined set of rules. When girls are left alone to play games on the other hand, they will tend to gravitate towards co-operative ones where the aim is not to win, but rather to strengthen relationships, and where rules are less important.

Every summer when I was a child, tennis fever would descend on the nation during Wimbledon fortnight. In June or July, all the kids in my town would be grabbing racquets and heading out to knock a ball around. I remember going out to play tennis with my sister one summer and being frustrated because she only ever wanted to "play rallies." That is, work together to keep the ball going back and forth for as long as possible without hitting the net. She didn't want to keep score, she wasn't interested in creating a winner or loser, and she wasn't much interested in rules. For example, if the ball landed outside of the boundary line, it didn't matter to her. She just wanted to keep the ball going. She just wanted to co-operate. As a boy, I didn't understand this. Nobody wins? What's the point in this? I remember imploring her just to play one competitive set.

I liked playing tennis with my best friend, Brendan though. With him, things got competitive. We would play regulation rules and if there was any dispute about line calls, the whole match would have to stop until we resolved it. That we were playing fair with each other–that *Justice* was done–was very important. Also, at the end of the day one us would win, and the other would lose. We didn't mind if that created inequality and if one of us felt bad about it. It just made us more determined to win the next one.

Back in my childhood, I also remember watching girls playing co-operative skipping games while chanting in unison. I remember they used to do a hand-patting game that I later discovered was called "Pat-A-Cake." The aim was to mirror each other's movements and chant a rhyme together. I remember they used to like taking care of dolls and play fantasy games around inviting friends for tea or getting married. As they grew a little bit older, I remember they would sit in huddles simply having conversations–often about boys and relationships. And they began to mirror each other in their clothes too. It seemed that once one girl wore something to school, the others would soon appear wearing the same item. Girls instinctive play behaviour was centred around mirroring each other, creating unity, forming bonds, and being relational.

I remember being genuinely baffled about the appeal of Pat-a-Cake in particular. Why are they patting their hands together? What's the purpose? At the same age, my friends would be trying to beat one another at football, in video games, racing bikes, or even just fighting! I remember being at Brendan's house having just watched wrestling on TV, and deciding to try "Figure of Four" moves on each other. The idea is that if you inflict a Figure of Four on your opponent they experience pain, but it's possible for them to flip-reverse it, and if they manage, the pain transfers back to you. We would spend ages trying to outmuscle one another to flip each other over.

I also remember cycling along the street with friends in those days and suddenly a race to the next lamppost would be announced. Boys are always testing themselves against each other and that's where the fun lies. I remember being at Brendan's eating crisps and drinking juice and him suddenly deciding upon a game where we had to throw a crisp into each other's glass from across the table. The loser had to eat the soggy crisp. When it happened, we couldn't stop laughing. And I have to keep emphasising the importance of *Justice* to boys too. I well remember when boys were arguing about whether someone had broken a law of the game, nearby girls would get upset about the conflict: *"What does it matter! It's only a game!"* In other words, *"who cares if that person bent the rules a little bit. Let's just all get along!"* This doesn't compute with a boy. Of course it matters! If we don't settle this, then we won't know who has won and who has lost. That's the point of playing!

In adulthood, neither men or women deviate much from these early behaviours. Men can obsess about sporting decisions

Trench

for years, and argue with each other all night about whether a player's foot was over the line, and whether a referee made the right call. And while they're doing that, women are still more keen to watch TV shows that centre on relationships, or be on the phone to a friend, or planning a social gathering.

We'll return to this subject later in the book, but for now I just needed to broadly establish the femininity of the *Soft Virtues* and the masculinity of the *Hard Virtues*. These are generalisations, and not every man or woman is going to fit the mould presented here. However, I hope we can see there's an essential truth to all this. If we do, it's going to help us immensely going forward.

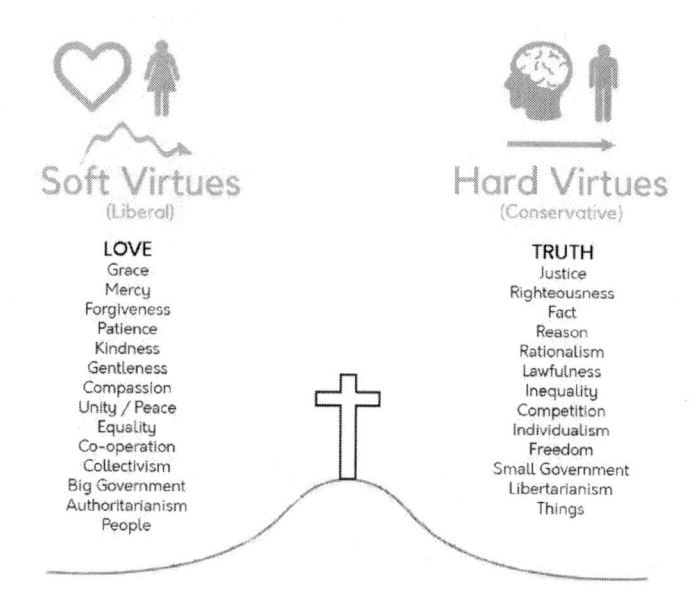

## Soft Virtues
(Liberal)

LOVE
Grace
Mercy
Forgiveness
Patience
Kindness
Gentleness
Compassion
Unity / Peace
Equality
Co-operation
Collectivism
Big Government
Authoritarianism
People

## Hard Virtues
(Conservative)

TRUTH
Justice
Righteousness
Fact
Reason
Rationalism
Lawfulness
Inequality
Competition
Individualism
Freedom
Small Government
Libertarianism
Things

NB: As well adding the female and male stick figures, I've now added "People" to the Soft side and "Things" to the Hard side.

# 13
# Disconnected.

There is one final point I want to emphasise about the *Hard* and *Soft Virtues*, and how they interplay with one another, before we move forward to the next section. It's a point I've made already but I need to make it clear in our minds before we proceed.

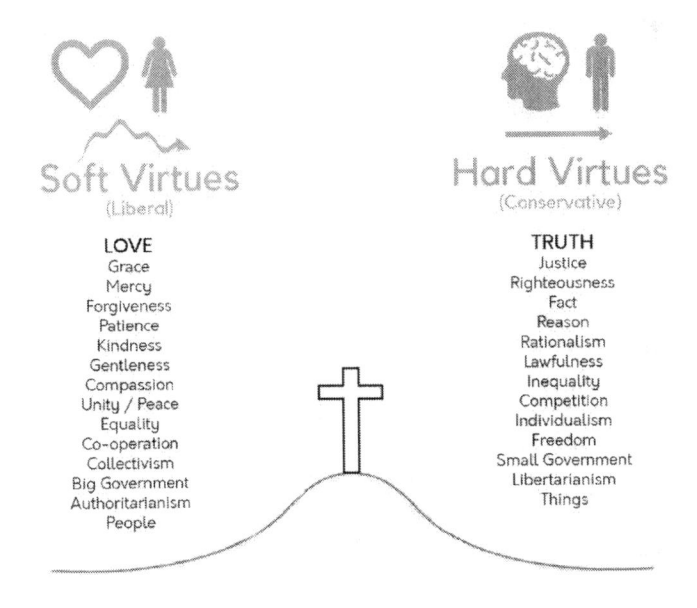

## Soft Virtues
(Liberal)

**LOVE**
Grace
Mercy
Forgiveness
Patience
Kindness
Gentleness
Compassion
Unity / Peace
Equality
Co-operation
Collectivism
Big Government
Authoritarianism
People

## Hard Virtues
(Conservative)

**TRUTH**
Justice
Righteousness
Fact
Reason
Rationalism
Lawfulness
Inequality
Competition
Individualism
Freedom
Small Government
Libertarianism
Things

It's difficult to say succinctly but let's try it like this:

*Love* without *Truth* ceases to be *Love*.
*Righteousness* without *Grace* ceases to be *Righteousness*.

In other words, a virtue from one side divorced from the values of the opposing side turns that value into a vice. It stops being the thing you were aiming for. I might be able to explain this using a couple of examples.

## Love Without Truth Is Unloving.

Imagine a man is on the way to jump off a bridge because he believes he's a bird and he wants to fly south to Africa for the winter. Now, let's say the man meets a Liberal along the way and he tells the Liberal about his plans. Since the Liberal only believes in the *Soft Virtues*, he can only respond to this man using a limited set of tools. These tools are things like *Love, Grace, Kindness,* and *Gentleness.*

The Liberal may therefore think, *"I want to love this person. I want to be kind and gentle. I don't want to hurt his feelings by telling him the Hard Truth that he's not a bird. That would upset him. It may cause conflict."* So the Liberal replies to the man, *"Of course you're a bird, and of course you can fly. You're the best bird I've ever seen. I just want you to know that I love you, and support you. I affirm you, and accept you as you are."* The Liberal then walks off feeling rather pleased with himself at his kindness.

But has he really been kind? Not really. Because the man then jumps off the nearby bridge and dies. Because he's not a bird. He's a man. He really needed someone to tell him the *Hard Truth* that men can't fly before he killed himself. Sure, it would have been uncompromising, hurt the man's feelings and caused some momentary conflict, but ultimately it would have saved his life. So you see, *Love* without *Truth* ultimately becomes unloving. At some point, if you really love someone and want the best for them, you've got to speak plainly.

I'll give another example from real life. At the moment, England has an obesity problem where 28% of the nation are considered dangerously fat.[1] Now we know that obesity causes many serious health conditions such as diabetes, heart disease, strokes, some types of cancer, and that it undoubtedly diminishes the quality and length of a human life. And the problem is exacerbated by the fact that many obese people are in denial and don't realise just how overweight they've become.

Now traditionally, if someone went to a doctor with an obesity related health complaint, the doctor would speak plainly and tell them their weight was the problem. In recent years however, there have been a rise in complaints to the NHS from some of these patients who felt "fat-shamed" by their doctor. In other words, it had hurt their feelings to hear the *Hard Truth*.

In response, doctors were issued with a new piece of instruction to be more "loving" and "kind" with their patients going forward. This essentially meant to avoid giving the *Hard Truth*. *"Don't tell them they're fat. Don't use that word. Try and be more loving."*

But is it really loving to avoid speaking plainly? If a doctor says to a morbidly obese patient, *"Your weight is fine! I just want to love you, and support you, and affirm you are you are. You are big and beautiful and don't let anyone tell you otherwise!"* What happens? Well, the obese person leaves the doctor's office feeling a false sense of security. Their health problems are going to deteriorate, they'll get diseases like diabetes, heart disease, cancer, or have a stroke, and they'll live diminished and shortened lives. Simply because nobody gave it to them straight. *Love* without *Truth* ceases to be loving. This is why Tam Fry of the National Obesity Forum, after hearing about these plans for NHS doctors to go more softly said, *"A lot of people are in denial about their weight and doctors should not shy away from telling them home truths."*

There are a hundred examples we could think of. If you have a child who gets involved with cigarettes, drugs, or gangs, is it more loving to gently affirm these choices or is it more loving to speak some *Hard Truths*? If that child is insolent and rude in their behaviour towards others, is it more loving to kindly pat them on the head, or is it more loving to break out the hard-edge of discipline so they learn to treat people with respect? The Bible famously says, *"Those who spare the rod of discipline hate their children." (Proverbs 13:24)* Refusing to break out the hard-edge isn't loving in the end—it's *hateful*. You have to hate a person to have a *Truth* that could improve or save their life and not share it.

## Righteousness Without Love Isn't Righteousness.

Meanwhile, the reverse is also true. The *Hard Virtues* you aim for cease to be virtuous if you detach them from the *Soft*. For example, *Righteousness* divorced from *Love* stops being *Righteous*. Jesus often had to deal with this problem in his time on earth. There were a group of zealots in his day called the Pharisees who believed themselves to be particularly righteous. They observed moral laws meticulously and believed in severe punishment for those who didn't.

Now one of these laws stated that no work should be done on the Sabbath. The Sabbath was designated by God to be a day of rest. But being particularly righteous, the Pharisees went hard in observing this law. In fact, in the passing of time, they kept evolving it to make it more restrictive and turned it into something unloving and cold–something it was never meant to be. Mark's Gospel records this story: *"Jesus went into the synagogue again and noticed a man with a deformed hand. Since it was the Sabbath, Jesus' enemies watched him closely. If he healed the man's hand, they planned to accuse him of working on the Sabbath.*

*Jesus said to the man with the deformed hand, "Come and stand in front of everyone." Then he turned to his critics and asked, "Does the law permit good deeds on the Sabbath, or is it a day for doing evil? Is this a day to save life or to destroy it?" But they wouldn't answer him.*

*He looked around at them angrily and was deeply saddened by their hard hearts. Then he said to the man, "Hold out your hand." So the man held out his hand, and it was restored! At once the Pharisees went away and met with the supporters of Herod to plot how to kill Jesus.'* (Mark 3:1-6)

Jesus wanted to compassionately heal this man's deformed hand, but because it was happening on the Sabbath and therefore breaking the rules, the Pharisees wanted to kill him. You see how imbalanced they had become? In their pursuit of *Righteousness* they had forgotten *Love*, and so actually became unrighteous.

In a similar episode, *"Jesus was walking through some grainfields on the Sabbath. His disciples were hungry, so they began breaking off some heads of grain and eating them. But some Pharisees saw them do it and protested, "Look, your disciples are breaking the law by harvesting grain on the Sabbath."* (Matthew 12:1-2) It's the same problem. In their determination to keep rules, the Pharisees would rather people go hungry. In their singular pursuit of *Righteousness*, they had forgotten *Love* and so become unrighteous.

That's all I wanted to clarify in this chapter before we move onto the next section, and it only confirms something I've been saying since the start–that in order to be considered good, we need to retain a respect for both the *Hard* and *Soft Virtues*. One virtue monomaniacally pursued to the point it divorces from the other side turns that virtue into a vice. It leads to corruption and evil, and it ceases to be the thing you were aiming for.

This is why the Bible says, *"Instead, we will speak the **Truth** in **Love**, growing in every way more and more like Christ, who is the head of his body, the church."* (Ephesians 4:15)(capitalisation and emphasis added) To be like Christ, we must blend *Truth* and *Love*.

And with that, we can now move on to Section Two. Hopefully at the end of this first section, the basics of the "*Trench Theory*" have now been established in your mind and has given insight into how all the values on each side are connected. For example, once you make *Love* the most important virtue, that necessarily leads to *Compassion*, and a desire for *Unity*, which leads to a focus on *Equality* and *Co-operation*, which leads to *Collectivism*, which leads to *Big Government*...and so on. Once you decide upon one value, that necessarily introduces the rest. And the same is true on the *Hard* side.

Now from here, the next step is to discover how this "*Trench Theory*" makes sense of world history, and more importantly, the society we live in today.

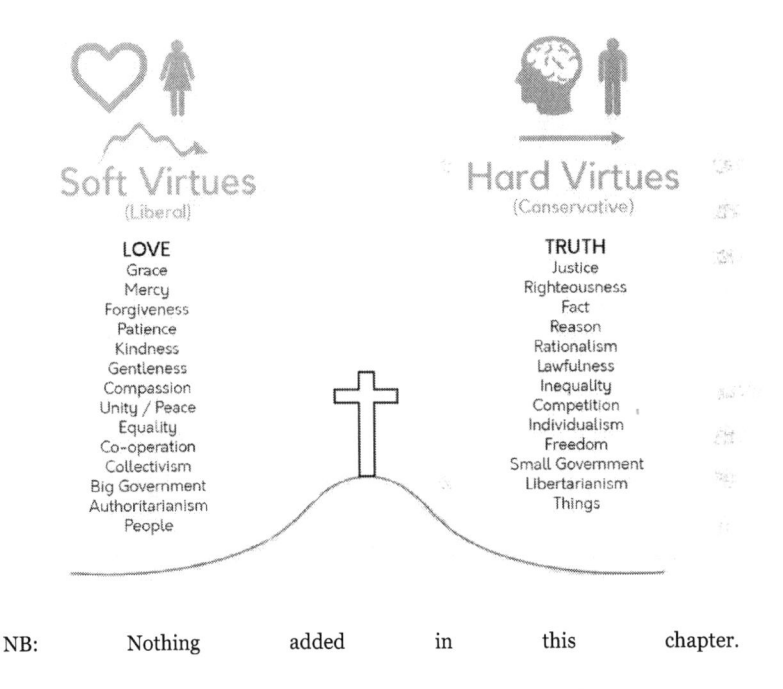

## Soft Virtues
(Liberal)

**LOVE**
Grace
Mercy
Forgiveness
Patience
Kindness
Gentleness
Compassion
Unity / Peace
Equality
Co-operation
Collectivism
Big Government
Authoritarianism
People

## Hard Virtues
(Conservative)

**TRUTH**
Justice
Righteousness
Fact
Reason
Rationalism
Lawfulness
Inequality
Competition
Individualism
Freedom
Small Government
Libertarianism
Things

NB: Nothing added in this chapter.

# Section Two.
## THE AGES

# 1
# Three Ages.

I'm going to start this section by saying we can very broadly divide the past two millennia of Western Civilisation into three eras.

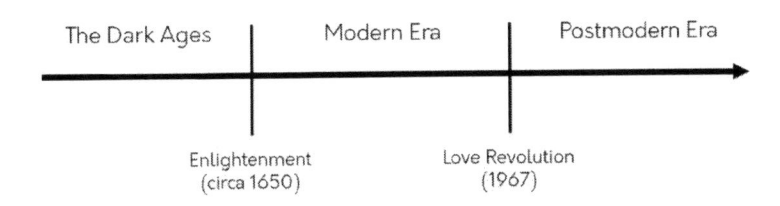

```
The Dark Ages    |    Modern Era    |    Postmodern Era
─────────────────┼──────────────────┼──────────────────▶
                 |                  |
            Enlightenment       Love Revolution
            (circa 1650)           (1967)
```

We are currently living in the **Postmodern Era** which began with a cultural revolution in 1967. For the purposes of this book, I'm going to call that the *"Love Revolution"*.

Before this, there was the **Modern Era**. It too began with something of a revolution—a 17th Century intellectual movement called *"The Enlightenment"*.

Before that, there had been **The Dark Ages.**[1]

Now as we proceed, it's important to remember that a new era always comes into existence in *reaction* to the one that went before. The Postmodern Era is a reaction against the Modern Era, and that in turn had been a reaction against The Dark Ages.

We're not going to spend too much time in The Dark Ages as they're not particularly important to this book, but we'll start the journey there to give us some context.

# 2

# From Darkness to Light.

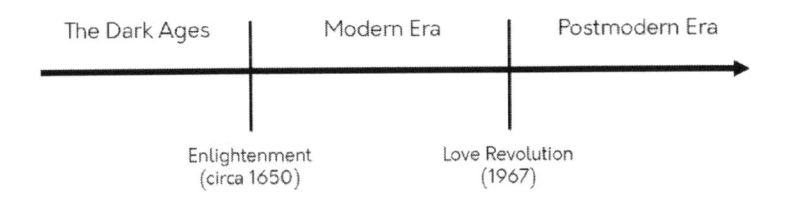

```
The Dark Ages      |     Modern Era      |      Postmodern Era
───────────────────┼─────────────────────┼─────────────────────▶
                   |                     |
              Enlightenment         Love Revolution
              (circa 1650)             (1967)
```

*"The Dark Ages"* refers to a period between 476AD and 1000AD and it was largely characterised in Europe by intellectual ignorance. Indeed, the *"Dark"* in *"Dark Ages"* refers to a darkness of the mind.

There was little scientific or cultural advancement during these centuries. The printing press hadn't been invented yet so books were not widely available. The vast majority of people couldn't read or write. Most didn't receive any formal education at all. As such, the masses were reliant on a select few at the top of society–those who could read and write–to hand down information. What's more, since the general population had no way of independently verifying the information they were given, they had to accept everything on blind faith.

Within this vacuum of ignorance, religious leaders became extremely important gatekeepers of knowledge. The Roman Catholic Church was the dominant religious organisation in Europe in those days, and the Pope was considered to be the mouthpiece of God on Earth. The priests who worked within the organisation were some of the very few in society who had received a formal education. Not only could they read and write both in English and Latin, but they also had the luxury of access to books. Therefore, whatever the priests taught the people was taken as gospel truth, and whatever the Pope decreed went largely unchallenged. In fact, so powerful was the Catholic Church in those days that even the Kings and Queens of Europe bowed the knee to the Pope. Kings and Queens may have reigned over temporal kingdoms, but the Pope was the gatekeeper of an eternal one. He imposed his will on monarchs by explaining that if they displeased him, he would excommunicate them from the church, thus effectively banishing them from heaven, and denying them eternal life.

The Catholic clergy quickly became corrupted by this unfettered power, and as *The Dark Ages* developed, the priests realised that they could use the people's ignorance to their advantage. Indeed, they could tell the masses almost anything and have it be believed. Therefore, they began twisting the truth for their own selfish ends. For example, they told people that forgiveness of sins could be bought with money. Johann Tetzel, a Roman Catholic friar said, *"As soon as a coin in the coffer rings, the soul from purgatory springs."*[1] Purgatory was an invention of Catholicism with no Biblical origin that said imperfect dead souls would stay in limbo somewhere between heaven and hell until the priests were given money. Only after this payment would he say a few magic words that would open up the gate to eternal life. None of this has any Biblical foundation of course, but without a means of fact-checking, it became a very profitable racket for the priests. The population would hand over huge sums of money in the hope it would smooth a dead relative's, or indeed their own, path to heaven. The Catholic church soon became exceedingly rich by such deceptions and the clergy realised that *"scientia sit potentia"*–knowledge is power. If they controlled what people knew, they controlled what people did. The populace could be bent to their will.

Now into this vacuum of ignorance, you can imagine that many other fanciful ideas took root. Superstitions were rife. There was a lot of mysticism and quackery, especially in the medical field. Tall stories abounded. Fear controlled. That's often what *The Dark Ages* became known for. It wasn't all bad, of course, and there was some beauty in the era too, but whichever social problems they had–whether it be poverty, bad hygiene, disease, violence, corruption or inequality–they largely stemmed from a lack of understanding. Indeed, life in those times tended to be short and relatively unpleasant. During this period in Europe, the average life expectancy was only around 30-35 years.[2]

## The Enlightenment.

But then gradually, came the Enlightenment. I say "gradually" because although the Enlightenment happened quite specifically in the middle of the 17th Century, the event that made it possible–
inevitable even–actually happened around 200 years before.

It was the invention of the printing press. From that moment in 1436, literacy levels began accelerating in Europe–

doubling on average every century—and the cost of sharing information through books and pamphlets began falling rapidly. This meant that where knowledge had once been concentrated in the hands of a few gatekeepers at the top of society, it was now quickly becoming democratised. Soon, the majority would read and write; soon, the majority would have first-hand access to books; soon, they would be able to share ideas, and think, and understand for themselves. This led to a period called The Renaissance where people began taking a renewed interest in intellectual pursuits. And as time progressed, this interest in philosophy, art and literature created huge rewards for society.

It was bad news for the Roman Catholic church though, of course. They who had held so much power as the controllers of information were not excited about this development at all. They knew that once people had independent means to learn, they would become less dependent on the clergy and their power and wealth would subsequently diminish. They were especially nervous about what would happen when people read the Bible in their own language. Centuries of Catholic lies and corruption would then be exposed. Purgatory? The people would discover it's not in there. Paying money for salvation? They would find the Bible specifically denouncing the idea: *"May your money be destroyed with you for thinking God's gift can be bought!"* (Acts 8:20)

The Catholic church did everything they could to stop their corruption being laid bare. They opposed the printing of the Bible in English and they hunted down those responsible for translating and smuggling it into the country. They burned the Bibles they discovered and anyone found reading one was killed.

However, it was no use. They couldn't hold back the tide of progress. By 1517, there were enough copies and enough literate people that could now read the Bible for the Reformation to happen. This was the moment when hordes of people, aghast at how they had been duped, rebelled against the Catholic system. Access to the truth had set them free from this corruption.

All this set the stage for the Enlightenment. By the 1600s, a highly educated intellectual class had emerged in Europe and they were wondering what other benefits may come from the pursuit of truth. What other tyrannies and corruptions might be exposed? What other misconceptions was mankind living under? What other kinds of progress could be made? The pursuit of truth may still yet reap many more rewards. Indeed, since ignorance had been the primary cause of so many of the problems in *The Dark Ages*, surely pursuit of truth would be the cure? As truth spread throughout society, enlightening all our minds, the intellectual classes believed lies, superstitions, quackery and mysticism would disappear forever. The mind of humanity would be liberated by knowledge and the end result of this enlightenment may even perhaps be a perfect world–a sort of Utopia.

So this became the primary goal of the Enlightenment– to pursue knowledge. Fact. Truth. Reason. These were the only things that mattered now. Indeed, the time became known as "*The Age of Reason*." And for many Enlightenment thinkers, pursuing these things meant going further than merely abandoning the Catholic system–it meant abandoning Christianity entirely.

To them, there was no argument that the Bible contained a great deal of moral truth which they liked. But by the same token, the Bible contained talk of the supernatural. Angels. Demons. Healings. Miracles. These were the sorts of things they associated with the Catholic church in the bad old days. And furthermore, belief in those things required faith. They didn't want faith anymore–when they'd taken things on faith in the Dark Ages, they had been duped and taken for fools. They wanted to get away from all that now. What they wanted in the *Age of Reason* was hard, solid, rational, empirically verifiable facts. That's all. They wanted things that could be seen, touched, tasted, felt and processed through the powers of the mind.

In a sense, the mind became deified in the *Age of Reason*. The mind was the arbiter of all truth. The final word on reality. The French philosopher Rene Descartes famously said in 1637, "*Cogito Ergo Sum,*" or in English, "*I think, therefore I am.*" This sentence summed up the Enlightenment philosophy. It is man's ability to reason that assures him of his own existence and therefore it is his ability to reason about the world around him that assures him of its existence too. Something is real as soon as you can *reason* that it exists. If something cannot be explained by reason alone, then it doesn't exist and should be thrown out.

Can we know that fairies exist by reason alone? No? Then we don't accept the existence of fairies. Can we reason that ghosts exist by science alone? No? Then we don't accept the existence of ghosts. Can we know that angels exist by science alone? No? Then we don't accept the existence of angels. That's the idea. We only accept what the rational mind can understand.

Obviously, God himself is not fully comprehendible to the human mind and is not observable through science alone, so the growing inclination of the Enlightenment thinker was to reject his existence entirely. However, there was a snag. They couldn't do it. They still needed God. Because without God, they had no rational explanation for how the universe could have come into being in the first place. If God didn't create all this, how on earth did we get here? Charles Darwin's Theory of Evolution was still a century or two away, and even that wouldn't be able to provide an answer to this question, so they needed some kind of logical explanation. As they looked for a compromise between faith and rationalism in those days, they settled on a blended idea called Deism.

Deism said that a god of some kind clearly made the universe in the first instance, but since the Enlightenment thinkers didn't want to have to deal with a supernatural being, they proposed that he played no further active role. Therefore, there are no supernatural activities in this world–no answered prayers, miracles, prophecies or healings, and no supernatural agents like angels or demons either. Instead, their view was that God was perhaps like a watchmaker. He created the thing, wound it up, and then left it alone to run its course. That seemed a decent compromise for the Enlightenment mind. Acknowledging God meant they had an explanation for the origin of the universe–the First Cause–but it also meant you didn't have to deal with him in a personal or supernatural sense. You could essentially now do away with active faith. There was no use trying to reach out to him with prayer because he wouldn't respond. Instead, the Enlightenment mission was simply to focus efforts on attaining knowledge of what God had made–his material world. They would learn about him through his creation. Therefore, what they needed most of all, they decided, was *science*.

There was an excitement about all this. A sense of adventure. Who knew what wonderful advancements would lie ahead as they began unlocking the secrets of the universe? As they journeyed from the darkness of ignorance to the light of knowledge, the future seemed bright! They would gradually unlock all the secrets of nature until a perfect understanding of all things was achieved. When they reached full enlightenment, then Utopia would come.

## The Utopian Dream.

It makes a certain amount of sense. Once they knew everything about anatomy, hygiene, and biology, surely they could create a society of perfect health. No longer would people live to the mere age of 35, but for much longer. Maybe even forever? Once they knew everything about psychology and sociology, surely they could create a perfect form of government and all oppression and tyranny would cease. Once they knew everything about chemistry, they could devise everlasting forms of energy. Once they knew everything about economics, they could devise a perfect financial system. All that was required was truth. Knowledge. Facts. Science. Reason.

So that's what the Modern Era became defined by–the pursuit of knowledge. And over the next few centuries, there was indeed an explosion of scientific and technological advancement.

There were huge leaps forward in mathematics, physics, biology, and astronomy to name just a few disciplines.

It was the age of discovery too. Famous explorers, inspired by the spirit of the times, traversed the planet in the quest for knowledge and answers. They found new materials and uncovered unknown civilisations. There was a romanticism in it. Young kids dreamed about becoming explorers who would spend their lives mapping the world, charting new animal species and meeting lost tribes with hidden secrets. And every time a mystery was unlocked and brought within the comprehension of the human mind, the impossible began to seem possible.

By the time the 19th Century had given way to the 20th, the progress had been truly astonishing. The Industrial Revolution after 1760 in particular, had caused a sudden surge in our technological evolution. The truth uncovered in these times meant we could now build vast bridges over previously impassable bodies of water. At first trains, and then eventually cars, enabled us to travel previously unfathomable distances in much shorter times. We could fly in airplanes! We could literally fly. It was astonishing. Uninhabitable deserts suddenly sprang to life by the building of giant dams that could stop mighty rivers in their tracks. We could now harness their power to supply power and water to whole cities. We built skyscrapers that touched the clouds and we even went into space! I mean...space! And this was just the beginning! Who knew what else we could achieve as our knowledge grew. We were becoming masters of the universe.

The science-fiction writers of the Modern Era had a great time imagining what the future might look like as we evolved with ever better technologies and scientific breakthroughs.

Living in bubble cities under the oceans? Farming on desert land? Colonising new planets in outer space? Flying cars? Robot servants? Time travel? Clean, free, everlasting sources of energy? Immortality? All impossible now perhaps, but not in the future when we have unlocked the secrets of the universe! *Nothing* will be impossible for us then. If we can dream it, we can do it. All we need is The Truth.

Now here's what I want us to notice about all this.

Truth. Reason. Facts. Rationalism. Improvement of the mind. What kind of virtues are these?

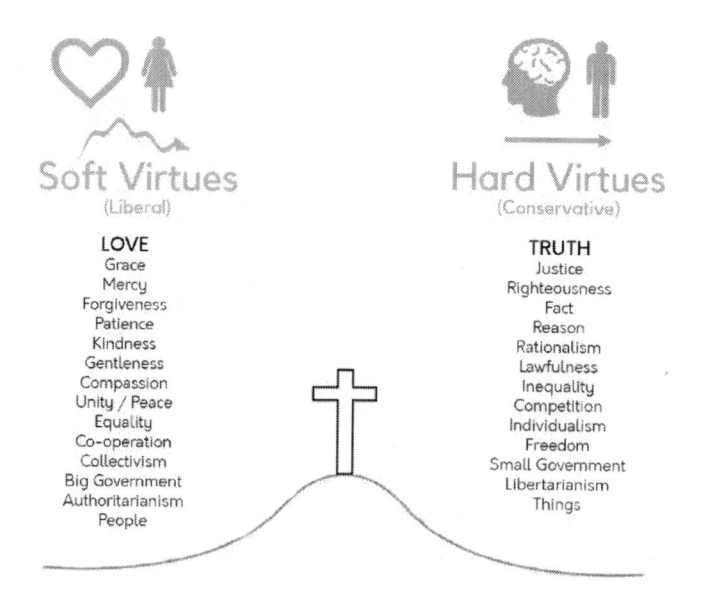

## Soft Virtues
(Liberal)

**LOVE**
Grace
Mercy
Forgiveness
Patience
Kindness
Gentleness
Compassion
Unity / Peace
Equality
Co-operation
Collectivism
Big Government
Authoritarianism
People

## Hard Virtues
(Conservative)

**TRUTH**
Justice
Righteousness
Fact
Reason
Rationalism
Lawfulness
Inequality
Competition
Individualism
Freedom
Small Government
Libertarianism
Things

These are *Hard Virtues*. The Modern Era was created and defined by the pursuit of the *Hard Virtues*.

## From Darkness to Light

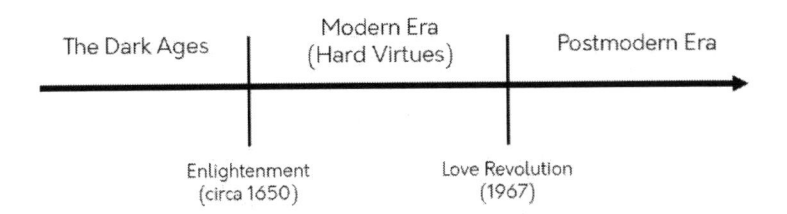

```
The Dark Ages    |    Modern Era      |    Postmodern Era
                 |    (Hard Virtues)  |
─────────────────┼────────────────────┼──────────────────────►
                 |                    |
            Enlightenment         Love Revolution
            (circa 1650)             (1967)
```

# 3

# Faltering Modernity.

Now we know there are benefits to prioritising the *Hard Virtues* and the Modern Era certainly experienced them. By focusing on *Truth*, they began pursuing an inequality of ideas, separating good ideas from bad ones. And through this they grew in knowledge. There was a lot of competition in the free market economy too which meant there were both winners and losers. Therefore, that promoted hard work, discipline, innovation, skill, excellence, imagination, unlocking potential, mental fortitude, humility, resilience and courage. These are all great things.

However, we know that by pursuing these *Hard Virtues*, there are pitfalls involved, especially when they are detached from the *Soft*. For example, we know that *Truth* is exclusive by its nature and to deal in it is to deal in something divisive. Remember Bob at the party making *Truth* claims about illegal immigration and religion? How he was thrown out for offending everyone? This gives us a picture by which to understand what happened in the Modern Era. Yes, we were advancing in knowledge, but at the same time, there was a lot of conflict along the way.

You see, although everyone in those days agreed that pursuit of *Truth* was clearly the answer to society's problems and through it Utopia could be built, people didn't always agree on what the *Truth* actually was. Throughout this period, all kinds of people from different fields of expertise began proposing theories about the *Truth*. And quite simply, these competing theories tended to clash with one another.

It's for this reason that the Modern Age became the age of the "isms". There were at least 234 isms that arose in these centuries—each one claiming to be the lens through which the world could best be understood and the method by which it could best be ordered. We had things like Absolutism, Academicism, Aestheticism, Anarchism, Casualism, Catastrophism, Cosmism, Determinism, Fascism, Nazism, Authoritarianism, Communitarianism, Communism, Pantheism, Republicanism, Syndicalism, Deconstructionism, Determinism, Freudianism, Hegelianism, Logicism, Expansionism, Marxism, Rationalism...and so many more.[1]

Now some of these *Truth* theories were good and some were bad, but the important point here is only that they were *contradictory*. For example, some said the theory of Capitalism represented the best way to model a society's economy, but then followers of Karl Marx later proposed Communism, which said the polar opposite. Both theories claimed to be the *Truth* and because *Truth* claims are exclusive by nature, that led to arguments between Capitalists and Communists. These arguments then spilled over into wars.

Therefore, although the Modern Age pursuit of *Hard Truth* led to incredible technological progress as we have seen, the same pursuit also led to arguments and division. Now again, I must keep repeating that as we saw earlier, division isn't necessarily a bad thing. If, in the process of argument and debate, you are able to divide bad ideas from the good, that's what drives progress. Exclusion isn't necessarily a bad thing if what you're excluding is false. And inequality isn't necessarily a bad thing if you're elevating good theories above bad ones. There's a reason after all, that the heart of free democracies are debating chambers. But again, the point I only want to make here, is that when you deal in *Hard Truth*, there *will* be debates along the way. There will be arguments. There will be conflict. And if you detach entirely from the *Soft Virtues* of *Love* and *Compassion*, you can start to become heartless towards ideological opponents and your arguments can spill over into war.

## Truth Wars.

In the Modern Era then, all this arguing about *Truth* and "isms" did lead to war. And as time passed, the wars tended to become more bloody. You see, with all this technological progress we were making, we could now kill more easily and in greater numbers. Our growing knowledge meant the bows and arrows of *The Dark Ages* had soon given way to guns, then cannons, then machine guns, then tanks and bombs. Indeed, much of our most rapid technological progress in the Modern Era came specifically *because* of wars! We developed new technologies specifically because two sides were in the middle of an argument for ideological supremacy and wanted to develop the means to win it. For example, radar, walkie-talkies, night vision, duct tape, jet engines and satellite navigation were all initially invented for the purpose of war. They were then only repurposed afterwards for peaceful means.[2]

*The Modern Age* then, was even more bloody than *The Dark Ages* had been. Hundreds of millions died in the battle to establish the supremacy of their "isms". And things only seemed to deteriorate as the years passed. By 1914 we had the First World War–a thing of unspeakable horror in which 17 million died and a further 20 million were wounded.[3] And then just a couple of decades later, in 1939, we had the outbreak of the Second World War. That was fuelled by a few particularly nasty 'isms'–namely Fascism, Nazism and Anti-Semitism. Because of these ideologies and the battle to defeat them, between 6-11 million Jews were killed in concentration camps and over 60 million died altogether throughout the course of the war–3% of the entire world population at that time.[4]

The prospects for the future didn't look promising either. By the end of the Second World War, the ideological competition had led the United States to develop and deploy the atomic bomb. It was dropped on Hiroshima, Japan on 6th August, 1945, and in a few seconds, an entire city was flattened. The whole population, numbering around 135,000 was incinerated with one blow. Atomic weaponry had proven extremely effective at winning arguments. But on this trajectory, it was clear that mankind would soon have weapons so destructive, they could potentially annihilate the whole world.

# 4
# Heartless.

As the Modern Era generation pursued *Truth*, they did often seem to be forgetting *Love*. They were becoming smarter, but in the process their hearts seemed to be growing harder.

## Soft Virtues
(Liberal)

**LOVE**
Grace
Mercy
Forgiveness
Patience
Kindness
Gentleness
Compassion
Unity / Peace
Equality
Co-operation
Collectivism
Big Government
Authoritarianism
People

## Hard Virtues
(Conservative)

**TRUTH**
Justice
Righteousness
Fact
Reason
Rationalism
Lawfulness
Inequality
Competition
Individualism
Freedom
Small Government
Libertarianism
Things

Therefore, as European explorers set off across the world to discover new lands, materials and ideas...they discovered them. They came across things like cotton, tea, silk, sugar, salt, spices, dye, and precious metals. Quickly realising their potential, they sought to advance civilisation by utilising these things. They established companies overseas to develop and transport these goods around the world, and to do it as cheaply as possible, they decided to use slave labour.

In stark terms, they would kidnap local people from the African continent in particular, would place them in chains, and force them to work in colonies and plantations, often to the point of death. They were treated as nothing more than cattle–often worse. To transport them from Africa to the Caribbean, up to 450 could be shackled and stowed on tiny shelves in ships.[1] These journeys could take around a month to complete–sometimes more–and during that time they were unable to move much or even go to the bathroom. It was so inhumane that around 15% of slaves consistently didn't even survive the journey. But to the slave traders, they were simply a means to an end. If pursuit of knowledge and progress got us to Utopia faster, and if some slaves had to be used and lost along the way, then it was a price worth paying. It was truly heartless behaviour. For those who survived the journey to the Caribbean, their fate was often even worse–being worked to death in plantations with no rights or dignity afforded to them whatsoever.

The natural world suffered in a similar way from heartlessness. All this pursuit of progress and knowledge meant destroying natural habitats like rivers, forests and oceans. Some animal species became extinct. Some were trophy hunted simply for the sport. Others were stolen from their natural environment and their families to be put in zoos or circuses. Many who did this were motivated by intellectual curiosity to learn more about these animals and yet there was often not much compassion for how they were treated.

I guess the question during the Modern Era became, *"What are we progressing towards here, exactly?"* People were becoming worried. All this emphasis on *Truth* was certainly bringing benefits and expanding our knowledge. Technologically, we were coming forward in leaps and bounds. But in the process, we seemed to be losing our humanity. We were becoming smarter, true. But our hearts were growing colder. We were using our new-found knowledge to enslave and kill each other. We were moving forward in the sciences, but then using that science to drop bigger bombs on each other. We were broadly agreed that *Truth* was the answer, but then we were fighting about what the *Truth* was. We understood more about our world than ever before, but in the process of discovering it, we seemed to be destroying it.

I recently came across a video of children in 1966 being asked what they believed they'd be doing in the year 2000. One encapsulated the times perfectly when he said, *"I'll probably be in spaceships going to the moon dictating to robots...or if something's gone wrong with the nuclear bombs I may be hunting and living in a cave."*[2] In this answer, he references both the pros and cons of modernity. They were becoming smarter yes, but on the other hand, there were growing dangers associated with it that threatened life itself. The next young girl said, *"I don't like the idea of waking up in the morning and eating a cabbage pill for breakfast. I don't think it's going to be so nice. Machines everywhere doing everything for you. You'll get all bored."* Clearly this girl believed that technological progress would one day mean pills replacing real food and robots doing all the work. The next boy said, *"I think all these atomic bombs will be dropping around the place and the whole world will melt, and the world will become one vast atomic explosion, and it will become like a supernova."* There's that fear of atomic warfare again. The next girl said, *"some madman will get the atomic bomb and just blow the world into oblivion."* The next said, *"there's nothing you can do to stop it. More people will get bombs and somebody's going to use it one day."*

By the middle of the 20th Century then, for all the progress, clearly people were beginning to get scared. It didn't seem like pursuit of *Truth* was going to create the Utopia that the Enlightenment thinkers had envisaged at all. Having already endured two world wars between 1914–1918 and 1939-1945, the Korean war between 150-1953, and with the US entering the Vietnam War in 1964, by the time these kids came along in 1966, there didn't seem to be much hope for the future. Indeed, it seemed there was going to be no end to the wards and the destruction. Remarkably, the United States was born right in the middle of the Modern Era in 1776, and had then found itself at war for an astonishing 93% of its entire existence.[3] People began to think there must be a better way than this. They wondered, *"Can we not learn to live in peace? Indeed, is world unity not the most important thing?"*

Enough was enough. No more fighting. No more bickering over *Truth*. No more division over "isms". The world was becoming too heartless and violent. If we didn't put a brake on things now, we may end up blowing the whole thing up. *"What we need,"* people thought, *"is more Love. We need more peace and unity. Love will save the world."* And with that, in 1967, the West suddenly decided it was going to abandon the

Trench

pursuit of the *Hard Virtues*, and it was going to aim only for the *Soft*.

The Enlightenment thinkers had been wrong. *Truth* wasn't all we needed at all; *Love* is all we need. The stage was set for the "*Love Revolution*."

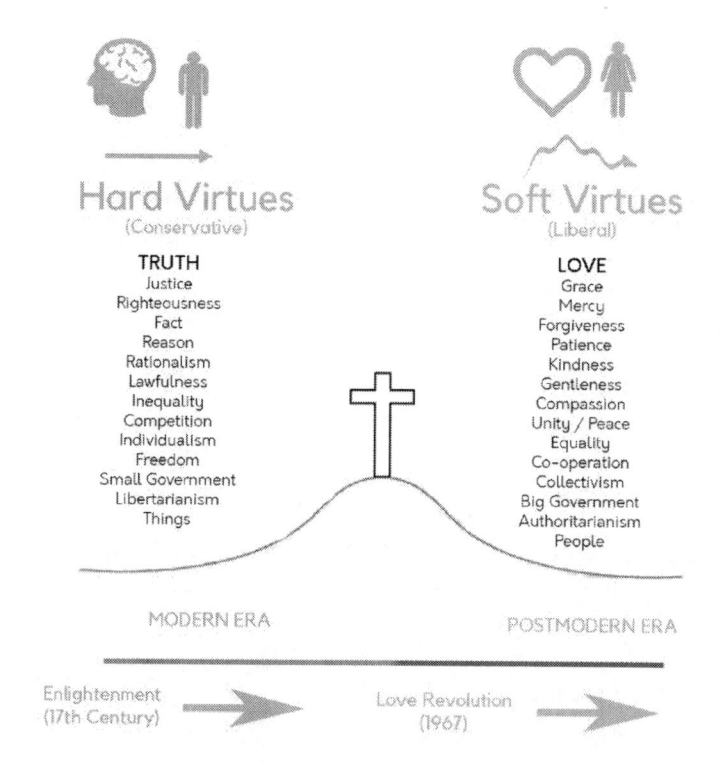

## Hard Virtues
(Conservative)

**TRUTH**
Justice
Righteousness
Fact
Reason
Rationalism
Lawfulness
Inequality
Competition
Individualism
Freedom
Small Government
Libertarianism
Things

MODERN ERA

## Soft Virtues
(Liberal)

**LOVE**
Grace
Mercy
Forgiveness
Patience
Kindness
Gentleness
Compassion
Unity / Peace
Equality
Co-operation
Collectivism
Big Government
Authoritarianism
People

POSTMODERN ERA

Enlightenment (17th Century) → Love Revolution (1967) →

NB: *To keep the diagram as clean as possible, you may notice that I've now flipped the Hard and Soft Virtues. The Hard is now on the left, and the Soft is now on the right. This means that it aligns with the timeline that has now been added at the bottom.*

# 5
# The Love Revolution.

To recap, *The Dark Ages* was characterised by ignorance so the Enlightenment tried to remedy that with *Hard Truth*. The pursuit of *Truth* in the Modern Era brought advantages like intellectual and technological progress, but also problems like division and war. Therefore, the people of the 1960s decided to remedy that problem with *Love*. And it's only once we understand the Postmodern Era is centred on a pursuit of the *Soft Virtues* that it begins to make sense.

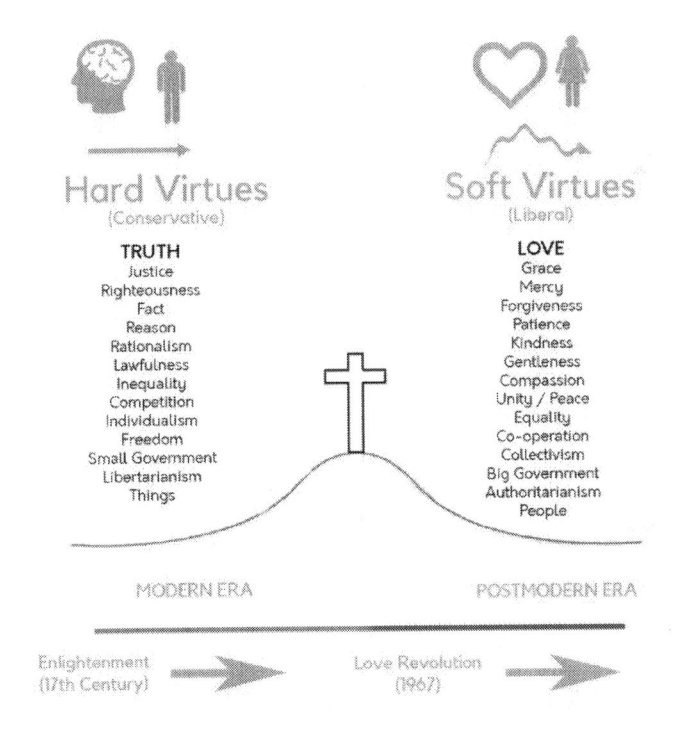

### Hard Virtues
(Conservative)

**TRUTH**
Justice
Righteousness
Fact
Reason
Rationalism
Lawfulness
Inequality
Competition
Individualism
Freedom
Small Government
Libertarianism
Things

### Soft Virtues
(Liberal)

**LOVE**
Grace
Mercy
Forgiveness
Patience
Kindness
Gentleness
Compassion
Unity / Peace
Equality
Co-operation
Collectivism
Big Government
Authoritarianism
People

MODERN ERA — POSTMODERN ERA

Enlightenment (17th Century) → Love Revolution (1967) →

## The Summer of Love.

Those who were there at the dawn of this "New Age" were conscious of the change of focus and it was quite deliberate. The astrologers of the day called it the ending of the *Age of Pisces* and the dawning of the *Age of Aquarius*, and through this revolution the fear of the future seemed to give way to one of hopeful anticipation. I'm going to refer to it in this book as *"The Love Revolution."* It's more commonly known as *"The Summer of Love."* But whatever we call it, that event in 1967 changed the course of Western civilisation. It represented a concerted attempt to rebel against the *Hard Virtues* of the previous generation, and to re-centre the whole of society around the *Soft Virtues* instead. Again, this was specifically because the old way had been causing division, and as people looked ahead, they believed it was beginning to threaten the very existence of life on earth. They began to dream instead of a future defined by *Love, Peace* and *Harmony*. Indeed, the most popular song of 1967 was called *"Age of Aquarius"* and the lyrics boldly declared, *"When the Moon is in the seventh house and Jupiter aligns with Mars then peace will guide the planets and love will steer the stars...this is the dawning of the Age of Aquarius."*[1]

The epicentre of the whole movement was the West Coast of the United States, and more specifically, the Haight-Ashbury district of San Francisco. Around 100,000 people congregated there that summer, and a local newspaper invited crowds from far and wide saying that, *"A new concept of celebrations beneath the human underground must emerge, become conscious, and be shared, so a revolution can be formed with a renaissance of compassion, awareness, and love, and the revelation of unity for all mankind."*[2] It's a rather opaque sentence but it had all the key words that were becoming attractive to that generation–compassion, love, unity. And so they came.

People were also invited through the lyrics of Scott Mckenzie's song, San Francisco, which was released in May 1967. He sang, *"If you're going to San Francisco be sure to wear some flowers in your hair. If you're going to San Francisco, you're going to meet some gentle people there. For those who come to San Francisco, summertime will be a love-in there. In the streets of San Francisco, gentle people with flowers in their hair. All across the nation, such a strange vibration, people in motion. There's a whole generation with a new explanation, people in motion..."*[3]

The movement did indeed then spread across the nation to New York City on the opposite coast, and then beyond to London, England. The people who participated became known as "hippies" and the word just meant something like, *"someone who is fully up-to-date."*[4] In other words, someone who had fully embraced the new set of values that would rule the New Age. They were also sometimes also referred to as "flower children" because of the propensity for wearing flowers in their hair and they talked about little else than "peace" and "love," to the point they became almost caricatures.

## The Role of New Media.

In the same way that the invention of the printing press had played an indispensable role in making the Enlightenment possible, fuelling literacy and allowing the spread of ideas, the invention of new forms of media did the same thing to spread the ideas of the Love Revolution. Commercial radio had become a mature medium by the 1960s, as had vinyl records and cinema, while television was beginning to become popular and affordable too. This meant that the New Age message could be spread around the world very easily–far more easily than ever before. A word spoken on one side of the planet could very quickly be heard millions on the other. And it was through these mediums, as well the older types of print media such as newspapers, books and magazines, that Western civilisation developed its shared concept of what must happen to build Utopia.

And what must happen? Well of course, that old divider, *Truth* must be banished immediately–even the very idea of it. From now on, nothing can really be known. Nothing is true. Nothing is real. In the February of 1967, The Beatles had already released "Strawberry Fields Forever," in which they sang, *"Nothing is real. And nothing to get hung about."* If there's nothing objectively true then there's nothing to get worked up about, or indeed fight about. Which means, peace and love will prevail. These words travelled around the world on vinyl records and through radio transmitters and were imbibed by millions of teenagers everywhere. Nothing is real. Nothing is true. Strawberry Fields Forever.

During the Summer of Love proper, on June 25th, 1967, the world's very first live, international satellite television broadcast occurred. The program was called "Our World", and various countries were asked to contribute something from their culture to the show. It would be beamed live to 24 nations simultaneously and reach between 400-700 million people. Nothing like this had ever been possible before. The British contribution was offered by The Beatles, who were the biggest cultural phenomenon of the day. They closed the broadcast with a live performance of "All You Need Is Love". The lyrics stated that nothing really matters except that we love one another. Love is all we need. Hundreds of millions of people watched and imbibed this message simultaneously. Nothing matters but love. Love is all we need. All we need is love.

Bob Dylan was another influential artist of the period who heralded the New Age. He sang, *"Come mothers and fathers throughout the land, and don't criticise what you can't understand. Your sons and your daughters are beyond your command; your old road is rapidly aging. Please get out of the new one if you can't lend a hand, for the times they are a changin'"*[5] Dylan spoke on behalf of the "Love Generation" when he told their parents, *"Your values are becoming obsolete. In the coming New Age, we are creating a world centred around love, and if you won't be a part of it, and if you can't lend a hand, get out of the way and be left behind. We, the youth of today, are beyond your command, know better than you, and have found the answer!"* Hundreds of millions of people imbibed this message around the world. The New Age is coming. Be a part of it or get out of the way and be left behind. The times are a-changin'.

The rebellion against *Truth* meant there was even a brief dalliance in this period with rejecting formal education altogether. It was considered by many hippies to be unnecessary and even counter-productive to the world they were trying to build. Timothy Leary was an American psychologist who was a thought-leader of the movement and he coined the phrase, "turn on, tune in, drop out." Dropping out of school became popular among high-school and college kids that summer, as they sought to reject conventional education with its hard, divisive, restrictive facts. Instead they tried to pursue a more "free" and "open-minded" avenue. Many of these hippies later became parents and chose not to set any boundaries with their own kids at all, preferring to let them run "wild and free." Certainly, there was a rejection of the sciences with all its hard edges. Instead, people of the time began to gravitate towards creative pursuits like poetry, music and art, because these are subjects with no right or wrong answers.

As far as religion went, the spirit of the age said that all religions were equal and nothing was really true. *"Let's all just be nice to each other...peace and love man."* New Age religion centred around blending philosophies together—a bit of Hinduism, a dash of Buddhism, a shake of Islam perhaps. Whatever you wanted. Eastern religions were especially embraced because they were believed to be centred on peace and love, and though each person concocted a different blend, and though these blends were internally contradictory, and contradictory of each other, in the end, it didn't really matter.

And finally of course, the New Age meant rebelling against *Hard Righteousness*. It hurt feelings when people were told they had sinned against God and his moral law–it made them feel unequal and upset. And it was divisive to consider that some people might go to heaven and others to hell. Therefore, the very idea that *Righteousness* existed was thrown out.

For example then, whereas in the Modern Era, based upon a Biblical foundation, sex was promoted as an activity to be enjoyed only within the confines of a lawful, life-long commitment of marriage, as far as the hippies were concerned the shackles were off. They talked instead about "free love," which essentially just meant having sex with anyone you wanted at any time. After all, the world can never have too much love, right? In Haight-Ashbury this attitude led to orgies and all kinds of deviant sexual practices. In order to accommodate this shift, 1967 was also the year that abortion was legalised in the UK through the Abortion Act.

Copious amounts of drugs were also taken at Haight-Ashbury that summer. LSD in particular was believed to have mind-expanding capabilities that would help free your mind of all the old rules and restrictions. Taking them was promoted through music and art.

And finally of course, because the *Soft Virtues* are embodied in femininity, the 1960s also saw the rise of Feminism. That was another feature of the New Age. The people of the revolution saw a female future where women would come to the fore to lead and re-shape Western civilisation.

All in all, the Love Generation were every bit as excited about their revolution as the Enlightenment thinkers had been about theirs. They were full of optimistic hope that the future was going to be bright, and that a Utopia centred around peace and love lay ahead. That's what they thought, anyway. But unfortunately, they were also every bit as naïve and imbalanced as the revolutionaries of old.

# 6
# Warning Signs.

The warning signs that the Love Revolution wasn't going to end well were there from the very start. And because we now understand *"The Trench Theory,"* I'm sure you can see why.

## Hard Virtues
(Conservative)

**TRUTH**
Justice
Righteousness
Fact
Reason
Rationalism
Lawfulness
Inequality
Competition
Individualism
Freedom
Small Government
Libertarianism
Things

## Soft Virtues
(Liberal)

**LOVE**
Grace
Mercy
Forgiveness
Patience
Kindness
Gentleness
Compassion
Unity / Peace
Equality
Co-operation
Collectivism
Big Government
Authoritarianism
People

MODERN ERA → POSTMODERN ERA

Enlightenment (17th Century) → Love Revolution (1967) →

After all, if it was inevitable that the Modern Era pursuit of the *Hard Virtues* would make people heartless, isn't it clear that the Postmodern pursuit of the *Soft Virtues* would make people brainless? If you abandon the concept of absolute *Truth* because

*Truth* divides, you will stop dividing truth from lies and become susceptible to falsehoods. If you choose to know nothing saying "nothing is real," then will become ignorant of reality. If you avoid dealing in facts because facts hurt feelings, you will become naive. If you hate rationality, you will become irrational. If you hate reason, you'll become unreasonable. If you won't identify bad ideas and exclude them, you'll have bad ideas. Hatred of *Truth* creates a lot of problems!

And that's only Truth. What about the other *Hard Virtues*? If you hate *Righteousness*, you'll become immoral. If you hate *Justice*, you'll become corrupt. If you hate *Competition* and prioritise only co-operation, you'll create a world devoid of hard work, discipline, innovation, skill, excellence, imagination, unlocked potential, mental fortitude, humility, resilience and courage. Indeed, if your *Love* detaches from *Truth*, it becomes unloving.

These are the problems that began developing for Western civilisation after the Love Revolution and there is much to say about it. Indeed, these problems have been compounding year-on-year through the Postmodern Era. We'll talk more about them in the third section. But even at Haight-Ashbury, right at the beginning of all this, it was clear to some people who witnessed it that humanity was on the wrong track.

## The Haight-Ashbury Midden.

The crowd that gathered in San Francisco in 1967 created something quite different from how it had first been imagined. The Beatles guitarist, George Harrison, visited Haight-Ashbury during the *Summer of Love* with his wife Pattie Boyd. As The Beatles had been great believers in the New Age philosophy and part of the vanguard that promoted its message, singing that "love is all you need" and "nothing is real", Harrison was excited to see what amazing things might be happening as a result of the movement. However, when they arrived in California, it was not as they had hoped. He said, "*We were expecting Haight-Ashbury to be special, a creative and artistic place, filled with Beautiful People, but it was horrible–full of ghastly drop-outs, bums and spotty youths, all out of their brains. Everybody looked stoned–even mothers and babies.*"[1]

Harrison thought he was essentially going to see a prototype for the Utopian community of tomorrow. A beautiful place full of love, creativity, music and art–a model community for all the world to follow. However, that's not what he found at Haight-Ashbury. I mean, he did find a prototype for what the world would become if it followed their example...but it was a midden. He found a stinking cesspool of immorality that depressed him so much, he couldn't leave fast enough. Indeed, almost as soon as they had arrived, Harrison and Boyd made an immediate escape and got right back on the plane to Britain again. They wanted nothing to do with it, and the experience was so shocking, they both agreed to stop taking LSD thereafter. The illusion had been broken.

If only the whole world had been able to have the same experience as George Harrison that day. Because unfortunately, everyone else is still pursuing the philosophy that made Haight-Ashbury such a depressing scene. The world is still living under the illusion that the *Soft Virtues* alone will create peace on earth, and that love is all we need. The world is still labouring under the pretence that *Truth* doesn't really matter and that we need only be nice; that *Righteousness* doesn't matter and that we only need be kind. Western civilisation continues to forge deeper into this Left trench ethos with every passing year.

The Love Generation kids of 1967 grew up to become parents. They taught their children the values they'd imbibed from those days. Those children in turn, grew up to become parents and passed the message onto their children too. With each new generation, the message has multiplied and become compounded. With the passing of the years, the Modern Era has faded further into the rear-view mirror, along with the people who knew it and who once held to its values. All the positions of power and influence in the Western world have gradually became occupied by people who have inherited a belief in the Left trench ethos. Therefore, the ideology now dominates the cultural narrative. And whether it be in the field of education, technology, politics, law, or in the media, the policy makers and the agenda setters all now sing from the same Leftist hymn sheet.

## 55+ Years of The War on Truth.

As I write this book, we are now over 55 years into the Postmodern odyssey and our culture is beginning to show quite severe signs of deterioration. In the next section, we're going to explore what has happened so far, and what we can expect to happen in the coming years if the *Trench Theory* holds true.

# Section Three.
## THE LEFT TRENCH

# The Story So Far.

In the first section of this book, we laid the foundational understanding for the *"Trench Theory"*, explaining what I mean by *Hard* and *Soft Virtues*.

### Hard Virtues
(Conservative)

**TRUTH**
Justice
Righteousness
Fact
Reason
Rationalism
Lawfulness
Inequality
Competition
Individualism
Freedom
Small Government
Libertarianism
Things

MODERN ERA

Enlightenment
(17th Century)

### Soft Virtues
(Liberal)

**LOVE**
Grace
Mercy
Forgiveness
Patience
Kindness
Gentleness
Compassion
Unity / Peace
Equality
Co-operation
Collectivism
Big Government
Authoritarianism
People

POSTMODERN ERA

Love Revolution
(1967)

In the second section, we took a brief walk through history to explain why the Modern Era could be said to be defined by the *Hard Virtues*, and why our Postmodern Era, which began in 1967, is being defined by the *Soft*.

In this third section, I next want to explain what will happen in our generation if we continue to fixate upon the *Soft* to the detriment of the *Hard*. My hope is that through this part of the book, some confusing developments of Postmodernity will begin to make sense, and perhaps ultimately, the lens of this theory may even help us predict the end-game for this Age. If you've ever been tempted to ask, *"why has the world gone crazy?" or "where is it all going to end?"* I hope that section three will bring some clarity.

## 2
# Brainless.

Let's start at the top and discuss how a Postmodern rejection of *Hard Truth* is making this generation brainless.

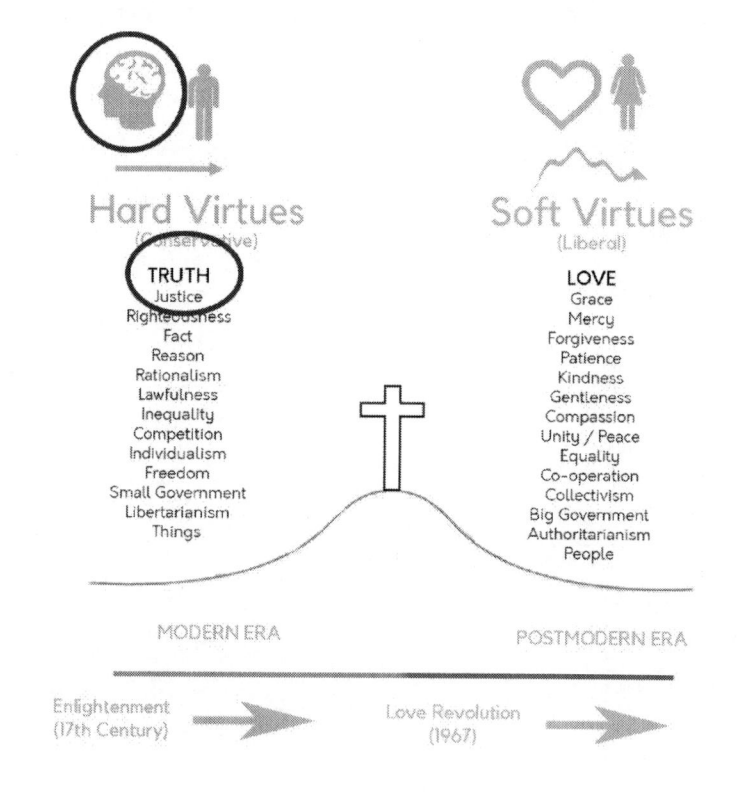

**Hard Virtues**
(Conservative)

**TRUTH**
Justice
Righteousness
Fact
Reason
Rationalism
Lawfulness
Inequality
Competition
Individualism
Freedom
Small Government
Libertarianism
Things

**Soft Virtues**
(Liberal)

LOVE
Grace
Mercy
Forgiveness
Patience
Kindness
Gentleness
Compassion
Unity / Peace
Equality
Co-operation
Collectivism
Big Government
Authoritarianism
People

MODERN ERA — POSTMODERN ERA

Enlightenment (17th Century) → Love Revolution (1967) →

## The War On Truth.

In December, 2015, a 52-year-old Canadian man called Paul Wolscht, who was then married and had seven children, suddenly felt that he was actually a six-year-old girl called Stefonknee.[1] In order to embrace this identity, he left his wife and children, started connecting with a transgender community in Toronto, and began living with an adoptive "mommy and daddy." His days were thereafter spent playing with dolls, colouring in pictures, and sucking on a dummy.[2]

Now, in a previous age when *Truth* was regarded to be important, Paul would have been clinically evaluated and some kind of mental breakdown would have been diagnosed. Because of course, Paul wasn't a six-year-old girl. However he felt about himself, and whatever he wished his identity to be, the fact remained that he was a 52-year-old man. It may have hurt his feelings to say it; he may have felt marginalised and offended; but nevertheless it would be the *Truth*.

In this *Soft* generation however, we have different priorities. *Love* is now our ultimate value and overrides the *Truth*. The Postmodernist believes it would be hurtful to tell Paul he's not a six-year-old girl, and therefore demands society play along with his delusion.

A similar story emerged in 2015 with a CrossFit enthusiast called Tyler DeYoung. Even though he was born in 1983 and was thirty-two-years-old, he decided to "transition" to the birth year, 2011, which at the time, would have made him four-years-old. Now of course, the fact is that you can't change the year of your birth—it's an immutable and fixed point in history. And in a previous age where *Truth* was regarded highly, Tyler would have been told as much. However he felt about himself, and whatever he wished his identity to be, he was thirty-two. It may have hurt his feelings to say it; he may have felt marginalised and offended; but nevertheless, it would have been the *Truth*.

In this *Soft* generation however, *Love* overrides *Truth*. Therefore, the people around him decided to affirm him in his identity as a four-year-old. He joined a CrossFit kids class and after dominating it, he made the news. Speaking to the media, he said, *"I wouldn't be here today if it weren't for everyone who has been supporting my transition."*[1] When his wife was asked for her thoughts she said, *"This is who he is, and celebrating that is more important than pressing him to conform to reality."*

In 2016, a 20-year-old Norwegian woman made the headlines not for swapping gender, but for swapping species. She decided that she didn't feel like a human at all but rather felt like a cat called Nano. She said, *"I realised I was a cat when I was 16 when doctors and psychologists found out what was the 'thing' with me. Under my birth, there was a genetic defect."*[1] Around the same time, another "transspecies" man called Tom began identifying as a dalmatian dog called Spot, while a PhD student in Arizona began identifying as a hippopotamus. Of course, none of these people really are cats, dogs or hippos and in a previous age where *Truth* was revered, we would have told them as much. However they felt about themselves, and whatever they wished their identity to be, the fact remained that they were all humans. It may have hurt their feelings to hear it; they may have felt marginalised and offended; but nevertheless it would have been the *Truth*. In the *Soft* Age, where *Love* trumps *Truth* however, our generation believes these people should all be treated as cats, dogs and hippos.

Some people have decided to identify as "transabled" too. A North Carolina woman, despite having perfect eyesight, decided to start identifying as a blind person. She began wearing opaque glasses so that she couldn't see, would turn off the lights, and used a white cane. She said, *"I really feel this is the way I was supposed to be born, that I should have been blind from birth."*[1] Another 61-year-old woman in Utah decided to identify as a paraplegic. Despite having the use of her legs, she began using a wheelchair and living as though she couldn't walk. Similarly, a man called Nick O'Halloran from Edinburgh, Scotland, made the news in 2017 because he identified as an amputee. He felt one of his legs didn't really belong to him and so chose to live as though he only had one.[3] Again, the plain *Truth* here is that all these people could see, walk and had all their limbs, and in a previous age where *Truth* was important we could have said it. However, in the *Soft* Age, feelings trump facts and this generation believes we should therefore play along with their fantasies.

Some people have even chosen to identify as inanimate objects. In recent years, a drag queen called Olympia made the news for identifying as household furniture while a man called Marco came to believe he is a cloud trapped in a human body. Marco said, *"I always sort of didn't fit my human body but I didn't realise the extent of it until about a year and a half ago. It's sort of like feeling a longing in a way, longing for a past life where I was a cloud...I have this fan in my room and sometimes I sit in front of it and imagine I'm flying again."*[1] There is also a case of a man identifying as an Apache helicopter.

Trench

I must repeat, as if it needs repeating, that none of these things are true. Whatever these people feel, and whatever they wish to be, they can't change reality. There was a time when we valued *Truth* and could have said it. But in the Postmodern Age, where *Love* is paramount, that old divisive *Truth* must be sacrificed. And so instead, we are told we must simply affirm fantasies. If a 52-year-old man feels he's a six-year-old girl then we'll affirm him in that. If a woman feels she's a cat, then she's a cat. If a man feels he's a dog or a hippo then he's a dog or a hippo. If someone feels they're a sofa or a cloud, then they're a sofa or a cloud. If someone feels they're an attack helicopter, then they're an attack helicopter.

The Postmodern world has become brainless in a manner that is almost beyond belief. If you'd told Modern ears that in the future, people would be running around pretending to be animals and bits of furniture and that huge swathes of Western civilisation would not only be playing along with the delusions, but even reconfiguring society to accommodate them and punishing those who object, they would think some madness had descended. Yet here we are, simply experiencing the outworking of the belief that "Love Is All We Need" and "Nothing Is Real." It started as a desire for peace but in abandoning the *Truth* that would disrupt it, we have become given to lunacy.

## Harm for the Individual

Is it really the worst thing in the world to let these people have their delusions, though? What's the worst that could happen? Well, remember earlier we talked about a man who believed he was a bird and planned to jump off a bridge so he could fly to Africa for the winter? He encountered a Liberal along the way and because the Liberal wanted to be kind, he merely affirmed the man in his identity. What happened next? The man jumped off the bridge and died. Because he wasn't a bird. He was a man. That's a picture–a parable if you like–of the problem here. *Love* detached from *Truth* becomes unloving.

Earlier, I mentioned a real-life example of how British doctors were instructed to stop telling obese patients the truth about their obesity in a bid to preserve their feelings. And what is the consequence? They develop health problems and die earlier than they should. Remember the North Carolina woman with perfect eyesight who identified as blind? Nobody confronted her with the hard Truth so she ended up pouring drain cleaner into her eyes and now is, in fact, blind. Nick O'Halloran, the man who identified as an amputee? He has gone to great lengths to damage his perfectly healthy leg so that doctors will agree to cut it off. He was even scammed out of £20,000 for a sham operation. These people have not been helped by having their delusions affirmed; it's ultimately led to their harm.

Likewise, there are many transgender people who feel a different sex from the one they really are. Rather than speaking *Truth* to them, helping them accept reality, and exploring the psychological reasons why they have rejected a part of their identity, it's commonplace for doctors today, in the name of compassion, to perform irreversible surgeries that mutilate their bodies. Some of these people are filled with remorse afterwards, but by then it's far too late. A woman from Newcastle, England, called Charlie Evans who "de-transitioned" back to her original sex after living for ten years as a man, spoke out about this in in 2019. She said that in response, hundreds of people had contacted her to say they were also experiencing regret.[8] These people needed counselling, not surgery. There are real consequences for people's lives when we pretend facts don't matter, and when we encourage fantastical delusions.

## Harm For Society.

Affirming fantasies has repercussions, not just for the individuals themselves, but also for wider society. In recent years, there have been a number of cases where male criminals, including sex offenders, have started identifying as transgender women so they can be transferred to female prisons. While there, they have quite predictably sexually assaulted the women inmates. Ignoring facts to affirm feelings has had severe consequences for these women.

A similar risk exists in other female-only spaces like public bathrooms and locker rooms. As JK Rowling, a survivor of domestic abuse herself, wrote, *"When you throw open the doors of bathrooms and changing rooms to any man who believes or feels he's a woman...then you open the door to any and all men who wish to come inside."*[4] The risk of attacks on women in these spaces could be greatly reduced if authorities simply adhere to biological realities. Ignoring facts has consequences.

Denying reality has an impact on female sport. Male-born athletes who self-identify as women now tend to be allowed participation in female sporting events. Since the biology of men gives them, on average, a 12% performance advantage in swimming and running, a 20% advantage in jumping events, and a 35% advantage in strength-based sports, women are simply unable to compete on level terms.[5] Even after surgery and with testosterone suppression, many male physical advantages remain, and when it comes to combat sports, these advantages go beyond unfairness and become dangerous.

In 2021, an MMA fighter called Alana McLaughlin, who spent 33 years as a man and who had previously been a soldier in the United States Special Forces, made a debut cage fight against a female competitor called Celine Provost. Due to his vastly superior strength and size, McLaughlin was able to dominate the fight before choking Provost into submission. Many who witnessed it voiced their horror at seeing a man beating up and choking a woman for sporting entertainment.

Indeed, the very first biologically male MMA fighter to be allowed to cage fight women under these terms was Fallon Fox, who made his debut at the Capital City Cage Wars. Fox brutally defeated a female opponent so badly, that the referee was forced to intervene after just two minutes. In that short time, the opponent, Tamikka Brents, had suffered a concussion and a broken skull that required seven staples. Brents said later, *"I've fought a lot of women and have never felt the strength that I felt in a fight as I did that night. I can't answer whether it's because she was born a man or not because I'm not a doctor. I can only say, I've never felt so overpowered ever in my life and I am an abnormally strong female in my own right. Her grip was different, I could usually move around in the clinch against other females but couldn't move at all in Fox's clinch."*[6] Ignoring facts has consequences.

I saw it said recently that, "you can ignore reality, but you can't ignore the consequences of ignoring reality." That's a concise way to put it. Put biologically male athletes into competition with women; into cage fights; into female prisons, and reality will intervene whether we like it or not. The consequences will be all too real for those involved. *Love detached from Truth becomes unloving.*

# 3

# Anti-Knowledge.

If there's an area of life that demonstrates our generation's growing hatred for *Truth* most clearly, it may be in regard to mathematics. Because in no other discipline are you so clearly dealing in hard, unyielding logic. After all, when you add 2+2, there can be no other answer than 4.

## The War on Mathematics.

*"What if a student believes it's 18 though?"* thinks the Liberal. *"We wouldn't want to marginalise that student. We wouldn't want to hurt their feelings by telling them they're wrong. We wouldn't want to create an inequality in the classroom where some students are considered better than others. So how do we solve this? Maybe we let 2+2 be whatever the student feels comfortable with?"*

Recently then, quite astonishingly, the Oregon Department of Education (ODE) released a document where they called for a move towards "Equitable Math." Essentially, this means pushing *Truth* to the side and simply focusing on making students feel good about themselves. Therefore, if one student feels 2+2 is 4, that's fine. But if another student feels the answer is 18, that's okay too. The ODE said, *"Upholding the idea that there are always right and wrong answers perpetuate objectivity."*[1]

The idea of "Equitable Math" is gaining traction. Back in 2018, educator Rochelle Gutierrez, whose speciality is "equity issues in mathematical education," gave a keynote speech called "Mathematx: Towards A Way of Being" at an educators conference in India. She said, *"to reconceptualise what mathematics is and how it is practiced, I argue for a movement against objects, truths, and knowledge..."*[1]

Wait a minute...a mathematics teacher openly stating at a global educators conference that she wants to argue against *Truth*? Against *knowledge*? As though those are bad things? Welcome to the Soft Trench. People are becoming so hateful of the *Truth* that they are actively *choosing* ignorance–choosing to know nothing–lest their knowledge create inequality.

Another teacher and PhD student, Brittany Marshall, gained a lot of attention on Twitter in 2021 for voicing her belief that 2+2 needn't equal 4. She said, *"Nope the idea of 2+2 equalling 4 is cultural and because of western imperialism/colonisation, we think of it as the only way of knowing."*[1] Although it's a ludicrous and historically illiterate statement, what became clear through the debate was that she had a lot of supporters. There are genuinely a lot of people in key educational positions today who would like to move away from exclusive statements around numeracy, driven by a misplaced desire to be kind to those who don't know the answers.

Sensible people may view these developments with bafflement. How on earth can Western civilisation have suddenly lost its mind like this? Throughout history there may have been some who said "nothing is real" and 2+2 has no fixed answer, but they would have been consigned to asylums and dementia wards...along with those who think they're cats, hippos, clouds and table lamps. But to live in a time where the view is held by *educators?* The *policy makers?* The *thought leaders?* The people who *run the show?* That's something else. How on earth did we reach a place in our development where educators have become hateful of *knowledge?* Of *facts?* Of *reason?* These are the things our forefathers prized more highly than anything else and that helped to build our civilisation! A pursuit of *Truth* is what brought us cars, planes, spaceships, heated homes, medicines, bridges, computers and the internet. What has happened?

I hope this book is beginning to bring some clarity. The great idea of our Age, held by those in the most important areas of power, is that Utopia will be built when there is *Equality, Unity and Peace*. And since *Truth*, by its very nature, brings inequality, arguments and division, we have decided we must reject the very notion of it. Our fixation upon the *Soft Virtues* is causing us to become anti-Truth and anti-intellectual. For this reason, it's accurate to called the Postmodern Age, the Post-Truth Age.

## More Harm For Society.

But remember, while you can ignore facts for a while, you can't ignore the consequences of ignoring facts. You can teach the next generation that 2+2 needn't equal 4, but there will be consequences further down the line for refusing to give them basic numeracy skills. Imagine in the future if an engineering company is tasked with building a bridge and all these students are now entering the workforce. One recruit thinks 2+2=18.

Trench

Another thinks it's 742. Another thinks it's -6. Does it matter now that everyone feels loved and included? Not so much. What matters is they measure the bridge properly using the correct numbers so they can contribute to the project and build it without it collapsing into a heap. If we stop teaching our children basic literacy and numeracy, we are failing to prepare them for the real world ahead. Our intended *Love* will become unloving.

# 4
# Tyranny.

So Postmodernity is, and will continue to be, increasingly marked by an anti-intellectual hatred for *Truth*. That naturally leads us onto another feature of the Age—that those who speak it will increasingly be reviled. As Selwyn Duke said, *"The further society drifts from the truth, the more it will hate those who speak it."*[1]

Trench

**Hard Virtues**
(Conservative)

TRUTH
Justice
Righteousness
Fact
Reason
Rationalism
Lawfulness
Inequality
Competition
Individualism
Freedom
Small Government
Libertarianism
Things

**Soft Virtues**
(Liberal)

LOVE
Grace
Mercy
Forgiveness
Patience
Kindness
Gentleness
Compassion
Unity / Peace
Equality
Co-operation
Collectivism
Big Government
Authoritarianism
People

MODERN ERA        POSTMODERN ERA

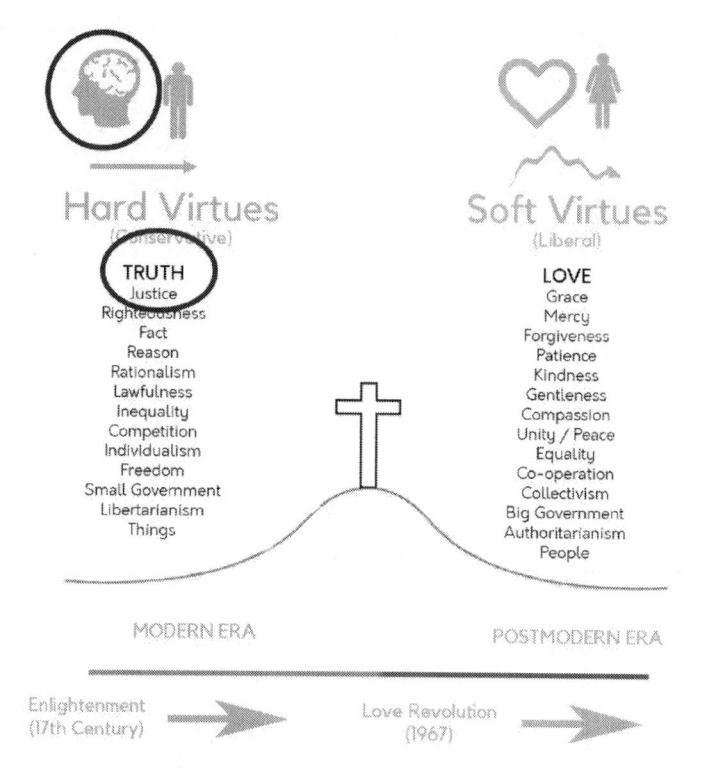

Enlightenment (17th Century) →     Love Revolution (1967) →

GK Chesterton made a prescient statement about the descending madness. He said, *"We shall soon be in a world in which a man may be howled down for saying that two and two make four, in which furious party cries will be raised against anybody who says that cows have horns, in which people will persecute the heresy of calling a triangle a three-sided figure, and hang a man for maddening mob with the news that grass is green."*[2]

It's almost uncanny how accurate this statement was. We really do now live in a generation where people are howled down for saying that two and two make four. Similarly, for stating other obvious facts, like 52-year-old men cannot be six-year-old girls. Or cats. Nor clouds or helicopters. Even though these things are basic, absolute, scientific, rational and self-evident, dealing in them makes you an enemy of Utopia, and so you will often be reviled for saying them.

## Cancelled.

When you get howled down and cast out of society for speaking plain facts, it's become known as being "cancelled." It happens regularly in our time. When someone deals in any kind of *Truth* that threatens to cause offence or inequality, Liberals tend to form aggressive mobs to ostracise that person from society.

For example, in the summer of 2018, a French teacher at West Point High School, Virginia—a man called Peter Vlaming—was cancelled for refusing to refer to a female student with male pronouns. He said he couldn't refer to her as male because truthfully she wasn't, and his religious beliefs forbade him from lying. Now even though Vlaming had basic, absolute, biological, rational and self-evident *Truth* on his side, he was still howled down by the Liberal mob for saying it, and he was fired from his job.[3]

A similar incident occurred in 2019 with a British Christian doctor called David Meckerith. As a man well-acquainted with biology, he said he simply could not refer to *"any 6ft tall bearded man as madam."*[4] He said to do so would be *"a ritual denial of obvious truth"* and that as a doctor, he knew maleness and femaleness are *"unchangeable and fundamental to who we are as people who were created in the image of God."* Again, he's biologically correct, but Meckerith was howled down and fired from his job too.

In another example occurring in 2021, Kathleen Stock, a professor of philosophy at the University of Sussex became the subject of controversy when she said that biological sex was immutable. She said that individual feelings about gender identities are *"not more important than facts about biological sex, particularly when it comes to law and policy."*[5] She too was howled down by students for stating plain, scientific facts. Indeed, such was the backlash against her statement, that she faced social isolation from colleagues and a co-ordinated campaign by students to have her fired from her role. Because of death threats, she was also advised by the police to install CCTV around her home and consider hiring bodyguards to protect her on campus.

When Professor Robert Winston, a renowned British doctor, scientist and television presenter, was asked for his views on Kathleen Stock's situation during an appearance on BBC's Question Time, he said, *"I'm about to say something that will probably want to make you edit the program when I'm finished. I will say this categorically: that you cannot change your sex. Your sex is there in every single cell in the body. You have your chromosomal sex, you have genetic sex, you have hormonal sex, you have all sorts of different kinds of sex...psychological, brain sex...they're all different. And we are very confused about this unfortunately. Regrettably, people will now accuse me of being transphobic. Unfortunately, you can't now say this publicly. This is one of the big problems. Saying this on this program undoubtedly will result in me getting a huge amount of hate mail–it always does....Overall, I think it's a very sad thing that we now can't discuss biological science without getting completely caught up emotionally with something which is completely wrong."⁶* Professor Winston was howled down for stating these facts, and it's unlikely the BBC will give him a platform to speak about the subject again. Simply because he dared to deal in reality.

## Chilled Speech.

Now if you know that speaking *Truth*, no matter how self-evident, is going to mean hate mail and death threats; the loss of friends; loss of platform; loss of opportunities; loss of livelihood; the pressure to stay quiet is obviously immense. After all, if Vlaming, Meckerith, Stock and Winston had only kept their mouths shut, they would have kept their jobs and had easier lives.

Many people are now being presented with this dilemma in the Postmodern Age, then. What do you do? Speak *Truth* and lose everything? Or bow to the mob, stay quiet, affirm delusions, and say things you know aren't true for self-preservation? Although Vlaming, Meckerith, Stock and Winston chose the former option, many of their colleagues consider the price of cancellation too big to pay and are choosing the latter. Indeed, many colleagues of these people apparently wrote in private to express their sympathies, but added they couldn't support them in public because they just couldn't afford to lose their livelihoods.

Therefore, we have arrived at a kind of tyranny. There is a figurative gun being pointed at everyone's heads which means that if anyone dare to speak plain *Truth* in public, or even to speak what they honestly think it may be, their lives will be actively destroyed. Many then, are intimated into silence. They refuse to say that two and two make four, and grass is green, or say what they really know about biology, because to do so would mean ruin.

On 26th September, 2021, the leader of the British Labour Party, Keir Starmer, was asked if it was right to say that only women have a cervix. Now there's a clear and scientific answer to this question and it shouldn't be controversial to say it. Indeed, that only women have a cervix was first documented over 2,000 years ago in the days of Hippocrates. And yet extraordinarily, when this question was put to Starmer he replied that it was, *"not right"* to say that *"only women have a cervix"*.[7] One week later, on 6th October, 2021, the British Prime Minister, Boris Johnson, was then asked the same question. During an interview with GB News, he was asked, *"Keir Starmer last week said it is not right to say that only women have a cervix. Do you agree?"*[8] Boris Johnson side-stepped the issue entirely, refusing to confirm or deny his position.

Why were they afraid to say it? Why had speaking the plain *Truth* become so utterly terrifying that they were prepared to affirm absurdities or say things they didn't really believe? Because of the fear of the mob. They knew that if they said it, there would be a wave of incandescent rage. They would be howled down and persecuted. Hate mail. Death threats. The loss of friends and colleagues. Demands for them to lose their jobs. The Liberal media machine would go into overdrive, attacking their character and capabilities. And in order to avoid this barrage, they simply bowed to the pressure.

## Big Tech and Government Censure.

Of course, people don't stop believing the *Truth* just because they're being intimidated. Everyone continues to know that only women have a cervix and nobody really stops believing in biological sex just because a gang with torches and pitchforks is metaphorically (or literally) standing outside your house. Instead, what happens is that *Truth* merely goes underground. People retain their independent thoughts and continue to speak their minds, but only behind closed doors and in hushed tones, amongst trusted allies. That alone is extraordinary. That we, in Western civilisation who used to pride ourselves on our freedoms, and whose culture was almost defined by them, now find ourselves behaving as if we were in Soviet Russia.

But as we journey deeper into the Postmodern Trench, and as our generation's hatred of the *Truth* grows, the trend of totalitarianism is only likely to grow with it. And what's especially sinister is the fact that social media companies and even police and government officials are falling in line with the Postmodern ethos.

A few years ago I made a video for The Fuel Project about transgenderism where I said it may be better to deal with gender dysphoria with counselling rather than performing irreversible surgeries. YouTube regarded it as "hate speech" and a strike was placed against the channel. Since YouTube operates a "three strikes" policy, it was effectively an intimidatory warning to stay quiet about transgenderism or else have my platform removed. I received a similar suspension from Facebook for a video that merely quoted passages from the Quran. Because it was ironically deemed offensive to Muslims who apparently were unaware of its violent content, I was again warned that future posts of that type would mean cancellation of my account.

It gets worse when the police are involved, and this is becoming increasingly common too. Police are now actively monitoring social media and taking action if anyone is deemed to have said something offensive. In January, 2019 for example, a man called Harry Miller was investigated by the police for a tweet where he questioned whether transgender women were real women. The police rang him to *"check his thinking."*[9] There are also many examples of Christian street preachers being arrested for quoting the Bible in public, or Christian café owners being warned to remove Bible verses from view.

Up until now, centuries old laws have protected freedom of speech and British citizens have generally escaped prosecution. The charges against Christian street preachers for example, have invariably been thrown out by UK judges until now. However, governments can always change laws. Therefore, at the time of writing this book, the UK government is attempting to pass an Online Safety Bill that would allow them to regulate and criminalise free speech on social media platforms. This would mean you don't only get thrown off the platforms by the companies themselves, but the police would have the power to go beyond intimidation and successfully prosecute.

In 2021, the Scottish government also sought to introduce a Hate Crime Bill to allow the police to successfully prosecute speech it offended another person. This far-reaching Bill proposed that people could be convicted whether or not offence was actually intended, and whether or not the offence could actually be proved. It extended into all areas of life—public and private—and included literature, plays, newspaper articles and works of art. In other words, if someone came to your home for dinner and you made a remark that offended them, the police would have grounds to prosecute you regardless of the fact it happened in your own home, regardless of whether it was meant to offend, and regardless of whether it could be proved you actually said it. Even worse, if someone came into your home and merely saw a book on a shelf that offended them, like the Bible, they could report you to the police and have you charged for possessing offensive material.

Now, thankfully that Bill was eventually watered down after a furore, but the mere attempt to pass it at all by the Scottish government shows which way the wind is blowing in the Postmodern Age. The government increasingly wants to make sure people are not just cancelled by the mob for the words they say, or simply thrown off social media platforms, but given criminal records too. Which clearly adds an extra layer of intimidation for the ordinary person. Can anyone really afford to speak the *Truth* anymore in this climate of fear, if it means not just the loss of opportunity and career, but jail too?

## Our Response.

We simply cannot submit to the encroaching totalitarianism. There are some principles in life—some transcendent causes—that are worth sacrificing comfort to preserve, even upon pain of punishment from the state, and freedom of speech is one of them. To give this up is to give up freedom itself. As Benjamin Franklin said, *"Whoever would overthrow the liberty of a nation must begin by subduing the freeness of speech."*[9] And as George Orwell said, *"If liberty means anything at all, it means the right to tell people things they do not want to hear."*[10] Once you lose the freedom to articulate your thoughts and express your beliefs freely, you have lost it all. It is the most fundamental of all the freedoms and the one upon which the rest depend. The fate of Western civilisation depends upon how readily we defend this right.

I read a tweet recently that echoed the spirit of the age when it said, *"I believe in freedom of speech but that doesn't mean saying things that others might find offensive."* That's literally what it *does* mean. That is the definition of freedom of speech. Now, that's not to say we should deliberately *try* to offend. That's not our intention at all. Indeed, the Bible tells us that when we are speaking *Truth*, we must be aware of its potential to hurt and so only to do so with the hearer's best interests at heart. It says, *"Instead, we will speak the **Truth** in **Love**, growing in every way more and more like Christ, who is the head of his body, the church."* (Ephesians 4:15) (emphasis added) As always, we are to blend both virtue sets, but at the same time, never give either of them up. We must defend *Truth*. To stay quiet or confirm absurdities just isn't an option. Submitting to tyranny never is. We speak the *Truth* in *Love*. But it is the *Truth* we speak nonetheless.

For that reason, I speak *Truth* to people who think they're cats, dogs, hippos, helicopters, or transgender, not because I want to be offensive but simply because I want to be truthful. Indeed, it's out of love that I think it's best they hear it. In the same way it's best to tell a man he's not a bird before he jumps off a bridge. In the same way it's best to tell morbidly obese people that their health is at risk. It's because I want their best that I believe they should be freed from delusions and conform to reality. Facts matter. They have consequences. Therefore, I encourage everyone else, as much as you are able, to resist the tyrannical intimidation too. Keep speaking things that you know are true, or even things you think may be true, and refuse to be cowed into silence. Refuse to echo lies. If you won't defend those freedoms now, they'll become harder and more costly to reclaim further down the line. And meanwhile, our society will not just sink further into absurdity, but also tyranny.

Either way, repressed speech and is something we can expect to see more of in the Postmodern Age if we keep pursuing the Soft Virtues. The further a society drifts from *Truth*, the more it will hate those who speak it.

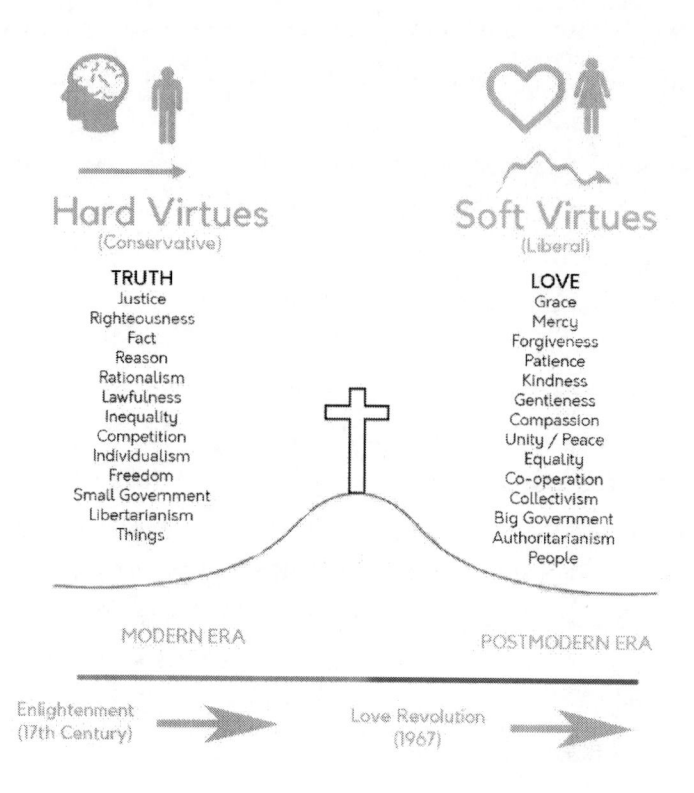

Trench

## Hard Virtues
(Conservative)

**TRUTH**
Justice
Righteousness
Fact
Reason
Rationalism
Lawfulness
Inequality
Competition
Individualism
Freedom
Small Government
Libertarianism
Things

## Soft Virtues
(Liberal)

**LOVE**
Grace
Mercy
Forgiveness
Patience
Kindness
Gentleness
Compassion
Unity / Peace
Equality
Co-operation
Collectivism
Big Government
Authoritarianism
People

MODERN ERA — POSTMODERN ERA

Enlightenment
(17th Century)

Love Revolution
(1967)

# 5
# Collectivism.

The desire for *Equality* and *Unity* that would see Postmodernists restrict freedom of speech is the same desire that would have them restrict all individual freedom of expression. Therefore, we can expect to see an increasing shift towards political "*Collectivism*" in the Postmodern Age.

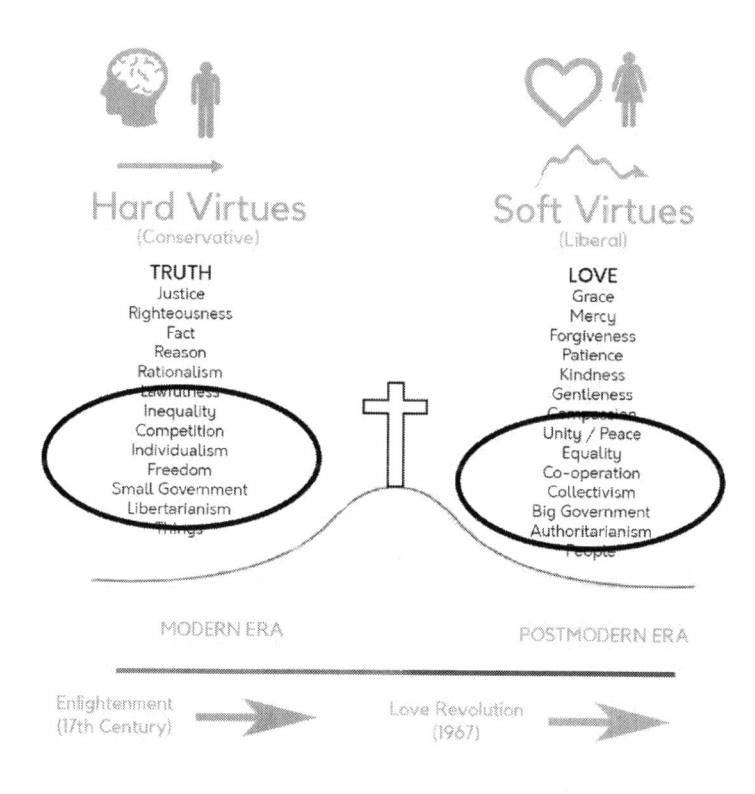

## Hard Virtues
(Conservative)

**TRUTH**
Justice
Righteousness
Fact
Reason
Rationalism
Lawfulness
Inequality
Competition
Individualism
Freedom
Small Government
Libertarianism

## Soft Virtues
(Liberal)

**LOVE**
Grace
Mercy
Forgiveness
Patience
Kindness
Gentleness
Compassion
Unity / Peace
Equality
Co-operation
Collectivism
Big Government
Authoritarianism

MODERN ERA → POSTMODERN ERA

Enlightenment
(17th Century) → Love Revolution
(1967) →

## Recap.

We covered this in the first section but we'll quickly recap for clarity the difference between Individualism and Collectivism. Individualists—that is Conservatives—believe that each human being is unique and should therefore be dignified as such. In other words, each person should have the individual freedom to speak and act according to their own beliefs as long as it's within the boundaries of the moral law and doesn't infringe on someone else's liberty to do the same.

Now, individuals speaking their minds and pursuing their own goals is obviously going to create conflict and competition. But as we've established, Conservatives don't mind that. They understand that verbal conflict i.e. debate, is how we separate good ideas from bad ones and advance in knowledge. They also know that competition, whether it be on the sports field or in the boardroom, develops character, hard work, discipline, innovation, skill, excellence, imagination, unlocked potential, mental fortitude, humility, resilience and courage.

Collectivists—that is, Liberals—have a polar opposite position. They believe people are not individuals but rather cogs in a bigger machine called society. And so that the cogs might fit well with one another, they prioritise *Equality* and *Unity*. This means no individual speech or behaviours can be allowed that disrupt the group.

Now, we've already noted that the Individualist worldview requires very little in the way of government. If people are to be left free to form their own opinions and pursue their own personal goals, then it's up to those individuals to choose what those opinions and goals will be. The Individualist ideally wants to be left alone by the government as much as possible. On the extreme end, they would want no government at all.

On the other hand, we've already noted the Collectivist worldview requires big, authoritarian government. If people are to be choreographed to move in harmony, there needs to be a grand choreographer. There needs to be a top-down power establishing what the collective goals of society will be and making sure everyone adheres to them. Under a collectivist system, the government decides what we must think and say to maintain peace and stay unified. Remember therefore, that Le Febvre and Franke discovered in their 2013 study that Liberals score much higher for dependence. Where Conservatives want to be left alone by the government, Liberals want to rely on it to direct their lives.

## Communism.

If the far end of Individualism brings us to no government at all, which is anarchy, the far end of Collectivism brings us to Communism—a government so big that it controls every aspect of human life, leaving no room for individual behaviours at all. Communism *"stresses not the importance of the individual, but rather the individual as a member of the collective. Thus defined, individuals only have the right to freedom of expression if it safeguards the interests of the collective...[People] have the right to express their opinion, but that opinion can only be expressed if it's in the general interests of society."*[1]

In Communist societies like these, nobody is allowed individual free speech because clearly that would disrupt social cohesion. Instead, the all-powerful state instructs people what they must think and say, and punishes anyone for deviating from the party line.

In Communist societies, nobody is allowed to express individuality through hairstyles or fashion either. In North Korea for example, there are twenty-eight state approved hairstyles and nobody can depart from them. Anything that would seek to differentiate one person from another is considered potentially divisive.

In Communist societies, nobody is allowed to generate their own income or own their own property. After all, people having their own businesses leads to financial inequalities. So that everyone may remain completely equal, the state owns all the property, means of production and wealth, which they distribute uniformly.

In Communist societies, so that everyone conforms exactly to the same ideology, there can be no higher authority than the state, and nothing that would compete for ultimate authority within people's hearts. Therefore, nobody is allowed to have a religion or independently worship God. After all, it would produce a conflict of interest if the state said one thing and God said another.

For similar reasons, Communist societies seek to destroy the family. Loyalty to parents and siblings may produce conflict with the demands of the government. Instead, the government must essentially become the father and mother of the nation. If there's to be complete cohesion, there must be complete reliance, dependence, and submission to this one, singular, all-powerful authority.

Communist countries go to extravagant and ostentatious lengths to demonstrate just how well their society has been choreographed to act in unison, as though it were the most important thing in life. In North Korea, for example, there is an annual gymnastics demonstration called the Arirang Mass Games. Of course, these mass games are not about competition but rather co-operation. In them, an entire stadium of up to 109,000 people are choreographed to dance and move in complete unison with each other. Videos are available on YouTube and if you care to watch, you will see in those demonstrations no individuals, but rather hundreds of thousands of faceless components making up a single organism.

## Our Direction of Travel

Now if we in the Postmodern Age keep pursuing *Unity* at all costs, and if equality and societal cohesion continue to be the only things that matter to this generation, we will drift towards this kind of Communism. We will find our civilisation increasingly handing over power to the state to choreograph us to move in unison. And that means that all individual thought, speech and behaviour will be discouraged and eliminated.

We're already seeing hints of this Communist creep, as we saw in the previous chapter. It's why the police have begun questioning people like Harry Miller, to "check his thinking" on transgender issues, and to make sure his thoughts align with the state-approved position. It's why Christian street preachers and café owners are being intimidated by the state to renege on their faith and instead conform their ideology to the government's. It's why social media platforms are threatening to punish disruptors who express unsanctioned ideas. It's why the Scottish government feels emboldened to introduce Hate Speech laws that convict people for having the wrong opinions, or owning the wrong reading material, even within their own homes. And it's why the UK government feels empowered to introduce the Online Safety Bill that seeks to control what people say online. It's all designed to produce a conformism of ideas, choreographed by the state, so that ultimately there might be *Unity*.

## Dehumanisation.

Obviously, the problems with moving towards such complete collectivist authoritarianism are many, as will become apparent as we progress in this book—we'll specifically get into the problems of Communism soon. But I think the most obvious problem that may be coming through in this chapter is dehumanisation. Collectivism ultimately means dehumanisation of the individual. After all, if people are denied the chance to think and speak freely, and act upon their most dearly held beliefs in the name of conformation, they are treated as robots.

What does it mean to be human, after all? Human beings are the only creatures on earth that pursue knowledge for its own sake so that we might form ideas about the world. That's a uniquely human trait. To deny us the freedom to independently pursue knowledge and make up our own minds about it is to deprive us of our humanity.

We are the only beings on God's earth with a larynx (voice box) by which we can articulate our thoughts and beliefs. To deprive us of free speech to express our ideas is to deprive us of our humanity.

We are the only beings on earth that have the ability and desire to express ourselves through fashion, art, music, drama, and books. To deny us free creative expression is to deprive us of our humanity.

We are the only beings on earth with an awareness of something transcendent, and the ability to think and reason about the meaning of life—the only ones to have an awareness of God and a desire to form a relationship with him. To deny us the freedom to worship and speak about that God is to deprive us of our humanity.

World peace sounds like such a noble thing, doesn't it? But when you understand that to have complete peace, you must have complete unity; and to have complete unity, you must remove all individualism; and to remove all individualism, you must have an authoritarian power clamping down on all free expression, it starts to sound less appealing. Is that kind of peace really worth it if it means reducing humans to robots—worthless, disposable, replaceable cogs in a totalitarian machine? Objects who have no reason for their existence other than to serve the purposes of the authoritarian state?

It's no way to live. And the evidence from Communist experiments around the world is that humans are not capable of such complete conformism anyway. Not really. Those who are subjected to extreme collectivist regimes find it unbearably oppressive and cannot leave fast enough. In the old Soviet Union, the government had to build walls to stop people escaping to the freedom of the West. That's still the case in places like North Korea today. And if people can't find a way to escape over the walls, they just find a way to express their individuality in secret, behind closed doors.

The point though, is that they shouldn't have to. People shouldn't have to live under tyranny, in fear of their government. Afraid to express an unsanctioned opinion. And if we in the West don't want to find ourselves in that position in the years to come, we must change trajectory quickly. I watched an interview recently from Ai Weiwei, a Chinese artist who escaped his home country where he had been persecuted for being critical of the Communist regime. Speaking to the American PBS channel he said, *"In many ways, the United States is already in the authoritarian state, you just don't know it. Many things happen in the US now that can be compared to the Cultural Revolution in China."* When pressed to give an example he said, *"Like people trying to be unified in political correctness. That is very dangerous."* This is a man who grew up and lived in Communist China, saw it first-hand, has now moved to the West, and sees the same fundamental ideas about social-cohesion-above-all taking root here. As we keep pursuing the *Soft Virtues* in Postmodernity, this will only become more apparent.

The 1967 Love Revolution isn't sounding like such a great idea anymore, right? We started off pursuing *Peace*, *Love* and *Unity* and on the surface it sounded good and we could understand the motivation, but taken to extremes, virtues become vices. Monomaniacal fixation upon the *Soft Virtues* is creating a society of anti-intellectualism, ignorance, tyranny, authoritarianism, and a growing collectivism that is tending towards Communism. And we're just getting started on the outworkings of the Left trench ethos.

# 6

# Globalism.

The fullest expression of Collectivism isn't just Communism—it's *global* Communism. After all, true collectivists don't just want *Unity* in local communities—they want *Unity* across the whole planet. Not just peace but *world* peace—that's the dream. They want everyone speaking with one voice and acting with one mind. Therefore, almost without exception, you will find people in the Left trench not only advocate for more authoritarian governmental control, but on an increasingly global scale.

## Individualism Stands In The Way.

Now again, the barrier to world peace is individualism. There's a quote that has been attributed to Brock Chisolm, the first Director General of the United Nations World Health Organisation (WHO), in which he says, *"To achieve world government, it is necessary to remove from the minds of men their individualism, loyalty to family traditions, national patriotism, and religious dogmas."*[1] This quote is controversial because closer investigation reveals he never actually said it word-for-word. Rather, it's more of a paraphrase of an essay Chisolm wrote in 1946 called, *"The Reestablishment of Peacetime Society."* It was after the horrors of World War II that people began dreaming about what world peace might look like and what Chisolm actually said in his paper, is that humanity is being *"crippled by local certainties, by gods of local moralities, of local loyalty..."* Therefore, although it's often challenged as a fake quote, in truth the paraphraser hasn't done a terrible job. Chisolm was indeed saying that world unity is being crippled by local loyalties, and that world peace would only be achieved when they were replaced with collective global ideas.

Now globalists have identified three types of individualism they find especially divisive. These are in regard to:

- Religion
- Nationality
- Possessions

Globalists believe that as long as people have independent ideas about God, they'll keep fighting about whose concept is true and there can never be world peace. They also believe that as long as people around the world have different national identities, there will always be tribalism and war between states, and there can never be world peace. And finally, as long as people own their possessions, there will be greed and inequality, and there can never be world peace.

If there is an anthem for this Era then, it would be John Lennon's *"Imagine."* Released in 1971, the lyrics specifically talk about trying to build a global Utopia unburdened by local loyalties to these three things:

*"Imagine there's no heaven*
*It's easy if you try*

*No hell below us*
*Above us only sky*
*Imagine all the people living for today, I*

*Imagine there's no countries*
*It isn't hard to do*
*Nothing to kill or die for*
*And no religion too*
*Imagine all the people living life in peace*

*You may say I'm a dreamer*
*But I'm not the only one*
*I hope someday you'll join us*
*And the world will be as one*

*Imagine no possessions*
*I wonder if you can*
*No need for greed or hunger*
*A brotherhood of man*
*Imagine all the people*
*Sharing all the world, you*

*You may say I'm a dreamer*
*But I'm not the only one*
*I hope someday you'll join us*
*And the world will live as one*

This song encapsulates the globalist sentiment so well that the United Nations released a new version of it in 2014–indeed, it could almost be considered the UN anthem.

## Global Religion.

You'll notice globalists making strong efforts in these three areas in particular then. In regard to divisive independent ideas of God, there are attempts to collectivise them into a One World Religion. Although John Lennon had sung that he wanted to get rid of God altogether, and although many globalists would agree that's the ideal scenario, many are content to simply homogenise our concept of who he is. Belief in a God isn't really the main problem; belief in *different* gods is the problem. If globalists can just get everyone in the world to put aside their *individual* beliefs and come together under a One World Religion, their theory is that it would clear the path to world peace.

For that reason, world religious leaders now regularly attend interfaith conferences that are ultimately designed to blend the world religions together. The UN is of course at the centre of these efforts with their annual World Interfaith Harmony Week. There's the G20 Interfaith Forum too, as well as many other independent events. These conferences always try to convene leaders around the idea that independent *Truth* claims made by each religion, which divide one from another, are unimportant and that all we really need to agree on is *Love*.

## Global Citizenship.

In terms of nationality, globalists increasingly advocate for the end of national borders and promote the idea of collective global citizenship. If you've been to the European Union recently you'll know that there are attempts to completely eliminate national identities and instead form a collective European one. To that end, there's a common currency, you can now travel quite freely around the continent without having to show a passport, and it's increasingly ruled from just one location. Globalists love this experiment and are keen to have it rolled out across the world.

This is why Liberals treated Brexit as such a tragedy in 2016. For Britain to pull out of the European Union and reassert national borders is a clear step backwards. For the Left, Brexit is something they have never come to terms with and can never accept. They are determined that Brexit mustn't be a success, lest it encourage other European nations to follow their lead and reassert their own national sovereignty too. This is why many globalist politicians have been overheard talking about the need to "punish" Britain for pulling away.

In the United Kingdom itself, there are now official organisations like No Borders UK, who in their own words, *"struggle against borders and immigration controls and strive for freedom of movement for all."*[2] This is one reason why Liberals have no problem with the influx of illegal immigration that we talked about earlier in this book. Indeed, on 13th November, 2021, the Director General of the UK Border Force, Paul Lincoln–the man in charge of keeping British borders secure–was revealed to be not much of a believer in borders himself. After doing hardly anything to stop 23,500+ immigrants from reaching UK shores in 2021 alone, he made an outgoing speech to friends and colleagues saying, *"We're all human beings, we're all mammals, we're all rocks, plants, rivers. B\*\*\*\* borders are just a pain in the b\*\*\*\*\* a\*\*\*...people are talking about immigration, emigration and the rest of the b\*\*\*\*\* thing. It's all b\*\*\*\*\* c\*\*\*."*3

In the United States, nothing caused as much consternation about Donald Trump's presidency for globalists than the idea that he was going to build a wall along the southern border with Mexico to keep illegal immigrants out. Globalists have the motto, "build bridges, not walls." They want to make it easier to travel freely; not more difficult. It's taken a while for the American Left to fully commit to the borderless idea, mind you. In the 1990s and into the early 2000s, Democrat politicians such as Barak Obama and the Clintons were still on record making speeches about the importance of border security. However, as we journey deeper into the Left Trench, the full outworking of the *Soft* philosophy is coming into view. What was once considered a radical idea is starting to become mainstream.

## Collectivised Economy.

And then finally, in terms of possessions, you will notice globalists increasingly experimenting with collectivist economic ideas that cause people to become increasingly dependent on the state. There are a few developments worth mentioning here in particular that are currently getting the Left excited.

Universal Basic Income (UBI) is one idea that is being toyed with. It means that everyone in society gets an equal monthly handout from the government on which to live, regardless of whether they've worked for it or not. This isn't an entirely new idea but it's experiencing a resurgence of interest in the Postmodern Age. Finland, India, Spain, South Korea, Kenya, Germany and Wales amongst others have recently tested versions of it. Switzerland put it to a vote but it didn't pass. During Covid-19, the UK government launched "The Furlough Scheme" which habituated people to the idea of receiving payments direct from the government specifically for not working. Interestingly, many people decided that once they'd tasted this life of leisure, staying at home and being paid for it, they quite liked it. Therefore, the furlough scheme helped break down some of the resistance that may formerly have existed to state dependence.

There's a theory that in the future, technological advances and automation may mean there simply aren't enough paid work positions for everyone on earth. If that were to transpire, the obvious question becomes, *"How will the economy work? What will we humans do with ourselves? How would we occupy our time?"* Many predict a future whereby the government simply issues everyone in the world a monthly Universal Basic Income.

A UBI is especially appealing for collectivists when they consider that the technology now exists to implement it as part of a cashless society. At the time of writing this book, something called Central Bank Digital Currency (CBDC) is being developed, and the exciting part for globalists is that such digital currency is programmable. In other words, governments could control where, how, and if the money is spent. According to the Official Monetary and Financial Institutions Forum (OMFIF), 60% of banks are already experimenting with this technology.[3] They say, *"Programmable money is designed with in-built rules that constrain the user. These rules could mean that money expires after a fixed date or its use is restricted to certain sets of goods."* This appeals to the authoritarianism in the globalist. What if the government holds all the wealth, distributes it equitably each month, and then that which hasn't been spent expires so that no individuals can hoard more than someone else? What if it means nobody can keep a separate supply in a biscuit tin under the bed? Or invest in things that grow their wealth beyond that of others? Indeed, this system has all the ingredients a Leftist desires– equality, dependence on the state, and authoritarianism.

The Leftist's excitement only increases when they consider you could easily build a social credit system into programmable money. In other words, people could be rewarded for collectivist behaviours and punished for individualistic ones. If someone behaves as the government desires, they may release extra credit to your account, but if someone rebels, the government may withhold or block that person from spending. Through this, people could be trained into obedience like animals.

The World Economic Forum, established in 1971, is a leading part of the effort to create this world without possessions. Every year, the richest and most powerful people in the world come together at the forum to talk about how they'll shape the future, and in recent times they've begun talking about the need for a "Great Reset"–the complete deconstruction of the current economic system and another one built along globalist lines. They infamously released a video in 2016 predicting that by 2030, *"you will own nothing and be happy. Whatever you want, you'll rent."*[4] The obvious question is, *"if we won't own our own things, who will we be renting from? Who will own everything?"* And the most obvious answer is, the state.

This video caused such a storm of protest upon its release that they have since removed it from YouTube. And this often happens. The Liberal elites who are pushing the globalist agenda in Postmodern life occasionally show impatience or overestimate how ready the world has become for their Utopian vision. They will sometimes reveal too much of their intentions too quickly, and then if there's a furore, they'll row back a bit to let more time pass. It's a bit like the end of *Back to the Future* when Marty McFly plays Johnny B Goode at the school dance. When the crowd recoils with horror he replies, *"I guess you guys aren't ready for that yet…but your kids are going to love it."*[5] This is what the globalists believe. It's just a matter of time. Maybe this generation doesn't want to give up faith in our God, or our national identity, or our capitalist economic system yet, but it's going to happen one day and our kids are going to love it. Or maybe even their kids. Or their kids. However long it takes, they're sure there's a generation who will arrive who will embrace the vision wholeheartedly. For that reason, they'll keep testing the waters occasionally until we're ready for it–a One World Religion, no borders, and no possessions, choreographed by a One World Government.

And I believe they're right. I mean, I think they're going to get their wish. If the Trench Theory is correct, then as the Postmodern Age develops, it seems fixation upon the *Soft Virtues* and a corresponding rejection of the *Hard* will develop these outcomes. Which means we're not only travelling on a trajectory towards anti-intellectualism, ignorance, tyranny, authoritarianism, and communism in the West, as we have already seen, but if the Liberal elite has their way, these things will happen on a *global* level.

Will we pull back before we reach that point? Maybe. But in the same way the Modern Era didn't end until its values had been pursued to their fullest extent, I think the Postmodern Era will only end when we've pursued these values to their fullest extent too. Only then will we realise that Utopia doesn't lie down this path. Only then will we realise what a mistake this whole generation has made. And a bit like George Harrison running away from Haight-Ashbury, we'll want to do the same thing. I guess the question is, if the whole earth succumbs to such a masterplan, to where would we run?

# 7
# Inevitable Globalism.

I hope it won't confuse too much if I pause in this chapter to give four more reasons why I believe collectivist, authoritarian globalism is the almost inevitable outcome for our Postmodern Era. I'm going to call these reasons:

- Moral
- Historical
- Geographical
- Prophetic.

Let's briefly walk through each of them.

## The Moral Reason.

The reason that Leftists fear individualism is because they think that if people are left free to speak their own mind and pursue their own ends, it leads to selfish behaviour that causes inequality, conflict, and exploitation. That's where the fundamental desire for a top-down control comes from…to keep everyone in line.

Now certainly, there is a risk of this happening. Earlier we saw how extreme individualism in the Modern Era led to exploitation and slavery. And it's true that human beings have a sinful nature from birth that skews us towards selfishness. The

Bible says, *"For I was born a sinner–yes, from the moment my mother conceived me."* *(Psalm 51:5)* Later the Bible describes the outworking of that sinful nature saying, *"When you follow the desires of your sinful nature, the results are very clear: sexual immorality, impurity, lustful pleasures, idolatry, sorcery,* **hostility**, **quarrelling**, **jealousy**, *outbursts of anger,* **selfish ambition***, dissension,* **division***, envy, drunkenness, wild parties, and other sins like these."* *(Galatians 5:19-21)(emphasis added)* So the Bible confirms that we have a sinful nature from birth and that if we follow it, it will lead to selfish behaviours which produce hostility, jealousy and division. So the Leftist isn't wrong with their initial premise.

However, to counter this problem, Conservatives have always believed you can put a control on the sinful nature at a local–that is, individual–level. Indeed, you can override the sinful nature in the hearts of human beings so that they independently choose to behave in selfless and sacrificial ways, without external compunction. How have we typically gone about this in Western civilisation? By imbuing hearts with Christian faith.

For the largest part of Western civilisation's existence, its citizens have lived freely with little or no governmental control on their speech or behaviour at all–free to speak their mind and pursue their own dreams. And yet for the majority of that time, the West remained a pleasant and happy place to be, full of neighbourliness, honesty, charity and decency.

How was this possible if people have a sinful nature and it naturally skews us towards selfishness? Well, firstly because the majority of people were having their moral compasses regularly calibrated by church attendance, Bible teaching and reading. The Bible trained people to be charitable and generous in contravention of their natural sinful desires. For that reason, the Bible says, *"All scripture is breathed out by God and profitable for teaching, for reproof, for correction, and for training in righteousness."* *(2 Timothy 3:16)* People were being trained in righteousness through exposure to the scriptures.

But even more than that, the Bible also makes it clear that when people give their hearts to God, he sends his own Spirit to dwell within their hearts, and this power is strong enough to overcome the sinful nature. The Bible says, *"you (that is, Christians) are not controlled by your sinful nature. You are controlled by the Spirit if you have the Spirit of God living within you...Therefore, dear brothers and sisters, you have no obligation to do what your sinful nature urges you to do. For if you live by its dictates, you will die. But if through the power of the Spirit you put to death the deeds of your sinful nature, you will live. For all who are led by the Spirit of God are children of God."* *(Romans 8:9,12-14)*

Now God promised the power of this Holy Spirit long ago in Old Testament times saying, *"And I will give you a new heart, and I will put a new spirit in you. I will take out your stony, stubborn heart and give you a tender, responsive heart. And I will put my Spirit in you so that you will follow my decrees and be careful to obey my regulations."* *(Ezekiel 36:26-27)*

When Jesus arrived on earth, he repeated the promise saying that the Holy Spirit would come after his resurrection: *"But the Helper, the Holy Spirit, whom the Father will send in my name, he will teach you all things and bring to remembrance all that I have said to you."* (John 14:26)

After Jesus' death and resurrection, the Apostles were then told to wait in an upper room for the Holy Spirit on the Day of Pentecost. They were told, *"... you will receive power when the Holy Spirit comes upon you..."* (Acts 1:8)

After this Holy Spirit had been made available to the church, Paul was then able to write to the Ephesians saying, *"I pray that from his glorious, unlimited resources, he will empower you with inner strength through his Spirit."* (Ephesians 3:16)

So yes, the Christian believes that we receive training in moral righteousness through reading the Bible and church attendance, but even more than that, we believe God uniquely empowers Christians through his own Spirit to overcome the sinful nature, and to be selfless, good and kind. John writes about the switch from selfishness to sacrifice that should then be evident saying, *"...because Jesus gave up his life for us...So we also ought to give up our lives for our brothers and sisters. If someone has enough money to live well and sees a brother or sister in need but shows no compassion—how can God's love be in that person? Dear children, let's not merely say that we love each other; let us show the truth by our actions."* (1 John 3:16-18)

There are many more verses along these lines, exhorting Christians to put to death their selfish sinful nature and to live selflessly. Which is why the early church, without external compunction or government interference was found freely and generously sharing their possessions with one another. The Bible says of the early church, *"And all the believers met together in one place and shared everything they had. They sold their property and possessions and shared the money with those in need. They worshipped together at the Temple each day, met in homes for the Lord's Supper, and shared their meals with great joy and generosity—all the while praising God and enjoying the goodwill of the people."* (Acts 2:44-47)

Do you see what's happening here? The early church had complete freedom to do as they wished, but instead of using their freedom to do evil, and exploit, and be selfish, they used their freedom to be kind and generous. Paul wrote to the Galatians, *"For you have been called to live in freedom, my brothers and sisters. But don't use your freedom to satisfy your sinful nature. Instead, use your freedom to serve one another in love."* (Galatians 5:13) That's exactly what the early church did. The Bible says, *"But the Holy Spirit produces this kind of fruit in our lives: love, joy, peace, patience, kindness, goodness, faithfulness, gentleness, and self-control."* (Galatians 5:22-23)

Now because Western civilisation was built upon Christian ideals, being trained in righteousness by the Bible, and many receiving the power of God's Holy Spirit into their hearts, they often emulated the early church by using their freedom to serve. That's what made Western civilisation such a beautiful place to live. Everyone had individual freedom to think, speak, and act as they chose, and were at liberty to pursue their own goals, yet the Leftist fear that all society would then automatically descend into selfishness and exploitation didn't materialise.

Indeed, although it's true that extreme individualism had caused people to exploit and enslave one another in the Modern

Era, it was the Christian influence that was responsible for ending those things. William Wilberforce, Thomas Clarkson and their community of saints, known as the Clapham Sect, were the driving force behind hundreds of social initiatives that led to revolutionary social changes we take for granted today. Wherever Christianity was most closely followed, it changed hearts and caused people to act in more selfless ways.

By Victorian times, the saying had emerged that although there was nothing wrong with making money, a man was a failure if he died rich. The wealthiest in society instead made sure to use their wealth to build and fund hospitals, schools, charitable initiatives, and food programmes. Remember, this all happened organically, without any compunction from external, authoritarian forces. This is what people *wanted* to do because of Biblical training and Holy Spirit power. Which is why most of the biggest charitable organisations in the world, even today, have a Christian origin.

Now after the two world wars in the middle of the 20th Century, Christianity began sliding out of favour in the West. Gradually, people stopped attending church in the same numbers, and Bible reading and teaching went into decline. Indeed, faith in Jesus himself began diminishing. It's no coincidence that from that moment then, collectivist tyranny slowly began to emerge.

Edmund Burke wrote, *"Men are qualified for civil liberty in exact proportion to their disposition to put moral chains upon their own appetites...Society cannot exist, unless a controlling power upon will and appetites be placed somewhere; and the less of it there is within, the more there must be without. It is ordained in the eternal constitution of things, that men of intemperate minds cannot be free. Their passions forge their fetters."*[1]

The less that individuals are willing or able to restrain their own sinful nature at an individual level, the more selfishness comes to the fore, and the more problems that creates for the collective. And therefore, to keep some kind of cohesion in society, the more the state will grow in power to restrict and enforce behaviour from without.

Indeed, human beings essentially have two options. Either put moral controls on your own appetites and live free; or follow your selfish, sinful nature and watch authoritarianism grow. Either govern yourself well from within or watch a government grow in strength to coerce you from without. It's no coincidence that wherever God is most visible, people are more free, and where he's least visible, authoritarianism expands.

This is a reason why I believe we are on an inevitable slide towards authoritarian globalism in the Postmodern Age. Because the West has turned its back on God, and since there doesn't seem to be any indication of repentance in the near future, we will keep sliding towards corruption, and in response, authoritarian governments will find more excuses to take more control for themselves and impose tighter rules. If you'd like to find more information on this mechanism between righteousness and freedom, I did a whole book and video series on the subject called, *"Stay Free – Why Society Can't Survive Without God."* You can find it at thefuelproject.org.

## The Historical Reason.

The second reason I believe a slide towards authoritarian globalism is inevitable is because if you look at world history, the arrow of time seems to point undeniably in that direction. This is another concept I've mentioned in previous projects but will quickly re-emphasise here. And the example I always use to make the point is from my own country, Scotland. It's an ancient country with a long history so it works well for this purpose.

If we were to go back two thousand years, Scotland didn't exist as a single, unified nation. Instead, the land was divided into hundreds of small pockets that were each controlled by family tribes called "clans." Each clan had a chief who was the head of the family. He would generally build a castle in the middle of his territory and from that stronghold, he would rule the area within his borders. Clans were often at war with their immediate neighbours, attacking each other, stealing livestock, and trying to take control of nearby lands. There were so many of these clans that in Aberdeenshire alone, just one region of Scotland, there are the remains over 300 castles. We'll call this the age of **local governance**.

Now, as time passed, an existential threat to all the clans arose from the South, in the form of an English king called Edward I, also known as "Longshanks." Around the 13th and early 14th century, he hoped to take advantage of this lack of unity north of the border by conquering the lands and bringing them all under his rule. In response to this threat, the Scottish clan chiefs suddenly had to put their petty squabbles aside and work together. People around the world came to hear of this story through the movie, Braveheart. It was William Wallace and then Robert the Bruce who were successfully able to unite the clans into one nation called Scotland, so that they might collectively be strong enough to fend off the invasion from the South. They defeated the English army in 1314 at the Battle of Bannockburn, and it was by working and fighting together against a common enemy that a national identity was forged.

And so we moved from the age of **local governance** to the age of **national governance**. Instead of hundreds of clan chiefs ruling over small pockets of land, Scotland now had one king—Robert the Bruce—ruling over the whole nation. England, of course, had the same setup. And the two nations were intermittently at war for many years to come.

Indeed, it wasn't until 1603 that the two countries joined together under a single monarch—King James VI of Scotland and I of England. This is the king who also commissioned the famous King James Bible. And it wasn't until 1707 that the two parliaments of Scotland and England joined together, along with Wales, to create a single political entity—the United Kingdom of Great Britain. There were a few reasons for this union but partly, Scotland faced the existential threat of bankruptcy due to a failed investment in something called The Darien Scheme. There were also growing military and economic threats coming from mainland Europe. Mighty nations like France, Spain and the Netherlands were building empires and they became a threat to Britain, who were building an empire of their own. Therefore, it made sense for Scotland, England and Wales to pool resources together and come together as one. It was largely by fighting side-by-side in these battles against foreign empires that a sense of collective British identity was formed. And of course, never was that more true than when Great Britain entered the First and Second World Wars. We'll call this age of empire, the age of **supra-national governance**–one throne ruling over many nations.

Now, after all the fighting between empires, and especially after World War II, global leaders decided that even more unity was required. They decided that such tragedies must never happen again, and that there must be greater cohesion. Out of that conflict then, came plans for the European Union. The aim was to unite all of Europe together under one political, judicial and economic system. Indeed, by 2009, the position of President of the European Council was created for the first time. We'll call this the age of **continental governance**.

That brings us up to the present day and I want us to notice a trend here. With the passing of time, power is becoming concentrated in increasingly few hands. When Scotland was full of tribal clans, there were hundreds of clan chiefs with small amounts of power controlling tiny pockets–*local governance*. A few centuries later, all of Scotland was being ruled by just one king who had much more power–*national governance*. A few centuries later, both Scotland and England along with Wales were being ruled by just one king who had more power still, even over an empire–*supra-national governance*. A few centuries after that, all of Europe now has a centralised government ruling over the entire continent–*continental governance*.

So what comes after local, national, supra-national and continental governance? Probably global governance. The arrow of time seems to be pointing in a clear direction–it seems there's an inevitable flow to all this. At some point in the future, if history is any guide, there will be a global political system and a World President. And since the Postmodernist wants globalism so badly as a fulfilment of their Utopian dream, I see no reason why the final step towards global governance wouldn't happen at the culmination of this very Age.

All I would add here is that the big lurches forward always tend to happen in response to existential crises like economic collapses and wars. Therefore, before the final leap toward global governance happens, I would expect there to be something like that—an economic Armageddon or World War III perhaps.

## The Geographical Reason.

As for the geographical reason why world government seems inevitable, and why it probably would be authoritarian, it has something to do with population growth. It seems that the more people there are on the earth, the more potential for conflict there is, and the more we create authorities to mediate.

Imagine going back to the beginning of human history and the immediate descendants of Adam and Eve. Let's say specifically to the time there were only one hundred people living on the earth. It's clear that a hundred people on this whole planet could live pretty much however they wanted. What I mean is, they could hunt and fish all day every day, and never come close to depleting food sources. They could fell as many trees as they needed for shelter and fuel, and never make a dent on the forests. And so clearly, there would be no need to manage these resources—no need for fishing and hunting permits, or logging regulations.

What happens if a hundred people don't get on with one another? What if there's friction and arguments? Well, they can simply move a hundred miles in any direction and claim a whole new territory for themselves. In fact, if they moved a few hundreds miles more, they may be able to claim a whole continent for themselves. They could continue to live freely without impinging on anyone else. And so clearly, there isn't much need to manage friction through community bylaws, court arbitration, police forces and other such things.

As the planet's population grows to the billions however, it seems clear that some organisational structures become inevitable. Billions of people can't hunt and fish all day, or fell trees at will, because then they would begin to cause extinctions and eradicate forests entirely. Therefore, some kind of authority is needed to monitor populations and make sure resources are managed in a sustainable way. Which means laws, permits, zoning, application processes, suitability assessments, renewal fees, bureaucracy and such like. We tend to create centralised controlling powers in response to growth.

Likewise, once the population reaches the billions, people can't just respond to friction by moving a few hundred miles away. Because whichever direction they travel, they'll find millions more people to rub up against there too. And even if they move to a different continent, they'll find millions again. Therefore, because people will always have disputes, it seems clear that organisational structures are then inevitably going to be created to govern. Which means more laws, rights, a police force and judicial system.

In other words, there seems to be a certain inextricable link between population growth and centralising control. Especially when, as we saw before, people don't have the governing power of God in their hearts, and therefore tend to selfish behaviour.

## The Prophetic Reason.

And then finally, and most importantly, I believe the move towards authoritarian globalism is inevitable because the Bible prophesies it quite clearly. If we turn to the thirteenth chapter of Revelation, we read that there will one day arrive a global ruler called the "Antichrist," and that he will be given *"authority to rule over every tribe and people and language and nation."* (Revelation 13:7) In other words, there will be a World President of sorts. The Book of Daniel tells us that under this global system of governance, national borders will be eradicated and instead the world will be divided into just ten regions, with a governor placed over each one.

This World President will present himself as the return of Christ, a man of peace, and the figurehead of a One World Religion. The Bible says he will have a right-hand man, sometimes referred to as the "False Prophet." He will *"exercise all the authority of the first beast. And he required all the earth and its people to worship the first beast..."* (Revelation 13:12)

The economic system will be reformed under an authoritarian model, controlled entirely by the Antichrist. The Bible says, *"He required everyone—small and great, rich and poor, free and slave—to be given a mark on the right hand or on the forehead. And no one could buy or sell anything without that mark, which was either the name of the beast or the number representing his name."* (Revelation 13:16-17) This is especially interesting in light of banks developing programmable digital currency. People who pledge allegiance to the global society will be allowed to participate, but those who don't will be blocked.

The end-time world presented by the Bible matches very closely to the one currently being pursued by Postmodern globalists. It's a One World system without national borders but instead ruled from one seat; a One World Religion; and a One World Economic system controlled by an authoritarian regime. It's the kind of world imagined by Lennon and Chisolm. I won't go into more detail here but if you'd like to know more about this subject, I did a comprehensive walk-through a few years ago called "Revelation: The Fuel Project Guide." You may also be interested in "The Coming Summer: Exploring The Signs of Jesus' Return." Both can be found on the website at thefuelproject.org.

# 8
# No Religion.

Having paused to expand upon the reasons why I believe authoritarian world government is inevitable, beyond the simple fact that Postmodern globalists are determined to pursue it in the name of world peace, let's look at what will happen if they are successful at bulldozing the three main obstacles they consider to stand in their way–those that John Lennon sang about in his song Imagine. These are individual religion, nationality and possessions. Let's start with religion.

## Godless Societies.

Will the world come together in brotherly love if we agree to do away with individual concepts of God entirely, like John Lennon imagined? The evidence from history says that's a naïve fantasy. Because this experiment you see, has already been tried. Based on the ideas of Karl Marx, the Soviet Union was formed on 30th December, 1922 and it was, *"the first state to have as its ideological objective the elimination of religion and its replacement with universal atheism. The communist regime confiscated religious property...and propagated atheism in schools."*[1]

It didn't create a peaceful Utopia though, nor a peaceful brotherhood of man. In fact, life in the Soviet Union without God quickly became hellish. During the eighty year period of its existence, people lived under dehumanising, oppressive state authoritarianism, and it's estimated that around 60 million people lost their lives at the direct hand of the totalitarian government.

The Russian author, Alexander Solzhenitsyn, who lived through those days, was once asked to account for the brutality that overtook his country. He replied, *"Over half a century ago, while I was still a child, I recall hearing a number of old people offering the following explanation for the great disasters that had befallen Russia: 'Men have forgotten God; that's why all this has happened.'*

*Since then, I have spent well-nigh 50 years working on the history of our revolution: in the process I have read hundreds of books, collected hundreds of personal testimonies, and have already contributed eight volumes of my own toward the effort of clearing away the rubble left by that upheaval. But if I were asked today to formulate as concisely as possible the main cause of that ruinous revolution that swallowed up some 60 million of our people, I could not put it more accurately than to repeat: 'Men have forgotten God; that's why all this has happened.'"*[2]

The Soviet Union is not an isolated example either. Everywhere nations have tried to banish God, they've sunk into misery. Mao Tse-Tung, for example, led a Marxist revolution in China where he closed down all churches and had religious leaders killed. Like John Lennon, Mao imagined that with no religion, no hell below us, and above us only sky, he could create a unified Utopia for the Chinese people. In reality however, it created one of the most oppressive and bloody regimes of all time. It's estimated that under Mao's reign between 1949-1976, around 45 million innocent civilians were either starved, worked to death, or just murdered by the state. To this day, the Chinese people live under an oppressive atheistic rule that denies their individual humanity.

Kim Il Sung had the same idea of a godless Utopia for North Korea. He ruled from 1950 to 1991 and rather than becoming a peaceful, harmonious society, it instead became one of the most dehumanising, oppressive countries in the world. Indeed, because it maintains that status under Kim Il Sung's offspring, it's difficult to know just what atrocities have been carried out there and how many have died—usually such things are only uncovered after the collapse of a dynasty. However, it's conservatively estimated that at least 3 million people died under Kim Il Sung's reign alone.

Another example of someone trying to banish God to create a godless Utopia was Pol Pot in Cambodia. He only briefly held power for about four years but during that time, he killed around 2.4 million people. Since the Cambodian population was only around 8 million at the time, this represents a quarter of the all the citizens in the country.

Earlier, I mentioned that the 20th Century was the bloodiest of all time, and yes, that was due to factions fighting over various "isms" as we have already discussed. But by far the most devastating of these "isms" was Communism. I've only mentioned four examples here, but there have in fact, been at least 28 attempts to create godless Utopias in the world and ruling over these, there have been more than 60 leaders. Combined, this handful of regimes has been responsible for the deaths of at least 110 million innocent people. Some experts place that figure much higher, at around 160 million. Indeed, statistically, if you live in a society where God has been shut out entirely, you are 58% more likely to experience oppression, corruption, starvation and murder at the hands of the state. Wherever God is side-lined, humans step into the vacuum and authoritarianism grows.

## Homogenised Religion.

What about the more moderate idea of simply blending the world religions into one, then? After all, the problem is less that people believe in God and more that they believe in *different* gods. That's what causes the division that thwarts world peace. What about homogenising them into a One World Religion?

Well, the bottom line here is that the idea of blending the religions together is only a good one if none of the world religions are true to begin with. If you have five types of dirt and you blend them together, it doesn't matter because at the end you will still have dirt. However, if you blend ice-cream with four types of dirt, you will destroy the one thing in the mix that was actually good to begin with. In the same way, blending religions together doesn't matter if all of them are false, but it's a terrible idea if one of them is true.

The Postmodernist believes in blending the religions together to form a New Age One World Religion because they don't really believe any of them are objectively true. And that's partly because they don't believe in objective truth at all. Ever since the New Age began in 1967 then, the attitude towards religion has always been to mix them together, taking the bits you like and leaving the bits you don't. A bit of Buddhism, a hint of Hinduism...it doesn't matter. The New Ager has always believed that as long as *Love* is the centre, nothing else really matters here. All the supposedly exclusive *Truth* claims that contradict each other in these religions can be ignored. Which is why we now have lots of interfaith conferences pushing that agenda.

But again, what if one of them really is true? The Bible makes some clear, exclusive claims about the primacy of Jesus. It says, *"There is salvation in no one else! God has given no other name under heaven by which we must be saved."* (Acts 4:12) Jesus said of himself: *"I am the way, the truth, and the life. No one can come to the Father except through me."* (John 14:6) These are hard claims. If Jesus is the only way, that means Muhammad is *not* the way; Buddha is *not* the way; the Hindu and Sikh paths are *not* the way. By asserting himself as the only path to God, Jesus himself is discarding the rest as false.

Now if these claims are true and Jesus is who he said he was—the only name under heaven by which we can be saved—clearly it would be folly to dilute or blend his words with the teachings of false prophets and false religions. It would be like blending ice-cream with dirt. You'd just end up with dirt. By blending Jesus' words with those of others, you would be abandoning something completely true for something less true, or even untrue.

## Unity Around Lies.

*Unity* isn't all that matters when it comes to our ideas about God. We need to make sure we are unified around the right ideas of God. Indeed, *Unity* without the prior establishment of *Truth* becomes *Unity* around lies.

I return to what I said a moment ago: If Jesus was telling the *Truth* about himself, and if he is indeed the only way, the only truth, and the only life, and if nobody comes to Father God except but through him, then to unite around any other belief is to unite around a falsehood. It's to unite around a path to self-destruction. It's to unite around false prophets and gods. It's to be unified on a pathway to hell.

This is why true Christians just can't be a part of the interfaith movement. To blend Christ with others is to mix our ice-cream with dirt. That being said, Liberal Christians are extremely seduced by the idea of a One World Religion centred upon nothing but *Love* and are gradually conforming to the ethos. At the beginning of the 21st Century, a movement called the "Emergent Church" began undermining the Bible's *Truth* claims and instead majored on the idea that *Love* and *Peace* was all that mattered. In 2011, a leader of the movement called Rob Bell, who was a pastor at the time, infamously released his book, "Love Wins." The message was that everyone could get to heaven via their own religious path as long as *Love* was at the centre. He was of course, simply absorbing the Postmodern New Age philosophy into his faith.

The Emergent Church has now given way to the term, "Progressive Church" but it's the same idea and it represents a big problem that so many are being seduced by the spirit of the age. Indeed, you will tend to find the church as a whole beginning to diminish the importance of the *Hard Virtues* and conforming to Postmodern thought. For example, many churches now approve of homosexuality. Even though the Bible is explicitly against it, they are willing to diminish the importance of *Truth* and *Righteousness* and fall in with the idea that Love is all that matters.

As one would expect, the Catholic Church is right at the centre of the interfaith movement to create a One World Religion centred on *Love*. In 2016, Pope Francis, released a YouTube video where he talked over a collection of leaders from the Catholic, Muslim, Buddhist and Jewish communities. He said, *"Most of the planet's inhabitants declare themselves believers...[though] many think differently, feel differently, seeking God or meeting God in different ways. In this crowd, in this range of religions, there is only one certainty we have for all: we are all children of God."*[3] The camera then cuts to a Buddhist who says, *"I believe in love."* Then a Jew who says, *"I believe in love."* Then a Muslim who says, *"I believe in love."* Then a Catholic who says, *"I believe in love."*

I would suggest that if Christians really want to love people, it's not by conforming to the New Age ethos, but rather it's by repeating boldly to the world that, *"There is salvation in no one else! God has given no other name under heaven by which we must be saved."* (Acts 4:12) It's difficult to keep holding fast to this position knowing that we are increasingly out of step with the culture, and increasingly reviled for even trying to deal in *Truth*. Nevertheless, that's what it means to be a Christian.

The Bible says, *"Do not be conformed to this world, but be transformed by the renewal of your mind, that by testing you may discern what is the will of God, what is good and acceptable and perfect."* (Romans 12:2)

We have two clear choices then. If we are not consciously following Jesus in spirit and in truth, then the default is that we will merely conform to the world around us. That will lead us away from Jesus and towards hell. That's the problem for the Progressive Church and the thing we must all consciously resist in the Postmodern Age.

And after all, if Jesus really is the only way to heaven, we love nobody by hiding that fact from them. It's like the Liberal who thought he'd be kind to the man who thought he was a bird and who planned to jump off a bridge. He wasn't really kind by hiding the *Truth*. The best thing he could have done was confront him with it and save his life. We need to confront people with the *Truth* about Jesus today, not just for the sake of their lives, but for the sake of their eternities.

As I mentioned before, we don't speak this *Truth* to deliberately be offensive. The Bible says, *"Instead, we will speak the* **Truth** *in* **Love***, growing in every way more and more like Christ, who is the head of his body, the church."* (Ephesians 4:15)(emphasis added) But speak the Truth, we must.

# 9

# Ice-Cream.

For many, I know the previous chapter just won't satisfy. I guess people may respond, *"How do we know for sure that Jesus was telling the truth about himself, though? How do we know that he is the only way, and that Allah isn't, or Buddha isn't? In other words, how do we know that Jesus is the 'ice-cream' to everyone else's dirt? The problem is that no human can point to their god and say, 'there he is' because they are invisible. Therefore, this seems to be an argument that nobody can ever win. If we don't blend the religions together into one, we seemed destined to fight between ourselves forever about unprovable things. Surely we can't countenance that. Isn't it better we just agree that nobody knows the absolute truth about this and come together around the concept of love in the meantime, for the sake of peace?"*

## Over-Estimating Religious Wars.

If that's your position, then I understand what you're saying. But first of all, I'd say that people tend to vastly overestimate how much conflict in the world is actually caused by religious arguments. Indeed, if you were to ask the average person on the street what the main cause of war in the world is, I'm betting the majority would say "religion." However, the reality is that out of 1,763 known wars throughout history, only 6.98% of them have had a religious cause.[4] Islam unsurprisingly accounts for over half of these, which means that if you remove it from the picture, the number of wars with a religious motivation is just 3.2%.

It's still something. But it's not nearly as big a problem as most tend to think. And why can't we debate these things in love? It's not a bad thing to try to establish the meaning of life. Indeed, is there anything really more important than figuring out who made us, why we're here, and what our purpose is? Discussions about these things doesn't necessarily have to spill over into physical conflict. The Bible says that when people debate about theology, it's like "iron sharpening iron." It helps us to think and develop our understanding. Therefore, rather than pretending there is no *Truth* for the sake of peace when clearly there must be, I would argue that it's worth the momentary debate to discover what the *Truth* is, so that we can thereafter unite around that.

## The Evidence for Jesus.

The next thing I'd say, is that although it's true nobody can point to their god and say, "there he is," that doesn't mean evidence isn't there and the debates must never end. It's like the wind. Nobody can see the wind, but we can all see the *effects* of the wind. And enough history has passed for us to see the effects each religion has had upon humanity. It's by examining this evidence that I think the case for Christianity becomes clear.

You see, for many centuries, the world was quite neatly divided into clear religious zones. The English speaking world and parts of Western Europe developed with a Reformed

Christian underpinning. In South America and Eastern Europe, the prevailing moral worldview was Roman Catholic. In the Middle East and North Africa, it was majority Muslim for many centuries. In India you had the prevalence of Hinduism. In the Far East it was various expressions of Buddhism. And then sprinkled across several countries since the 20th Century we've also seen attempts at Communist Atheism.

Now what has become very apparent in the passing of time is that the nations who have historically underpinned their society with Reformed Christian values have become the most prosperous, healthy, pleasant places to live. Indeed, a graphic I've often referred to is this one by Transparency International. This organisation annually produces a report listing all the nations of the world, ordered from least corrupt to most corrupt:

The text is too small to read, but the top twenty least corrupt nations in 2020 were listed here as:

| | | |
|---|---|---|
| 1. | Denmark | (Self-identified Christian 98%, Muslim 2%) |
| 2. | New Zealand | (Self-identified Christian 52.8%, none 32.2%) |
| 3. | Finland | (Self-identified Christian 84.7%) |
| 4. | Singapore | (Buddhist 42.5%, Muslim 14.9%, Christian 9.8%) |
| 5. | Sweden | (Lutheran 87%) |
| 6. | Switzerland | (Self-identified Christian 79.3%) |
| 7. | Norway | (Self-identified Christian 90.1%) |
| 8. | Netherlands | (Self-identified Christian 50%) |
| 9. | Germany | (Self-identified Christian 68%) |
| 10. | Luxembourg | (Self-identified Christian 87%+) |
| 11. | Australia | (Self-identified Christian 67.4%) |
| 12. | Canada | (Self-identified Christian 70.3%) |
| 13. | Hong Kong | (Local religions 90%, Christian 10%) |
| 14. | United Kingdom | (Self-identified Christian 71.6%) |
| 15. | Austria | (Self-identified Christian 78.3%) |
| 16. | Belgium | (Self-identified Christian 100%) |
| 17. | Estonia | (Self-identified Christian 93.9%) |
| 18. | Iceland | (Self-identified Christian 91.2%) |
| 19. | Japan | (Buddhist 84%) |
| 20. | Ireland | (Catholic 87.4%, Christian 4.8%) |

Alongside their corruption ranking, I have put the prevailing religion in each country in brackets. Now even though these percentages are only nominal and declining, a clear pattern can be seen—that the vast majority of the least corrupt nations in the world have had a traditionally Christian moral underpinning.

This isn't a coincidence. The Bible's moral instruction and the Holy Spirit's power has proven uniquely capable of restraining the sinful nature and beautifying human hearts. It's not as though Western people are intrinsically more moral or had a head-start of some kind. Indeed, prior to the arrival of

Christianity in the West, it was a truly savage place, with child sacrifice and ritual murder. For example, there's a well not far from me in Scotland where druids used to carry out ritual drownings. We have many stone circles around this area where pagan sacrifices were carried out too. We can only ascribe our moral advancement to the teachings of Jesus and the Spirit of God that we once embraced.

Most Westerners today don't even realise they inherited their morality from the Bible. They think it happened through some kind of natural evolution. I read a tweet recently that said, *"Interesting how unaware we are that so much of our cultural thinking in the West has come from Christianity. We assume forgiveness, sacrifice, love of one's enemies, sanctity of life come from inside us. They don't."* That tweet speaks the truth. We have inherited these things from a strong tradition of Christian faith, and yet we don't tend to realise it.

Now of course, as the West continues to abandon God in the Postmodern Age, the echoes from our Christian past will become increasingly faint. The power which once held the sinful nature at bay will be removed, and therefore, I expect corruption to start rising in the West in the Postmodern Age. Indeed, it already is rising. Whenever I refer to this Transparency International chart, I always have people replying something to the effect of, *"pfff, you think the West isn't corrupt??"* First of all, that's not what this chart is saying. This chart is saying that the West is merely *comparatively* less corrupt than the rest of the world. In other words, as corrupt as you think it is in the West, try Russia or China. But secondly, since the West is now abandoning Christianity, I agree we can now expect to see things deteriorating here in the times ahead. The West will become more corrupt on its current trajectory and this graphic will become less relevant. However, that's why it's important I present this information now. So that in the future, as we fall into that corruption, we understand that we were once ethical, and the decline is intrinsically connected to our rejection of God. Indeed, if in future years we find ourselves mourning the past and yearning for what we've lost, I want us to see that the only way we get those days back is by returning to Jesus. Whatever happens now, the fact will always remain that while the West adhered most closely to the Bible, and attended church, and embraced Jesus as Lord, our society became the most decent, pleasant and beautiful in the world–the envy of the world.

This is why illegal immigration tends to flow only in one direction–towards the traditionally Christian nations. There are no floods of Norwegians risking life and limb to get into Islamic Iran. There are not thousands of Canadians attempting to infiltrate Atheistic North Korea. No caravan of Brits desperate to reach Hindu India. Large scale immigration typically all flows in one direction–to Canada, the United States, New Zealand, Australia, the United Kingdom and Western Europe. And that's simply because people are drawn to the nations that have been founded upon Christian principles.

Indeed, only Japan, Singapore and Hong Kong buck the trend in the top twenty list of least corrupt nations. And since Singapore and Hong Kong were under the control of the predominantly Christian British Empire for 144 years and 156 years respectively, there may even be a Christian foundation to the morality in those places too.

I believe the evidence is clear that Christianity is the "ice-cream" of world religions, and that even if you don't believe that blending it with other religions is to blend something true with something untrue, you must still admit that blending Christianity with other religions is to blend something that works with things that don't work. Or at least, things that don't work quite as well. Islam, Hinduism, Sikhism, Atheism, and Buddhism have all had the same chance as Christianity to create societies in their image and the fact is they haven't been as successful at making happy, prosperous, healthy and free ones. Some of them have downright terrible records. When Afghanistan fell back into Taliban hands in 2021, people were scrambling to the airport, clinging onto planes for dear life, preferring to risk everything rather than live under strict Islamic law once again.

So again, why would Christians consider absorbing anything of those philosophies into our own way of life? Why, for example, would a Christian country blend anything of Islamic Sharia Law into their own civilisation, when by looking to countries where Sharia Law has prevailed for centuries, it has produced nothing but corruption and barbarism? Isn't it clear that would be an act of self-harm? Can't we see that the better idea is to dearly hold to the *Truth* that has served us so well? And even work to spread Christian ideas to other parts of the world so they can share in our blessings? So they can share, not only in what's true, but that which *works*?

If we are to unify around anything, then first of all let's unite around the *Truth*. And second of all, if you're not yet convinced that Jesus is the *Truth* as he claims, then at least unite around the thing that works. On both counts, you're going to end up with Jesus Christ.

# 10

# No Country.

The next thing that globalists believe stands in the way of world peace is national borders. As long as people have national identity, there will be tribalism and war. That's how the theory goes. So let's say the globalists have their way and erase them, and manage to create a One World system of governance. Would that help create Utopia?

## Power Corrupts.

It's a naïve assumption. A few chapters back, I talked about how rule over Scotland developed. Two thousand years ago, there were hundreds of clan chiefs ruling tiny pockets of land, and I called that the age of **local governance**. The clan chiefs then banded together under one King, Robert the Bruce and so began an age of **national governance**. From there, Scotland merged with England and Wales under King James VI & I, eventually created the British Empire, and I called that the age of **supra-national governance**. And then finally, after the Second World War, the European Union was formed and I called that the age of **continental governance**. From there, it seems inevitable that the next stage will be **global governance**.

What I want to highlight is that at every stage so far–from the local level to the continental level–there have always been corrupt and tyrannical rulers. Remember the maxim: Power corrupts. And absolute power corrupts absolutely. Wherever you find a concentration of power of any description, you will soon find people who enjoy wielding it a little too much.

In Scotland's days of **local** clan chiefs, there were corrupt ones amongst them. Evil ones. Brutal ones. I was recently at a castle called Auchindoun and its most famous story centres around the castle's chief, Sir Adam Gordon, riding to a neighbouring one at Corgarff in 1571 and killing everyone inside. However, at this local level, there was always a natural check on such corruption because if one clan chief acted in evil ways, there were hundreds of other clan chiefs of roughly equal status, resources and power who could fight back and put him down. Indeed, William Mackintosh avenged the events of Corgarff by destroying Auchindoun thereafter.

The same principle held true in times of **national** kings. In the succession of Scottish monarchs over the centuries, some of them were good but some of them weren't. Again, just recently I was at Drumin Castle that once belonged to Alexander Stewart, one of the sons of Scotland's King Robert II. He became known as the "Wolf of Badenoch" because of his notorious cruelty and rapacity. However, whenever there were evil rulers at that level, there were always other national leaders of roughly similar stature and power who could fight back and restore order.

The same held true in the times of **supra-national** rulers. For every Adolf Hitler who took it into his mind to form a coalition and subjugate a continent, there was a Winston Churchill of roughly similar power and stature who, with the help of his own coalition, could fight back and restore order.

Now we are currently in the age of something approaching **continental** governance. The entire European continent is coming under the power of a single government, and this has been done partly to compete economically with other vast entities like China, Brazil, the USA and India. Now let's say that one of these continental giants went rogue and started attempting to subjugate neighbours...and let's be honest, that could easily be China one day very soon. It's clear that even now, should a leader rampage around the world, there would be other leaders of other continental giants, who have similar stature, resources and power to fight back. One would imagine that if China ever launched an attack on the world for example, Europe, the United States, and other Western partners, would join forces and be more than a match.

But what if we then moved beyond **continental** governance and moved into an era of **global** governance, as the Postmodernists would like? And what if all the power in the world was concentrated in just one pair of hands? In truth, we could only be one more step away from that eventuality. Doesn't history show that at some point, the global government would become subject to a corrupt and tyrannical ruler? This is where the Liberal trait of dependence on government becomes very naïve. They are used to trusting the state to direct their lives in a kindly manner, but if you expand the power of government enough, corruption and tyranny is sure to emerge.

Of course, if this were to happen on a global scale, this time there would be nobody of equal power to match the tyrant and put him down. Indeed, as controller of all the world's resources, weapons and armies, nobody else could touch him.

## The Prophesied Future.

The Bible predicts this will happen. The Antichrist will rise to the top of global government and be given *"authority to rule over every tribe and people and language and nation."* *(Revelation 13:7)* Because he has control of all the world's resources, the people of the earth will say, *"Who is as great as the beast? Who is able to fight against him?"* *(Revelation 13:4)* He will be able to impose his tyrannical will without hindrance. The Bible says, he will *"wage war against God's holy people and conquer them."* *(Revelation 13:7)*

Do we still think removing all national borders and moving to a global system of governance is a good idea, then? You can understand why John Lennon said it, and why globalists want it. But it's simply naïve to think concentrating power in a few hands to choreograph the world in harmony is a recipe for world peace. It's a recipe for tyranny. Imagine someone like Adolf Hitler rising to the apex, not of a nation, but of a planet. Hitler was able to kill millions as the Fuhrer of just one country and it took six years of war for the rest of the world to get rid of him. Imagine someone of his disposition becoming Fuhrer of the world, then? Perhaps a more pertinent example is Joseph Stalin. As the leader of a totalitarian regime, he was responsible for the deaths of 60 million. Imagine someone like him having power, not just of an area like the Soviet Union, but the whole world? Imagine him having control of all the world's armies, weapons and resources. The potential for that to go wrong doesn't bear thinking about.

Of course, in the formation of a world government, the architects of it will attempt to put checks and balances in place, and those who put themselves forward to rule will fancy themselves incorruptible, but those checks and balances will fail, and leaders will be corrupted.

The Bible says that when global governance occurs, such will be the unrivalled power of the Antichrist, that Jesus Christ himself will have to personally return to depose him. This is the passage we looked at in Section One in regard to Jesus' harder side. The Bible says, *"Then I saw heaven opened, and a white horse was standing there. Its rider was named Faithful and True, for he judges fairly and wages a righteous war. His eyes were like flames of fire, and on his head were many crowns. A name was written on him that no one understood except himself. He wore a robe dipped in blood, and his title was the Word of God. The armies of heaven, dressed in the finest of pure white linen, followed him on white horses. From his mouth came a sharp sword to strike down the nations. He will rule them with an iron rod. He will release the fierce wrath of God, the Almighty, like juice flowing from a winepress. On his robe at his thigh was written this title: King of all kings and Lord of all lords."* (Revelation 19:11-16)

This is Jesus returning to defeat the totalitarian world regime that has been established by the Antichrist. And it's for this reason that again, I do sometimes wonder if the Postmodern Age is the last one. I don't know for sure, but it seems that the Soft Trench path we are on right now, if left unchecked, will eventually create the kind of world Revelation prophesied–the one that is in place prior to the return of Christ. Either way, I just want to highlight in this chapter that the peaceful Utopia Postmodernists think they're creating by erasing national borders is quite naïve. They just won't realise that until it's too late.

# 11

# No Possessions.

The final thing that globalists believe stands in the way of world peace is individual possessions, and so they could like to collectivise the world economy. The idea is that as long as people own their own things, there will be greed, inequality, and wars over resources. This is why remember, the World Economic Forum envisages a Communist future where the state owns everything and distributes it equitably. They think in this way, "you will own nothing and be happy."

## Lessons From History.

It's another very naïve idea. Inexcusably naïve, in fact. Because the Communist experiment has already been tried multiple times and we already know what the results are. To be clear, Mirriam-Webster defines Communism as, *"a way of organising society in which the government owns the things that are used to make and transport products and there is no privately owned property."*[1] That's what the elite globalists want and it's the fullest expression of their collectivist dream.

Have human beings ever been happy under such Communism, though? Never. Extreme collectivist societies have been responsible for more misery and deaths since their first implementation than all other ideologies put together. Indeed, earlier I mentioned that wherever collectivist societies have existed, the government has had to build walls around it to stop people escaping. I also mentioned how during the 20th Century, between 110-160 million people lost their lives at the hands of Communist regimes. And how as soon as your country embraces Communism, your chances of dying horribly at the hands of government instantly rises by 58%. It's such a dehumanising thing to treat people like cogs in a machine at any rate that most simply cannot accept it.

## Why Communism Fails.

Indeed, there are four major reasons why Communism fails and the most significant one is that it's incompatible with human nature. Human beings are simply not worker ants or cogs in a machine. It might make society more cohesive if we were, and it's true there would be peace if we all had the same thoughts and goals, but the fact is that we're not and we don't. Instead, we are all gloriously unique individuals, with our own thoughts, opinions, voices, hopes and dreams, who have an innate desire to express them and live free. No amount of coercion, training or force will ever knock that out of us. Indeed, throughout history, people have never fought more consistently or passionately for any other cause than liberty. History shows that most tend to think life's not worth living at all if it's not lived free.

Communism then, because it denies our essential human nature, and denies one of our most fundamental desires, can never stick long-term. People will always try to flee from it so they can be free, and if that's not possible, they'll still attempt to assert their individuality in some way. At that point, Communist leaders will be faced with a dilemma. They must either give up on the ideology entirely and admit it's incompatible with human nature, and let people express their independent thoughts, or alternatively, they must become persecutors of individualism in a neverendingly futile attempt to keep everyone restrained.

Since the rulers of the system are likely enjoying the power and don't want to give it up, and since they likely believe wholeheartedly that social cohesion matters more than individual identity, persecutors is what Communist leaders become. Always. Which is why collectivist regimes always end in coercion, tyranny and murder. In the Soviet Union, Joseph Stalin conducted the Great Purge to eliminate all dissenting citizens. Also known as the Great Terror, it's estimated he killed around 750,000 people between 1936 and 1938. In Cambodia, Pol Pot tried to eliminate all individual dissent through The Killing Fields. He murdered around 1.7 million during this time. Indeed, it's worth noting that the biggest atrocities in Communist societies don't happen in spite of the system; they're a natural consequence of the system. If you want complete cohesion, you must remove all individualism, and since people naturally are individuals, you must eliminate them somehow.

The second major reason Communism always collapses is because it requires the concentration of power into too few hands. To make Communism work, you need an authoritarian power controlling and choreographing the movements of society down to the last detail. And if you give anyone, or any regime, that kind of power, it will corrupt them. Democratic systems work because they disseminate power throughout the whole of society and even down to the individual level of the voter.

Although there is an ultimate authority in the form of a President or Prime Minister, the parliamentary system provides checks to their power. There are also term limits to make sure nobody stays in the position too long, and if they turn corrupt, there are ways to throw them out of office. In a Communist system however, power to choregraph for the ruler must remain absolute.

The third reason why Communist regimes always fail is because collectivising the economy destroys production incentives for ordinary people. Under an individualistic system, the harder you work and the more you innovate, the bigger your rewards. Under Communism however, it doesn't matter how hard you work because the benefits never increase. The government gives you the same amount of money each month whatever you do. So why bother working hard at all? Why not do the minimum you can? That's what happened in the Soviet Union. People tried to do as little work as possible because there was no advantage to doing more, and so the economic engine of the country ground to a standstill. There was saying that emerged in those days: *"We pretend to work, and they pretend to pay."* Communist nations will always become unproductive, and the economic system will always fail.

A fourth problem enters the mix in Communist societies. A capitalist free market economy works because it conveys vital information to both producers and consumers through the price system. Market prices tell producers how much people value their product, how much they therefore need to make, and how much they can sell it for. Under socialist central planning however, there's no substitute to convey this vital knowledge. As a result, socialist central planners tend to produce the wrong things in the wrong quantities. This is one of the reasons why Communist states routinely suffer from a shortage of basic goods, while simultaneously have too much of shoddy things that nobody wants.

## The Problems Are Innate.

It's important to state all this because the argument that Communists always make is that the ideology has never been properly implemented. They claim the dysfunctionality, the tyranny, dehumanisation and murder, were simply down to bad leadership, and that if we were to try again, things would be different. However, that is naïve thinking. We can understand the basic motivation for equality and the idea of a unified society is certainly enticing. However, when you enforce collectivism in the pursuit of those things, you are denying essential human nature in a way that can never truly stick, and which will always end badly.

Indeed, Communism has been in existence for well over a century now. It has been tried in a variety of countries, on different continents, with a variety of leaders, with a variety of personality types. It's been tried in European nations like Russia and Germany, Asian countries like China, North Korea and Cambodia. It's been tried in South American countries like Venezuela too. And it has always produced exactly the same results—repression, tyranny, killing, starvation, misery and ruin.

That's because the problem isn't the implementation, the geography, or the characters at the helm; the problem is

Communism itself. It has inherent problems that deny human nature and reality itself, so that however well intentioned, it will always end in absolute disaster. John Lennon sang about a world with no possessions. Trust over 160 million dead souls that we don't want that world. Madness is doing the same thing over and over and expecting different results. Pursuing Communism again would be the epitome of madness. And yet I repeat, because we live in a Left Trench Age, that's the direction we're heading in.

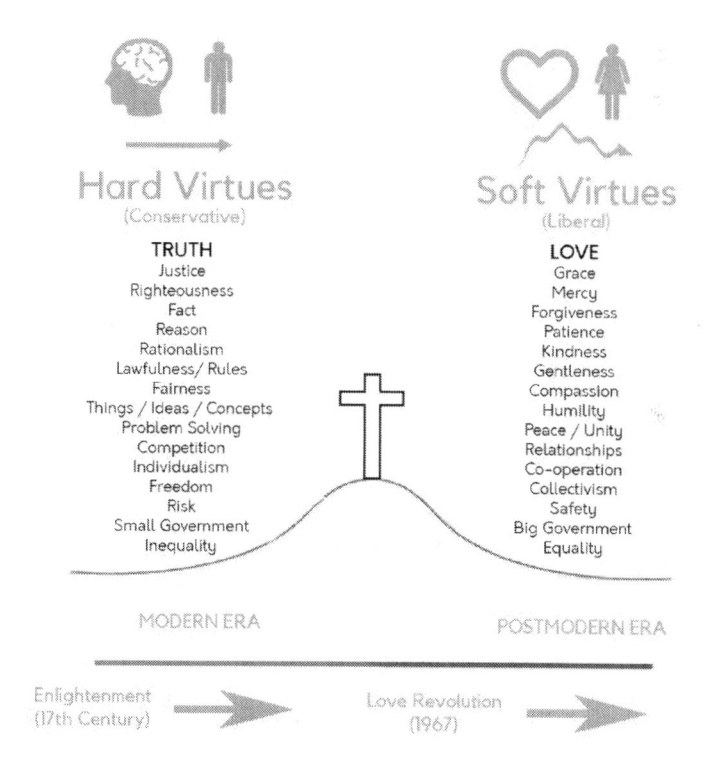

## Hard Virtues
(Conservative)

**TRUTH**
Justice
Righteousness
Fact
Reason
Rationalism
Lawfulness/ Rules
Fairness
Things / Ideas / Concepts
Problem Solving
Competition
Individualism
Freedom
Risk
Small Government
Inequality

## Soft Virtues
(Liberal)

**LOVE**
Grace
Mercy
Forgiveness
Patience
Kindness
Gentleness
Compassion
Humility
Peace / Unity
Relationships
Co-operation
Collectivism
Safety
Big Government
Equality

MODERN ERA  POSTMODERN ERA

Enlightenment
(17th Century)

Love Revolution
(1967)

# 12

# Hypocrats.

As we see a rise in authoritarian government in this Left Trench Era, we will see a corresponding rise of "Hypocrats." *"You mean, hypocrites, right?"* Well, yes. But in truth, I mean something more than that. Hypocrisy, yes. But, state-sponsored hypocrisy. Institutional hypocrisy. Hypocrisy of the ruling classes. A feature of oppressive regimes is that they never follow their own rules.

## The Pharisees.

Remember from Section One, the authoritarianism of The Pharisees? Paul, called them *"the strictest sect of our religion."* (Acts 26:4-5) Remember how they placed particularly impossible rules on the population regarding the Sabbath? They demanded people not even lift a jug of milk or a handful of figs on that day because it counted as work. Remember then, how when Jesus healed a man's deformed hand on the Sabbath, they were ready to kill him for not conforming? Remember how when Jesus' disciples then began breaking off some heads of grain as they walked through a field, the Pharisees called it 'harvesting' and were apoplectic with rage? They wanted people to conform absolutely and were ready to deliver the ultimate punishment upon anyone who stepped out of line.

Yet you can bet the Pharisees were making exceptions for own behaviour. Jesus said, *"You hypocrites! Each of you works* on the Sabbath day! Don't you untie your ox or donkey from its stall on the Sabbath and lead it out for water?" *(Luke 13:15)* Again he said, "Which of you doesn't work on the Sabbath? If your son or cow falls into a pit, don't you rush to get him out?" *(Luke 14:5)* The Pharisees were demanding an extreme collectivist pattern of behaviour and punishing people harshly for stepping out of line, and yet the rules were so draconian, they decided to exempt themselves.

Jesus therefore said, *"[The Pharisees] don't practice what they teach. They crush people with unbearable religious demands and never lift a finger to ease the burden. Everything they do is for show. On their arms they wear extra wide prayer boxes with Scripture verses inside, and they wear robes with extra-long tassels. And they love to sit at the head table at banquets and in the seats of honour in the synagogues. They love to receive respectful greetings as they walk in the marketplaces, and to be called, 'Rabbi.'*

*What sorrow awaits you teachers of religious law and you Pharisees. Hypocrites! For you are so careful to clean the outside of the cup and dish, but inside you are filthy–full of greed and indulgence! You blind Pharisee! First wash the inside of the cup and the dish, and then the outside will become clean too.*

*What sorrow awaits you teachers of religious law and you Pharisees. Hypocrites! For you are like whitewashed tombs–beautiful on the outside but filled on the inside with dead people's bones and all sorts of impurity. Outwardly, you look like righteous people, but inwardly your hearts are filled with hypocrisy and lawlessness.*

*Snakes! Sons of vipers! How will you escape the judgement of hell?"* (Matthew 23:1-34)(abridged)

With the image of unwashed cups and whitewashed tombs, Jesus is illustrating that although the Pharisees took part in performative public behaviours to give an illusion that they were following the rules like everyone else, in reality their demands were such a crushing burden that nobody could realistically keep them, and therefore behind closed doors they were complete hypocrites. This will always be the way. Wherever there is excessive legalism or authoritarian rule, you will find the leaders unable and unwilling to live underneath the burden of their own crushing decrees.

If we look at the authoritarian regimes of the 20th Century, this is plain to see. While the worker ants in the Soviet Union and Maoist China were forced to live by oppressive regulations that stripped them of their individuality and humanity, experiencing harsh punishments for the merest of individualistic infringements, that was never a problem for the ruling classes. Joseph Stalin and Chairman Mao demanded the little ants live in uniformly small, basic homes, yet they lived in palaces. They demanded the ants live on meagre food rations, yet they feasted like kings. They demanded the ants own no wealth of their own, yet they had vast hordes of it. They demanded the ants be not free to think or speak their mind, yet they exempted themselves of this restriction. Mimicking the Pharisees, Stalin and Mao crushed people with unbearable demands and didn't lift a finger to help ease the burden. They killed those who stepped out of line. They loved to parade in public and receive the adulation of the people. They loved to banquet and sit in the seats of honour. But they were like unwashed cups and whitewashed tombs. They were snakes. Sons of vipers. Hypocrites. Hypocrats.

## Postmodern Hypocrats.

Fast forward to 2020, and the emergence of Covid-19 saw Western civilization experiencing a lurch towards authoritarian rule with almost incomprehensible speed. Although you could say the "nanny state" had been gradually expanding ever since 1967, and people were definitely aware of growing government intrusion in their daily lives, it was in 2020 that our civilization crossed the Rubicon in a very sudden way.

It seemed that Covid-19 caught Western governments off-guard. There was a sense that every President and Prime Minister were initially clueless about how to respond, and in desperation, they began looking at each other to see who was putting together the most effective response—one which they could take inspiration from. And it was in the middle of this panic, that Communist China came to the fore.

The Chinese government were feeling pretty smug about themselves if the truth be told. Being a totalitarian state that had reduced their population to worker ants, they were able to order them all inside their homes as part of a national lockdown. Having done this, they subsequently mocked the West for its ideas of democratic individual freedoms that would restrict them from following suit.

Through their English language news outlet, Global Times, they taunted the West. One headline said, *"The world is now entering a global test of governance in which China is the leader."*[2] Another on 15th March 2020 read, *"Many Western governments ill-equipped to handle coronavirus."*[3] Still another from 22nd March said, *"Western political system gets a radical health check."*[4]

In one of these articles, they wrote, *"While the global health crisis may still have a long way to run, a number of things are already clear. First, viruses affect all nationalities. Second, China has done an impressive job with the pandemic. And third, other countries who don't follow China's lead have done a worse job—especially Western liberal democracies."* It continued, *"There is much to admire about the US and the individual liberties that are such a sacrosanct part of its identity, at least in theory."* This sentence is dripping with sarcasm. And responding to the idea that some Asian democracies had actually fared pretty well they said, *"While it's true that some Asian democracies such as Singapore and South Korea seem to have done a good job, that's only because they allow high levels of state intervention. Western democracies like Australia probably won't be able to follow that success."*

In other words, the Chinese government was taunting the West saying, "the only way you can handle a crisis like this is to become more authoritarian, more communist...more like us." The article finished by saying, *"China's response has been impressive but it's too soon to declare victory or be smug about the problems of the West."*

Now, back in the UK, these taunts were heard loud-and-clear, and the government bought the propaganda. This is why, under Prime Minister Boris Johnson, The Coronavirus Act

(2020) was swiftly introduced in the United Kingdom. This piece of legislation effectively suspended democracy and gave the government near unlimited "emergency" powers to rule by decree. Through this Act, laws could now be introduced without going through the normal democratic process of scrutiny, debate and votes. These decrees would be legally binding and arbitrary punishments could be dished out upon those who didn't comply. Britain effectively went through a very abrupt process of "Chinafication."

Indeed, using these new limitless powers granted to themselves through the Coronavirus Act, the British government then formally announced a Communist style national lockdown on 23rd March, 2020, that would force individuals to stay inside their homes 24/7. This happened just days after the wave of taunts that had come through the Global Times.

Further mirroring China, protests against these measures were banned. Complete compliance with the diktats was demanded. Anyone flouting lockdowns could be investigated by the police and duly punished. Drones and other forms of mass surveillance were used to monitor the population from the air and some were apprehended for merely walking their dog in the countryside. Government officials during this period encouraged people to snitch on their neighbours if they believed they were not conforming and leaving their home without government approval. Businesses and churches were forcibly closed and hefty fines were issued for those who didn't comply. The furlough scheme was introduced that made people dependent on government handouts for their income. A "Track and Trace" app was launch whereby individuals had to log their movements on government databases, detailing where they'd been and for how long. All the while, any free speech that contradicted the accepted narrative around Coronavirus was shut down. With the help of Big Tech and especially social media companies like YouTube, Facebook, Twitter and Instagram, people who asserted independent thought were considered dangerous dissenters, and were often censored or removed from the platforms, even if their assertions had scientific foundation. This was enacted so that only one type of thought could be heard online, so that all people of the world might be choreographed to speak in unison.

The almost instantaneous switch from free liberal democracy to authoritarian rule was staggering. Indeed, such was the scope of the power that the government granted itself, that when they first considered it, they didn't believe it would be possible in a country like the United Kingdom–a place with such a strong democratic tradition. Professor Neil Ferguson, part of the government's Scientific Advisory Group for Emergencies (SAGE) admitted in an interview with The Times in 2020, that it was by looking to Communist China that they were first given the idea. He said, *"I think people's sense of what is possible in terms of control changed quite dramatically between January and March (2020)."* After witnessing Communist China implementing lockdowns, they thought, *"It's a communist one party state. We couldn't get away with it in Europe...But then Italy did it. And we realised we could."*

Now under this severe and crushing authoritarian rule that demanded social isolation, separation of friends and families, even to the point of being banned from being with loved ones as they lay dying or attending their funerals, you can bet the rulers made exceptions for themselves. Even after Boris Johnson announced a national lockdown, you can be sure he permitted himself to keep going about his business as usual.

Even though the lockdown rules commanded that people not travel more than five miles from their door to exercise, Johnson himself was later spotted flouting the rules by riding his bike seven miles away.[5] Even though he had announced a lockdown on November 5th, 2020 and that remained in place into the following year, and although harsh penalties were being placed upon ordinary people for holding Christmas gatherings, it later transpired there were at least six or seven parties at his home at 10 Downing Street during that period. According to reports some of these, *"...occasions allegedly saw 40 or 50 people crammed cheek by jowl into a medium sized room."*[6] A witness said Johnson was present at one of these gatherings at least, *"and remarked on how packed it was."*[7] Johnson and his chancellor Rishi Sunak were also contacted by the "Test and Trace" app in July 2021, which for ordinary people meant remaining at home in quarantine. However, Johnson decided to ignore that rule when it applied to himself.[8] At the time of writing, many more stories like these are leaking into the public domain.

Government officials around Boris Johnson also routinely flouted their own rules. Although the first lockdown was announced on 23rd March, 2020, Johnson's chief advisor, Dominic Cummings, was caught out just four days later on 27th March. It transpired he had driven from London to Durham–a distance of 264 miles–to stay at a house near his parents. On 12th April, 2020, he had then driven for a day out at Barnard Castle, which was another some 30 miles away. And then on the 13th April, he had driven back to London again.[9]

The aforementioned Professor Neil Ferguson meanwhile, a member of SAGE and another key architect of the lockdown, was revealed on 6th May, 2020 to have been leaving his home regularly to visit his mistress. This was the same Neil Ferguson who had apparently *"been critical to Boris Johnson's decision to impose social distancing"* in the first place.[10]

Matt Hancock, the UK government Health Secretary at the time of the crisis, roundly criticised Ferguson for breaking Covid rules, saying *"his actions were extraordinary and appeared to suggest he should be prosecuted."*[3] Hancock, for his part, had become the face of the government during the crisis in the UK, as he was the one tasked with giving daily televised briefings on how the situation was being handled.

Although Hancock had used his daily updates to warn in the strongest possible terms that people breaking lockdowns and social distancing rules would be punished to the full extent of the law, and though he had demanded Ferguson be prosecuted, it later transpired in June 2021 that he had been breaking the rules as well. And for the exact same reasons. After hiring an aide called Gina Coladangelo at the taxpayers' expense, he had embarked upon an affair with her. They were filmed breaking social distancing rules by having a steamy clinch in his office. Later, Hancock was forced to resign for his hypocrisy saying, *"I accept that I breached the social distancing guidance in these circumstances. I have let people down and am very sorry."*[11]

In December, 2020, Nicola Sturgeon, the First Minister of Scotland, after regularly insisting the Scottish people were legally required to wear masks indoors, was photographed talking to three people at a funeral without one.[12] Catherine Calderwood, the Chief Medical Officer for Scotland, was caught out visiting her holiday house in April, 2020.[13] Margaret Ferrier, a Member of Parliament for the Scottish government, despite testing positive for Coronavirus in October 2020, promptly travelled by train from Scotland to London.[14]

The Welsh First Minister, Mark Drakeford, also imposed stringent social distancing and mask wearing rules upon ordinary people in Wales. He frequently warned that if people didn't obey his decrees, he would tighten the rules still further. And yet, on 16th November, 2021, he was filmed at a Diwali celebration dancing on a packed dancefloor, without a mask, and surrounded by others who weren't wearing masks either.[15]

Unwashed cups, all of them. Whitewashed tombs. Hypocrites! They crush people with unbearable demands and never lift a finger to ease the burden. Everything they do is for show. How they love to sit at the head table at banquets and receive respect and honour as they walk in the marketplaces. Snakes. Broods of vipers. Hypocrites.

## The Climate Crisis.

As I write this book, the Covid crisis is vying with another for the news headlines. Climate scientists have reached the conclusion that without immediate action to reduce carbon emissions, the world's average temperature is going to become so hostile that it threatens the very existence of life of on earth. And now that Western governments have discovered (very much to their surprise) that Left Trench citizens seem ready to accept authoritarian rule, you can bet they want to hold onto the power for the purposes of this crisis too. As the Conservative politician, Michael Gove said in 2009, *"The general rule over human history is that once powers as are yielded to the state at moments of crisis or emergency, it's never the case–or very rarely the case–that the state hands them back."*[16] With these wise words, it's amazing that Gove went on to become part of the UK government who implemented the Coronavirus Act (2020). But then people have a habit of softening their attitudes towards authoritarianism if they're the ones in charge.

Therefore, through Covid-19 first, and then climate concerns second, the elites have essentially made a power grab that threatens to remodel Western civilisation forever. World leaders have essentially concluded, *"do you know what? Those Chinese taunts really had some truth about them. Our liberal democracies really aren't effective for dealing with emergencies. We do need to be more authoritarian so we can respond more quickly, and it probably would be best for the world if we continue granting ourselves unlimited power, or at least keep it as an option going forward. The little worker ants really should learn to do what we tell them."* People in Western societies are now being conditioned to accept authoritarianism, and due to the prevailing Left Trench ethos, there are enough citizens who are now ready to go along with it.

But you can be sure the elites themselves are still not following their own rules. In November, 2021, COP26 took place in Glasgow. COP stands for *Conference of the Parties* and is an annual UN summit attended by nations who signed the United

Nations Framework Convention on Climate Change–a treaty that came into force in 1994 and which bound nations to work together to tackle climate concerns.

Now despite the elites telling the general public for years that air travel is one of the biggest contributors to carbon emissions and that we were all going to have to reduce or eliminate international travel in the future to save the planet, these same elites arrived in a parade of at least 400 private jets. These jets are estimated to have blasted a combined 13,000 tonnes of $Co_2$ into atmosphere–more gas than 1600 Scots would burn through in a year. The message seems to be that although us little people must forego foreign holidays in the future, the rules won't apply to the elites–they're too important so exceptions must be made. Indeed, as far as Jeff Bezos–the founder of Amazon–was concerned, only three months prior to attending COP26 in his private jet to make a speech, he had been the first man to launch himself into space using a private rocket ship. Unwashed cups. Whitewashed tombs. Hypocrites.

Another thing the elites have been telling us for years is that we must stop using private cars powered by gasoline, because they emit too much carbon dioxide into the atmosphere. Indeed, at the time of writing, the UK government has outlined plans to ban the sale of petrol cars from 2030. Instead, they insist we must learn to walk, cycle, and get used to the inconvenience of using mass public transport. Either that, or we must pay for electric vehicles that are far more expensive and, for the time being anyway, don't work nearly as well. Just days before his arrival at COP26 however, US President Joe Biden had used an 85-vehicle motorcade to meet the Pope in Rome. All of these cars ran on fossil fuels and not one with electricity. A number of other world leaders were spotted arriving at COP26 in fossil fuel vehicles, and these were also spotted clogging up the streets of Glasgow around the summit, even idling while stationary in backstreets. In other words, *"you little people can do without cars from now on, but the rules don't apply to us."* Unwashed cups. Whitewashed tombs. Hypocrites.

In recent times, the UK government has highlighted plans to ban the installation of gas boilers in new homes by 2025. Indeed, the International Energy Agency (IEA) has suggested that no new gas boilers should be allowed anywhere in the world from that year. Instead, it has been proposed that the general public switch to heat pumps that are costly to install and that in colder climates anyway, such as the UK, have been proven to be ineffective at warming homes. However, after demanding the general public make the switch, the Telegraph approached 30 serving UK government ministers to ask if they had done it themselves. Not a single one of them had. In other words, *"you little people need to move to an ineffective, inconvenient and expensive heating system, but the rules don't apply to us. We're too important."* Unwashed cups. Whitewashed tombs. Hypocrites.

What was even more galling about COP26 is that part of the authoritarian Covid-19 measures that had been introduced in Scotland were "Covid Passports." These effectively meant that if you hadn't received full vaccination and if you couldn't prove it with a government passport app, you would be barred from certain places and crowded events. However, none of the elites arriving in Glasgow for COP26 were asked to show such documentation. They could travel freely and participate in the conference, surrounded by thousands of other delegates without hindrance. Several photos emerged from the conference where the delegates weren't wearing masks either. One rule for the little people, but no rules for the elites. Unwashed cups. Whitewashed tombs. Hypocrites.

Indeed, over the two years between 2020 and 2021, as authoritarian rule was foisted upon the general population, many images emerged of officials ignoring their own rules. There have been videos of world leaders standing off-stage ready to make a speech without a mask, and merely putting it on briefly for show as they walk to their podium. More videos exist whereby they are schmoozing without masks, briefly put them on for photographers, and then remove them when the cameras have gone. It's all performative. "Everything they do is for show." Hypocrites.

On 26th October, 2021 it was announced that mandatory mask wearing rules that applied to staff in the House of Commons would not apply to MPs themselves. And although the government closed bars and pubs for the general population throughout the pandemic, the bar inside the House of Commons always remained open. Indeed, it was discovered that throughout 2020 since the first national lockdown was announced, parliamentary pub sales exceeded £280,000. Unwashed cups. Whitewashed tombs. Hypocrites! Everything they do is for show. How they love to sit at the head table at banquets and receive respect and honour as they walk in the marketplaces. Snakes. Broods of vipers.

The consistent pattern of behaviour for the two years between 2020 and 2021, firstly due to Covid and then latterly for climate concerns, was that though we must stay locked in our homes under authoritarian regimes, stripped of individual agency, masked, silenced, inconvenienced, micromanaged, controlled, sacrificing our income, the practice of our faith, connection with our friends and families, our travel, and even the warmth of our homes, no such rules apply to the elites. As we go deeper into the Postmodern Age, and as monomaniacal obsession with the *Soft Virtues* pushes us further towards collectivism and authoritarian governance, I believe this will become a defining mark of our time. State sponsored hypocrisy. Hypocrats.

# 13

# China.

The way that the West seemed to lose faith in itself throughout 2020—its long-cherished beliefs, values, freedoms, cultural norms, political systems and democratic structures, is most likely a huge turning point in the development of the Postmodern Era. Especially because we traded them specifically to follow the lead of China—a Communist authoritarian state. Indeed, there's a growing sense in our time that as the world moves towards globalism, China is hoping to mould the whole Postmodern Age in its own image.

The Council on Foreign Relations says, *"For more than two millennia, monarchs who ruled China proper saw their country as one of the dominant actors of the world. The concept of zhongguo—Middle Kingdom, as China calls itself—is not simply geographic. It implies that China is the cultural, political, and economic centre of the world. This Sino-centrist worldview has in many ways shaped China's outlook to global governance—the rules, norms, and institutions that regulate international cooperation. The decline and collapse of imperial China in the 1800s and early 1900s, however, diminished Chinese influence on the global stage for more than a century.*

*In the past two decades, China has reemerged as a major power, with the world's second largest economy and a world-class military. It increasingly asserts itself, seeking to regain its centrality in the international system and over global governance institutions.*

*The institutions, created mostly by Western powers after World War II, include the World Bank, which provides loans and grants to developing states; the International Monetary Fund, which works to secure the stability of the global monetary system; and the United Nations, among others. President Xi Jinping, the most powerful Chinese leader since Mao Zedong, has called for China to "lead the reform of the global governance system," transforming institutions and norms in ways that will reflect Beijing's values and priorities.*

*China is pursuing a multipronged strategy towards global governance. It supports international institutions and agreements aligned with its goals and norms, such as the World Bank and the Paris Agreement on climate change. Yet, on issues in which Beijing diverges from the norms of the current system, such as human rights, it seeks to undermine those values and create alternative institutions and models. In areas where norms and institutions are still being established, such as internet governance, China works with other authoritarian powers such as Russia to create standards that reflect their interests.*

*China has become a powerful force in global governance. Increasingly, its efforts appear to be deepening divides with other countries, particularly democracies that are committed to existing norms and institutions. Ultimately, this divide could make it harder for states to collaboratively address major international challenges. The divide could even create two distinct systems of global governance, badly undermining multilateral cooperation."*[1]

For their part, China don't see two distinct systems emerging on the global stage. At least, not permanently. They believe they will win the battle of ideas around what the globalised system should look like. Indeed, China only sees the West, with its freedoms and democratic values going into complete decline in the Postmodern Age, while their own political system rises to dominate the world.

China's English news website, The Global Times–the same channel the Chinese government used to taunt the West into adopting an authoritarian Covid response in 2020–makes no secret of the fact it wants to rule the world in the New Age. In one article from 13th November, 2021 they say, *"China has risen. We hold high the banner of people-centred socialism...The US and the West still regard their democracy as a hallmark. [But] Their political systems have been seriously ageing after hundreds of years...Western-style democracy [is] full of drawbacks such as populism, political struggles, derailed people participation, and manipulated misguided elections.*

*Western-style democracy is still able to have its say in the international public arena. It's because of the economic and social strength accumulated in history. Those countries are still the most developed ones, which has helped them conceal their ugliness and fool the world with sophistries and cover-ups.*

*However, some Western elites are now a little bit panicked. They know the West is plagued by problematic politics and a sluggish economy. Meanwhile, they have seen the fast development of China. After the outbreak of Covid-19,*

*China's "people first" political ideology has quickly transformed to great achievements in fighting the epidemic. They worry that if this continues, the fundamental flaws in their narratives about democracy will be exposed, and the perception that their political systems are "bad" will spread throughout the world.*

*The US and some Western countries in recent years have frantically increased their attacks on China's political system. Doing so is of no help to solve the decline of their own systems."*[2]

Unfortunately, China seems to be correct in saying Western elites are becoming panicked. Our leaders are losing faith in individualism, liberty and democracy. On 6th October, 2021, US President Joe Biden said, *"[The question] is whether or not we can function. There's a great debate going on and I'm not exaggerating this...all of you who deal internationally...there's a great debate going on whether or not, in the 21$^{st}$ Century...in the second quarter of the 21$^{st}$ Century...can democracies function with things moving so rapidly? And I can tell you that a couple of the folks I've spent a lot of time with of late—Mr Putin and Mr Xi Jinping—they really believe that autocracies are the only way forward, because they can act quickly and decisively. It's not a joke. And we're seeing the effects of this around the world."*[3]

Imagine a sitting US President wondering aloud whether democracy is fit for purpose, and pondering whether it can function in the future. George Orwell was right when he said, *"The real division is not between conservatives and revolutionaries but between authoritarians and libertarians."*[4] That is indeed the biggest battle of our time. Globalism is happening and I do believe a world government is inevitable, again probably preceded by a financial collapse or some other existential crisis like a war, but the question the globalists are asking themselves is, what kind of New World Order will it be when it arrives? Will it be one of individual freedom, democracy and political libertarianism? Or will it be one of group collectivism and political authoritarianism?

In the past, when the West believed wholeheartedly in individualism, freedom and democracy, there would be no question that we would fight to establish those things in a global age, and wouldn't countenance the idea of adopting a collectivist system. However, the rise of Communist China is happening to coincide with a West that is feeling increasingly comfortable with Left Trench values that point in China's direction. During Covid-19, Western leaders didn't look at China's authoritarian lockdowns and turn away in disgust–they copied them! They bought the propaganda. They saw what China was doing with their lockdowns and said, *"you know what, authoritarianism doesn't look too bad at all. Maybe we do need some of that in our civilisation. Maybe we do need to get rid of some democratic processes and rule by decree. Maybe that will allow us to adapt to rapidly changing problems more quickly in the future and maybe the idea of individual liberty is fundamentally flawed."* And from that came lockdowns, covid passports, police intimidation, elimination of counter-narratives, mass surveillance, and so forth.

Indeed, over recent months and years, we have seen Western governments acting in ways that would have previously been incomprehensible. Our society would seem almost unrecognisable to the generation who fought to protect freedom and democracy in World War II. I feel as though this book is going to age very quickly because events are happening at such a fast pace. But even as I write, European nations like Austria, Germany and the Czech Republic have just announced winter lockdowns for the unvaccinated only. Essentially they are creating a kind of two-tier society; a health apartheid. People are losing their jobs because they refuse to accept an experimental vaccine. Videos are emerging of police roaming the streets and wandering through shops and public areas looking for anyone who may be outside of their home without government approval. Austria has announced *compulsory* vaccines and Germany is following suit. Australia has established detention camps for those who refuse to get the jab and are tracking down people who try to escape. You could hardly imagine anything more dystopian than a state feeling it should have the power to inject its citizens with a substance against their will and locking them up for non-compliance. Completely unconscionable in previous times. But now, accepted. Now the elites have had a taste of these powers, a precedent has been set, and not only do they have no intention of giving them up, but they're feeling free to use them almost at will, expanding upon them, for a variety of different reasons.

In November, 2021, the Indian government announced that it was going to impose a lockdown on New Delhi, not because of Coronavirus this time, but because of heavy air pollution. They noticed the air was filling with smog, looked at what levers they had available to them, and realised Covid-19 had given them a new one to imprison people in their homes whenever they saw fit. If they could use such a power for one emergency, why not any other? Now they know they can "get away with it," as Neil Ferguson put it, you can bet lockdowns will become a regular part of life going forward, for a whole variety of things.

In March 2021, in the wake of the murder of Sarah Everard in London, Green Party peer Baroness Jenny Jones, saw it as an opportunity to call for a lockdown for all men after 6pm. She said, *"In the week that Sarah Everard was abducted and, we suppose, killed–because remains have been found in a woodland in Kent–I argue that, at the next opportunity for any Bill that is appropriate, I might put in an amendment to create a curfew for men on the streets after 6pm. I feel this would make women a lot safer, and discrimination of all kinds would be lessened."*[5] If people will accept lockdowns for one crisis, why not this one? This is why I described Covid-19 as the moment the West crossed the Rubicon. The very nature of our civilisation has changed because our government got a taste of authoritarianism and decided it quite liked it. From here, it's difficult to see a reversal in the Left Trench Age. As the world becomes globalised, it seems inevitable we will increasingly conform to an authoritarian Chinese model.

## Our Acceptance.

In many respects, the problem isn't so much that our governments are trying to implement these authoritarian measures–the problem is that we in the West are now so deep into the Left Trench mentality that we consider them reasonable. Locking people up in their homes? Reasonable. Injecting people against their will? Reasonable. Many don't see what we're becoming and where this path leads. Indeed, many are now so entrenched in the *Soft Virtues* that they actively *welcome* this level of government intrusion. They demand more! For the collective, you see. For the good of the whole. For the cohesion of the group. Regularly have we seen Left wingers in the media almost begging for the government to impose *more* lockdowns; *harsher* lockdowns; for a wider variety of things; and to punish more severely those who don't conform. At the merest hint of a rise in Covid numbers, left trenchers will flood social media with *demands* that the government lock them up and keep them safe!

In previous times, Western citizens simply didn't accept such things. For example, when King Charles I dissolved parliament in Britain in the 1600s to rule by decree, believing himself to be above the law, the people declared war on him and had him executed. The court convicted him saying, *"This court doth adjudge that he the said Charles Stuart, as a Tyrant, Traitor, Murderer and Public Enemy to the good people of this Nation, [and] shall be put to death, by the severing of his head from his body."*[6]

Many Western citizens don't value their individual freedoms enough to offer resistance anymore. Or to even be worried about what's transpiring. There are some protests taking place around the Western world, and at the time of writing they are growing, but they are generally ignored by mainstream media and not yet considered big enough to give the government pause for thought. Far from it—world leaders seems emboldened right now. The polls seem to regularly say authoritarianism is what the majority want, their power grabs seem to be met only with cheers and approval ratings boosts; and because every other world leader seems to be behaving in the same way, they continue to pursue these Chinese inspired policies. Every Western leader seems to be in a race to establish themselves as the one doing the most to keep their citizens safe.

At this present stage then, it looks like the boasts of China are going to prove correct. I don't know for sure what will transpire in the years ahead but the Trench Theory would suggest that as we venture deeper into the Postmodern Age, there can really only be one outcome—more people who welcome an age of collectivist authoritarian globalism. I hope I'm wrong for all our sakes.

## 14
# The Present Is Female.

I think we've said enough about the connected problems around collectivism, globalism, authoritarianism and communism for now. So let's move on and highlight some other features of the Postmodern Age that, if the Trench Theory holds true, will increasingly become visible in our time—starting with the idea that the Postmodern Age will become more feminine.

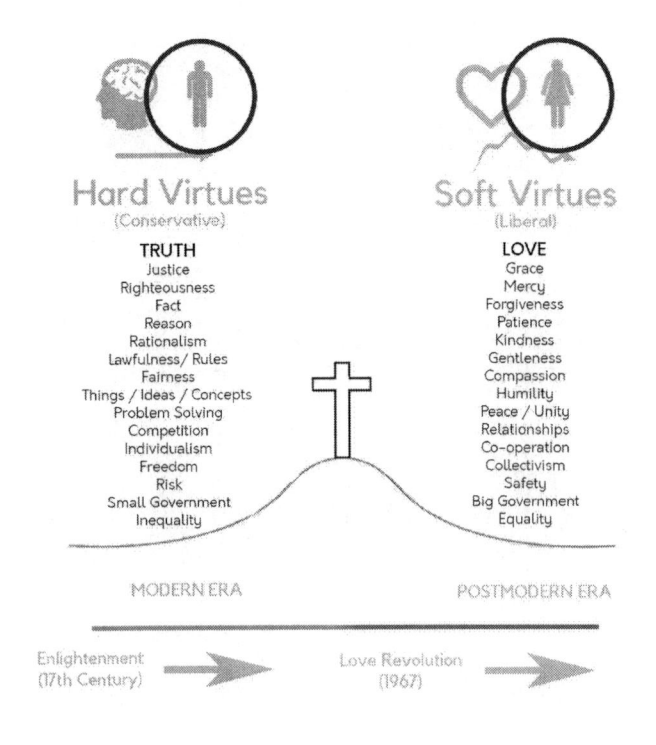

| Hard Virtues | Soft Virtues |
|---|---|
| (Conservative) | (Liberal) |
| TRUTH | LOVE |
| Justice | Grace |
| Righteousness | Mercy |
| Fact | Forgiveness |
| Reason | Patience |
| Rationalism | Kindness |
| Lawfulness/ Rules | Gentleness |
| Fairness | Compassion |
| Things / Ideas / Concepts | Humility |
| Problem Solving | Peace / Unity |
| Competition | Relationships |
| Individualism | Co-operation |
| Freedom | Collectivism |
| Risk | Safety |
| Small Government | Big Government |
| Inequality | Equality |
| MODERN ERA | POSTMODERN ERA |
| Enlightenment (17th Century) → | Love Revolution (1967) → |

Because the *Soft Virtues* are embodied by women, and because the *Hard Virtues* are embodied by men, femininity will be increasingly exalted in the Postmodern Age, while masculinity will be increasingly reviled.

## Toxic Masculinity.

I don't think this development is really in doubt. Feminism has experienced a gradual growth in support since the Love Revolution of the 1960s and although in this generation, you will never hear the term "toxic femininity," "toxic masculinity" is an idea very much in vogue. The term came to prominence in the 1980s and has seen a surge of usage from the 2010s. It's now thrown around in a rather blasé fashion whenever men are acting badly or even whenever men are acting like, well...normal men.

Now let's be clear about what the word "toxic" actually means. Some synonyms for "toxic" are *"deadly, harmful, lethal, noxious, pernicious, virulent, pestilential, poisonous, and venomous."*[1] Traditional expressions of masculinity are now seen not only as outdated, but something dangerous. Something threatening. Something deadly.

It's easy to see why our generation feels threatened by it. Natural masculinity seems to stand in opposition to everything the Postmodernist is trying to achieve. After all, while Postmodernists believe it's better to centre in the heart, men centre in the head. While Postmodernists want *Love* to prevail, men want *Truth* and *Justice* to prevail. While Postmodernists prioritise feelings over facts, men function in the opposite direction. While Postmodernists want harmonious co-operation, men are naturally competitive. While Postmodernists want equality, competitive men naturally produce inequality. While Postmodernists are comfortable with dependence on the state, men naturally want to strike out on their own, forge an independent path, and take responsibility on their shoulders. While Postmodernists want to be led, men want to lead. While Postmodernists are interested in relationships, men are more interested in things. While Postmodernists are uncomfortable with the hard edge in raising children, men require it. Men just don't fit the mould for the Soft Generation.

Indeed, how can we build a peaceful collectivist Utopia centred around the *Soft Virtues* with such things as men in it? They're getting in the way! They embody everything that this generation hates and has been trying to escape since 1967. To counter this problem then, for many decades now, there has been a concerted Postmodern attempt to change the image of what masculinity is. In short, men are being told they must become more like women.

From at least the 1990s, experts in the media began talking of the need to put men "in touch with their feminine side." This meant men were to be more emotional and relational like women. The term, "metrosexual" was coined around this time. A metrosexual man was a new kind of man who unashamedly enjoyed pursuits and activities more traditionally associated with women–fashion, shopping, skin care, beauty products, shoes, bags, make-up, and moisturiser. Their body hair was generally shaved too, conforming to a more feminine standard of beauty.

As we have moved into the 2020s, this has developed further and men are now frequently congratulated for wearing feminine clothing. In recent years, celebrities like Harry Styles, Billy Porter, Jaden Smith, Keiynan Lonsdale, Marc Jacobs, Brandon Wilson, Jonathan Van Ness, Jared Leto, Post Malone and Ezra Miller have all "challenged toxic masculinity" by wearing skirts and dresses. They have been lauded in the media for their "progressive" attitudes. Indeed, quite coincidentally, the day that I began writing this chapter, Arena Homme+ magazine launched a new edition with the professional footballer, Dominic Calvert-Lewin on the cover. He was wearing a schoolgirl uniform replete with grey skirt and blazer, long white socks, and a pink handbag. Anyone who expressed misgivings about the outfit on social media was predictably admonished for manifesting toxic masculinity. One wrote on Twitter, *"All the people saying he shouldn't wear that [schoolgirl uniform] are prime examples of toxic masculinity, we wonder why men's mental health is so bad and you look at these comments."*[2]

Now, although celebrities are renowned for attention-seeking behaviour and their fashion choices alone could not be considered evidence of a deeper societal desire to feminise men, in 2016 Jo Heywood, the headteacher of Heathfield boarding school made the headlines for encouraging the young boys in her care to start wearing dresses too.[3] She said, *"If a little boy wants to explore wearing a princess dress...that is to be encouraged. Have girlie make-up but let boys have it too."*[4] In 2019, ten Australian schools began encouraging boys as young as eight to start doing the same.[5] The same year, a school in Manchester updated their policy to allow boys to wear skirts.[6] And in 2021,

Castleview Primary School in Scotland *requested* that boys wear skirts for at least one day to show solidarity with a Spanish initiative called, "La ropa no tiene genero", which translates as "Clothes have no gender."[7]

If we were to look at any of these developments in isolation, like boys wearing skirts for a day, it could be seen as a harmless bit of fun. I'm sure such things have happened in the past in the name of charity. However, within the context of the Postmodern Age and understanding the Trench Theory as we now do, these things clearly mean more than that. They combine to represent a war on masculinity itself.

## The War on Boys.

It's no coincidence that Liberals are targeting schoolboys. If you want to change a culture, the best place to start is by targeting the young, who are more malleable and easy to influence. And after all, if you mould them, you mould the next generation. However, attempts to feminise boys are a misguided attempt to work against nature and are only leaving boys in trouble.

Back in 2000, Christina Hoff Sommers from the American Enterprise Institute wrote a book called, "The War on Boys–How Misguided Feminism is Harming Our Young Men," in which she talked about how our civilisation's restructuring around feminine ideals was beginning to harm the next generation. She said, *"Being a boy is a serious liability in today's classroom. Increasingly, our schools have little patience for what only a couple of decades ago would have been described as 'boyishness'. As psychologist Michael Thompson has aptly observed, girls behaviour is the gold standard in schools. Boys are treated like defective girls. As a result, these 'defective girls' are not faring well academically."*[8]

A major 2015 US report collected data from 5,000 subjects and supported her observations. It concluded that school environments were being tuned to fit "feminine-typed personalities," and while that was making it easier for girls to achieve better grades, boys were being left behind.[9] Indeed, boys were beginning to underperform significantly, failing to attain decent levels of proficiency in reading, being less likely to go to university, and being more likely to drop out altogether. In the United States then, girls now make up 60% of college enrolments, while men only 40%.[10] College enrolment as a whole has dropped by 1.5 million in the past five years, but males make up 71% of that drop. As of 2018, 76% of educators in the American system were also women. Research suggests that lack of male perspective in schools is part of the reason why natural boyish behaviour is often misunderstood.

For example, many teachers bemoan the fact that boys seem less interested in reading. However, it has transpired that they're less interested because the books being given to them in school today are simply more attuned to a feminine psyche. As Christina Hoff Sommers notes, boys generally won't be interested in reading if you're going to present them with Little House on the Prairie. However, if you give them a non-fiction book like the Guinness Book of Records, or something to do with sports statistics, boys will read voraciously. It comes down to treating boys as boys and not trying to mould them into the image of girls.

Often the boyish psyche is not only undervalued, but treated as dangerous. A story emerged some years ago of a third-grader in California called Justin, who loved science-fiction, pirates and battles. These are normal interests for a boy. Therefore, when he was asked to draw a picture for an assignment, he chose to draw a battle scene with a sword fight. However, this alarmed his female teacher so much that she called his parents into school. She expressed grave concerns about the boy's violent state of mind. From the father's perspective, however, he was equally concerned. Not about the picture, which he regarded as perfectly normal for a young boy, but that it had been misinterpreted by the teacher as concerning. In a similar vein, Hoff Sommers told of a Maryland boy called Josh Welch, aged seven, who was sent home from school one day because he merely nibbled his strawberry PopTart into the shape of a gun.

The feminisation problem extends into sports days, as we have already seen, as well as physical education and recess. Competitive games that boys enjoy tend to be banned from the Postmodern school playground. Dodgeball, red rover and even tag have largely disappeared. These are now considered too damaging to self-esteem or too violent. Coming from Scotland, I remember we used to enjoy a good snowball fight in the winter, but this was outlawed during my time because some kids got hit on the face and it ended in tears. From a personal perspective, we didn't care. The risk was worth the fun and it did no long-term damage. But the teachers considered it unacceptable. I have quite a big scar on my head too, because of playing football in the playground around the age of 10. I was knocked off balance and hit my head on the corner of the school. Thirteen stitches, it was!

Because of such incidents, teachers have banned these games and insisted boys play more like girls, in a peaceful and cooperative way. In fact, one popular American classroom guide even called for "tug-of-war" to be replaced with "tug-of-peace". I have no idea what that looks like but it sounds awful.

As Michael Thompson said, the school environment today idealises girlish behaviour as the gold standard and treats boys merely as defective girls, who must become moulded to be more like their female counterparts. It's impossible to change a boy's inherent nature though. And these attempts to feminise them only leave them confused and isolated. Indeed, without an outlet for their boyish interests and energy, many now attend school to a daily chorus of negative feedback that says, "Pay attention! Stop fidgeting! Don't touch that! Be more like the girls!" They come to regard school as a wholly unwelcome experience because nothing they do seems to be right. That's not to say that boys mustn't be disciplined and taught to harness their energies, or indeed learn to sit still and concentrate, but too many of their natural enthusiasms are being misunderstood as problematic in the Postmodern Age.

As Sommers says, *"If boys are constantly subject to disapproval for their interests and enthusiasms, they are likely to become disengaged and lag further behind. Our schools need to work with, not against the kinetic imaginations of boys."* She continues, *"As our schools become more feelings centered, more competition free, more sedentary, they move further away from the needs of boys. We need to reverse the boy-averse trends. Male underachievement is everyone's concern. These are our sons. These are the young men with whom our daughters will build a future. If boys are in trouble, so are we all."*

# 15
# The War Continues.

The war on masculinity doesn't end when boys leave their schooldays behind. It has become a constant barrage throughout life. The media for example, increasingly portrays traditional masculine roles in a singularly negative light.

In the 1960s, if you saw a father on television, he tended to be portrayed as wise and strong—a leader to turn to in times of difficulty. Throughout the decades however, the portrayal of fathers has increasingly morphed to that of a bumbling, infantile buffoon. It was already visible in the 1980s, but certainly from the early 1990s onwards, Homer Simpson became the archetype upon which television fathers would thereafter be modelled. A low IQ idiot, who is lazy, immature, and who is constantly making bad choices to the consternation of a long-suffering and far more sensible wife. Think of any American TV show with a family since that decade, especially in the comedy genre, and almost certainly, the father would fit the mould—Malcolm in the Middle, Everybody Loves Raymond, Family Guy—all of them. As author, Warren Farrell put it, if an alien came to earth and watched American television today, they would conclude that child development was simply about overcoming the stupidity of the dad.[11]

In advertisements, it's the same story. It's a common trope now for men to be the butt of the jokes in commercials in a way that would never be sanctioned in reverse. Typically adverts will show men being ignorant about the benefits of a product, while a woman in-the-know needs to show him the way. Men will be creating a problem that a woman will use the advertised product to solve, often with an eye-roll or shake of the head. Muller Yoghurts ran a campaign over a number of years where the punchline simply involved a glamorous woman yelling "fat free??" causing some startled and hapless man to fall over, get hit on the head with a ball, lose his clothes, or get splattered with sand or clay. Generally, the Postmodern Age had decided that men are there to be demeaned and made a fool of.

In movies, a thread of feminism now runs through a majority of stories coming out of Hollywood and people talk openly of "Smashing the Patriarchy," which more or less translates to destroying male leadership. It's generally believed that if women could be placed in leadership roles instead, that would be half the battle in creating paradise.

## Men As The Problem.

When Covid-19 struck, the media predictably began running stories that stated male leaders had performed significantly worse than female leaders in their response, merely exacerbating the problem rather than solving it. Politico ran a story at the end of 2020 with the headline, *"2020 Has Been Miserable. Is Extreme Masculinity To Blame?"*[1] Of course, you would never see a headline like that in reverse. Imagine it, *"2020 Has Been Miserable. Are Women To Blame?"*

Male leadership, and masculinity more generally, is typically blamed by the media for the "climate catastrophe" too. In July, 2021, The Independent and Guardian newspapers ran stories headlined, *"Five Ways Men Contribute More To The Climate Crisis Than Women"*[2] and *"Men Cause More Climate Emissions Than Women."*[3] Around the time of COP26, the media was flooded with headlines that said female leadership was needed to solve the problem. The Guardian declared, *"We Need More Female Leaders In The Fight Against Climate Change."* Vogue said, *"Why We Desperately Need More Female Leaders Making The Decisions on Climate Change."* Just the day before writing this chapter, BBC Scotland ran a news story that announced that women were likely to suffer more from the "climate emergency" than men. As ever, men are denounced as the cause of all problems and women the cure. Men are idiots and buffoons; women are wise and good.

Wherever there are mental health problems, typically the root cause will be ascribed to "toxic masculinity." The theory goes that masculinity is making people ill, and if we don't allow men in particular to become more feminine, they'll get depressed and want to commit suicide. Remember the Twitter comment in response to Dominic Calvert-Lewin dressing like a schoolgirl? *"All the people saying he shouldn't wear that [schoolgirl uniform] are prime examples of toxic masculinity, we wonder why men's mental health is so bad and you look at these comments."* Now, men are indeed increasingly plagued by depression and suicidal thoughts. In the UK, three-quarters of suicides are men. But our culture never allows itself to consider that part of the problem could be that a war is being waged on their very nature, and that it may not help to tell men their very nature is toxic, unwanted, and unnecessary.

In fact, whatever problems are currently perceived to be ailing the world, you can be sure there is a nearby journalist, reporter, columnist, or expert, fancying that masculinity is the problem and that femininity is the answer. If men could just stop being men for a moment, all our problems would be solved.

## Women As The Solution.

In March, 2020, UN Women shared a graphic of what their ideal global Utopia would look like. They called it "Equiterra."

It may not print very well but a closer inspection shows that women run this idealised society. If you look through the windows of the science lab, it's all women. In the top-right corner, a woman is chairing a company meeting. The bottom-left corner has a female boss being pronounced CEO of the year. Indeed, there doesn't appear to be male leadership represented anywhere in this image. Along the riverbank, there's a recycling plant where "toxic masculinity" is being dumped.[4]

UN Women also tweeted a list of ten things in December, 2020 that they felt could help create this ideal society. They recommended, "amplifying feminist voices" and "ending toxic masculinity."[5] More femininity and less masculinity is always the answer in Postmodernity.

## Hatred of Men.

Now, the further people delve into the Left Trench, and the more of this ethos they imbibe, the more hatred for men begins to swell in their hearts. On Twitter in 2021, the hashtag, #killallmen began trending. Around the same time, so did the hashtag, #menaretrash. This is truly venomous stuff. The Huffington Post reported on the phenomenon at the time saying, *"If you listen carefully on any given day, you'll hear the words 'men are trash' like a gentle hum vibrating across the globe. An anthem if you will...The phrase 'men are trash' can actually be directly translated into; 'masculinity is in transition and it's not moving f\*\*\*\*\*\* fast enough...When women across the land cry out, 'men are trash', what it really means is, your ideas of manhood are* *no longer fit for purpose."*[6] In other words, men are still being too masculine and getting in the way of Utopia. They need to hurry up and become more like women so we can get on with things.

## Struggling Men.

In the same way working against a boy's natural instincts leaves him confused and disengaged at school, constantly berating men for their masculinity has a similar effect in adulthood. Many men are struggling today, not really sure of their place in this society, their value, or even their necessity. They are consistently told from multiple angles that they're toxic dangerous idiots, and the world would be better off without them. Indeed, that their very presence is an unwanted hindrance to the world.

In response, men can sometimes try to fit in, becoming more feminine to fit in with Postmodern ideals. Alternatively, they can sometimes check out of society altogether. There's a movement called "Men Going Their Own Way," often shortened to MGTOW. It's a community of men who have decided that if nothing they do is right, and if they simply can't please women however hard they try, and if all of society is against them, they're going to separate themselves from women and from the whole system.

Society is missing out, however. We all lose when we attempt to eradicate masculinity. As we've already learned, it's a man's desire for competition that creates an environment that encourages hard work, discipline, innovation, skill, excellence, imagination, unlocked potential, mental fortitude, humility, resilience and courage. It's the same desire for competition that creates economic progress. It's a man's interest in things rather than people that mean they invent and build things like cars, planes and skyscrapers. It's a man's decisive and unyielding nature that makes him a good leader when the way ahead doesn't seem clear. It's a good man's harnessed aggression and desire for justice that makes him a great police officer or soldier, ready to take to the battlefield to defeat tyranny. It's a man's natural desire to take dangerous risks that mean he's also willing to take heroic risks, running into burning buildings to save people when his own safety isn't guaranteed. Masculinity, when properly harnessed and allied with moral goodness, is not something to be feared but something fundamental to a healthy and prosperous society. Masculinity at its best means leaders, protectors, providers, innovators, warriors, and self-sacrificial heroes. Strong families and communities literally depend on these things. And we could do with a bit more of them in a culture that's becoming overwhelmed by the worst excesses of the *Soft Virtues*.

In truth, both sexes know we need masculinity and lament its disappearance. Many women say they miss the old chivalry–the days when a man would typically take the lead; hold doors open for women; would take off his jacket to keep his wife warm; would sleep on the side of the bed nearest the door to be a first line of defence against intruders; would give up his seat on public transport; would walk on the kerb side of the pavement to shield others from puddle splashes or veering cars. It's the type of chivalry that meant when the Titanic sank, 75% of the survivors were women because the men sacrificed their spaces in the lifeboats to save their wives and kids.[11] But do you know why this kind of chivalry died? Because feminists told men it was demeaning, toxic, and they didn't want it. Feminism killed chivalry.

I read an article in the Guardian newspaper recently where a woman was complaining that men were now so scared of being accused of #MeToo harassment within the workplace that they'd completely checked out of flirting or even contact with women. This woman hated that development. She found that work, devoid of the subtle interplay between the sexes, had made her environment sterile and lacking some of its former fun. Indeed, there's a theory that the feminisation of men is what led to 50 Shades of Grey becoming so popular. Women were subconsciously, or consciously, missing strong men who take the lead, and were therefore turning to the realm of fantasy to find them.

Apart from anything else, what our society just hasn't figured out yet, although it will in the passing of time, is that going all-in with *Soft Feminine Virtues* and expelling all forms of *Hard Male Virtues*, isn't the answer. It's not going to create the Utopia they imagine. In fact, going extreme with the Left Trench is creating its own, very feminine problems.

# 16
# Toxic Femininity.

I really don't want to use the term, "Toxic Femininity." As I hopefully am making clear in this book, I don't regard either masculinity or femininity as toxic. Both are good, were made by God, and we need both qualities in equal measure.

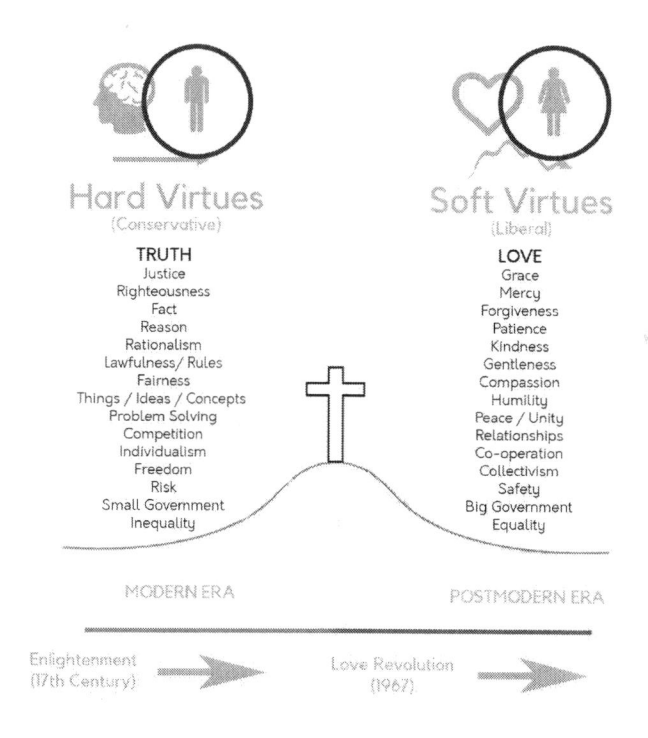

**Hard Virtues** (Conservative)

TRUTH
Justice
Righteousness
Fact
Reason
Rationalism
Lawfulness / Rules
Fairness
Things / Ideas / Concepts
Problem Solving
Competition
Individualism
Freedom
Risk
Small Government
Inequality

**Soft Virtues** (Liberal)

LOVE
Grace
Mercy
Forgiveness
Patience
Kindness
Gentleness
Compassion
Humility
Peace / Unity
Relationships
Co-operation
Collectivism
Safety
Big Government
Equality

MODERN ERA → POSTMODERN ERA

Enlightenment (17th Century) → Love Revolution (1967) →

Indeed, the central point of this whole book is that our only problem is extremism on either side. Problems arise when we go so deep into one trench that we detach from the values of the other. I only speak about "Toxic Femininity" here as a play on a pre-existing term, and because in our Postmodern Age, the biggest issues we're facing stem not from extreme *Hard Virtues*, but extreme *Soft*. Let's look at three examples.

## Cancel Culture.

Cancel culture could be said to be a result of "Toxic Femininity." Men and women tend to resolve differences with people of their own sex in very distinct ways. Men take a more direct, confrontational, and risky approach, by going into direct physical combat with an opponent. That is to say, they fight. Normally, these fights are short lived, and once they've been had, the matter is considered to have been dealt with.

Women deal with differences in a very different way. Remember, this is a sex who places the utmost emphasis on interpersonal relationships, co-operation, equality, and inclusion. These are female values. Within that context then, what is the ultimate punishment a woman deliver upon an enemy? Social *exclusion*. Denial of relationship. Character defamation. Women deal with rivals not through physical aggression, but through social aggression. Rather than fighting with fists, women wage a war of reputational destruction. They will gossip, whisper and spread rumours about their rival, hoping to create both a united group and an excluded foe.

They'll go to great lengths to make sure it happens. Very few things are considered off-limits in these psychological assassinations. Women will attack status, character, career, and any existing friendships or forms of support to make their rival feel completely ostracised. In many ways, a female attack can be much more considered and comprehensive than a male's. They don't just want to punch an enemy on the nose and be done with it; they want their enemy to feel mentally and emotionally alone.

There are many studies that have explored why women display aggression in this more subtle, yet comprehensive way. Paula Stockley and Anne Campbell produced a paper in 2013 on "Female Competition and Aggression." They concluded that females are primarily wired to survive, to compete for preferred mates, and to reproduce. They suggested that all three priorities make women more averse to risk, and this is perhaps why their aggression to other females is low risk and indirect. They said, female strategies in regard to a rival include, *"refusal to cooperate with them, destruction of their reputation (so that others will also refuse cooperation), and ultimately exclusion from the group. Indirect aggression (the use of pejorative gossip and social exclusion) is women's preferred aggressive tactic. Because harm is delivered circuitously and because it is executed simultaneously be several members of the community, it is a low risk strategy."*[7]

The study continues by saying, *"the strong bonds between women and their emotional interdependence make victimisation by indirect aggression a particularly painful experience, leading to depression and even suicide."*[7] This basically echoes what we've been saying already. That because women hold relational unity to be of paramount importance, and because women depend on one another for support, the most hurtful thing one can do to another is exclude and deny that relationship—to make someone feel like an outsider. Studies have shown that women's heart rates increase in response to the stress of social exclusion far more than in men. And indeed, social exclusion is far more costly for women, since men are less relational beings anyway, and rely less heavily on a friendship network.

Now because the Postmodern Era is essentially feminine, we are seeing this aspect of "toxic femininity" coming to the fore through "cancel culture." We've already discussed the problem of this thing but cancel culture is described by Wikipedia as *"a form of ostracism in which someone is thrust out of social or professional circles—whether it be online, on social media, or in person. Those subject to this ostracism are said to have been "cancelled"...[It] constitutes a form of boycotting or shunning involving an individual (often a celebrity) who is deemed to have acted or spoken in a questionable or controversial manner."*[8]

This is such a feature of our time that barely a day passes where some individual isn't having their lives brought to ruin because of being cast out in this very feminine way. Remember Peter Vlaming, David Meckerith, Kathleen Stock and Professor Robert Winston being "howled down" and losing their jobs for stating obvious truths? They were cancelled. This happens to ordinary people quite regularly now—being shunned, having their reputation shredded and their livelihoods destroyed, often just for speaking facts. Facts that may be divisive and that may hurt feelings, but facts nonetheless.

And that leads us onto the curious behaviour of "Virtue Signalling." Stockley and Campbell noted that women prefer to deliver harm circuitously, executed by several members of a community, because it's a low risk strategy. Therefore, in the feminine Postmodern Age, if someone comes across a *Truth* that they believe could hurt feelings or disturb the collective ideology, they put up a signal to wider society that effectively says, *"I've found a trouble-maker here! A traitor is in our midst! Someone here is refusing to conform!"* In response to this signal, a group then gathers round to either bully them into submission, or ostracize them completely from society.

The person who raised the flare in the first place has at least two solid motivations for doing it. Firstly, it's a low risk strategy for them. Often, virtue signalling is carried out online so there's no physical risk involved and again, it's delivered circuitously. Secondly, virtue signalling gains favour with the collective. It's a way of saying, "look how right-on my own opinions are. Look how they mirror the group orthodoxy. Look what a true believer I am." It helps bind a person to the group. Creating a common enemy in general is a good way to bind a group together.

Now of course, as we saw earlier, cancel culture creates a myriad of problems for society. People are having their lives and reputations utterly ruined merely for stating basic facts. They're being denied jobs, platforms and friends for departing from the group orthodoxy. In turn, this is leading to the criminalisation of free speech and the proliferation of absurdity. It's leading to collectivist government that stamps out individualism and dehumanises. And it's leading to tyranny. A very feminine, Left Trench type of tyranny.

## Lived Experience.

A second outworking of "toxic femininity" that we are experiencing in Postmodernity is the prioritisation of feelings over facts—what has become known as the primacy of "Lived Experience."

I'll give an example of this. Let's say that a black woman is walking down the street and she *feels* that a white man gave her a strange look. She interprets this look as being evidence of racism. Now it may not have been. The guy may have been grumpy with everyone that day; he may not have been looking at her at all and she may have misread the direction of his glance; she may have misinterpreted what it meant; or indeed, *she* may have been the irritable one that day. There are all kinds of possible explanations. But regardless of what the objective truth is, because she *feels* she has been a victim of racism, that goes down in the Postmodern parlance as her "Lived Experience." Which means that as far as anyone is concerned, she has now officially been a victim of racism. Even if she hasn't. In her eyes she has. And what she *feels* is sacrosanct. Nobody can invalidate what she *feels*. Her subjective feelings trump facts.

Many people in the Left Trench will now quite happily accept someone's *Lived Experience* as incontrovertible evidence. For example, if there's a company where one disabled person *feels* there's systemic discrimination against him, he might bring his complaint to the management. Now let's say the management take the complaint seriously and a review is launched, through which all the other disabled workers are asked for their opinion. Now let's say the other disabled workers reply that there is no discrimination as far as they're concerned. The management want to make absolutely sure though. So they conduct further checks to make sure there's no wage disparity or access problems. And there isn't. In other words, the hard data all says there is no systemic racism in the company. They go back to the original complainer and say that all the hard evidence points towards the fact there is no discrimination. The original complainer may now *feel* offended that his *Lived Experience* is being questioned and invalidated. He knows what he *feels*. And if he feels it, that is all that matters. Which means in the Postmodern Age, he is officially considered a victim of discrimination. Even if he isn't. Indeed, if he were to take his story to the media and tell them he feels discriminated against, they would generally have no hesitation in branding the company discriminatory. Even if they're not. That's what they'll be called. Because in the Postmodern Age, a person's *Lived Experience* simply can't be denied. His subjective feelings trump facts.

Quite irrational stuff, right? And this emphasis on subjective feelings over facts causes many problems for society. People and companies are now being vilified for things they have never done; being forced to apologise for things that never happened; being cancelled for attitudes they don't have; reprimanded for systemic problems that don't exist. And because people are now aware they can make others dance to their tune by claiming a negative *Lived Experience* without requiring any hard evidence to support it, it encourages people to make more of these spurious claims for personal gain. This irrationality, and elevation of feelings over facts, is a result of what could be called, "toxic femininity."

## Safetyism.

The third and final feature of "toxic femininity" I would highlight is something called, "Safetyism." This is a term that I first came across in a book called, "The Coddling of the American Mind" by Greg Lukianoff and Jonathan Haidt. It's such an important concept that we're going to end the chapter here and start a new one devoted to it.

# 17
# Safetyism.

In Psychology, neuroticism is described as one of the big five personality traits and it's *"the degree to which a person experiences the world as distressing, threatening, and unsafe. Each individual can be positioned somewhere on this personality dimension between extreme poles: perfect emotional stability versus complete emotional chaos."*[1]

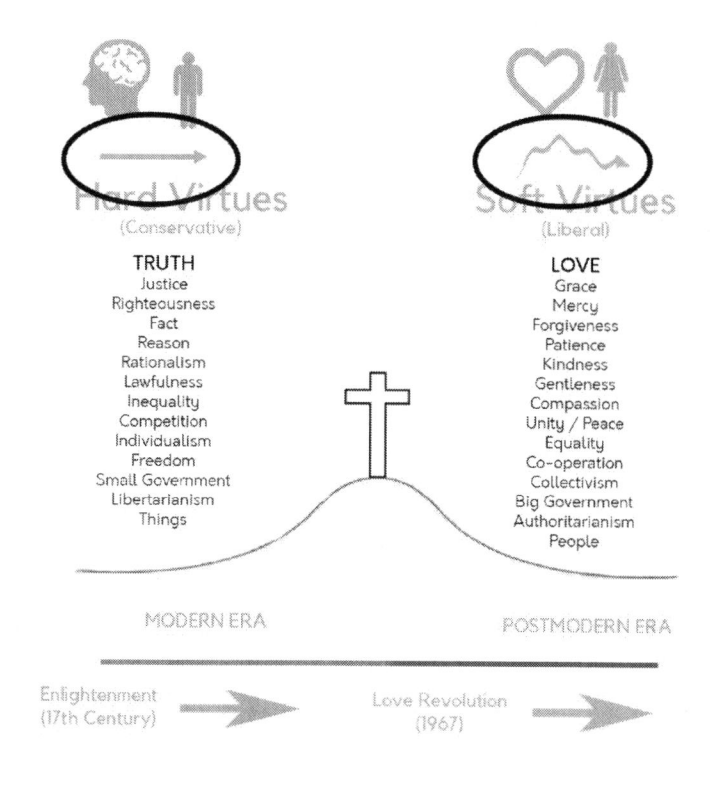

| Hard Virtues (Conservative) | Soft Virtues (Liberal) |
|---|---|
| **TRUTH** | **LOVE** |
| Justice | Grace |
| Righteousness | Mercy |
| Fact | Forgiveness |
| Reason | Patience |
| Rationalism | Kindness |
| Lawfulness | Gentleness |
| Inequality | Compassion |
| Competition | Unity / Peace |
| Individualism | Equality |
| Freedom | Co-operation |
| Small Government | Collectivism |
| Libertarianism | Big Government |
| Things | Authoritarianism |
|  | People |

MODERN ERA → POSTMODERN ERA

Enlightenment (17th Century) → Love Revolution (1967) →

Now as our graphic perhaps indicates, women as a whole tend to score far more highly in neuroticism than men, meaning women tend to be more fearful of pain, are more likely to anticipate it, and are more risk averse to things that may cause it. In contrast, because men score much lower in neuroticism, they less fearful of pain, are less likely to anticipate it, and are far more risk tolerant—even risk loving. In other words, while women may often overestimate dangers and be prone to worry unnecessarily, men may underestimate dangers and not worry when they should.

There are many studies on this but to highlight just a couple, a joint 2008 experiment between the University of Wroclaw in Poland and the University of Liverpool explored everyday situations like catching a bus and crossing a busy road. They discovered that although both sexes are competent optimisers of time and both aim to minimise their wait at the bus stop, *"single males pursue a more risky strategy than single females by cutting waiting times much finer."*[2] Also, when crossing a busy road they discovered men are more likely to take chances. They said, *"Males are more likely than females to cross busy roads when it is risky to do so."*

A similar study in 2006 by the University of California, San Diego examined the risks men and women are willing to take with a whole range of things including money, health, recreation and social activities, and on all fronts, women were more risk averse. They discovered that women were more likely to anticipate negative outcomes; their perception of how disastrous those outcomes would be was greater; and they anticipated less enjoyment from participating in a risky activity overall, even if they were to be successful.[3]

Now this tendency to overestimate danger has many advantages for women. For example, women statistically are safer drivers than men. With a heightened sense of peril, they drive on average 12% more slowly than men, meaning they need to hard brake 11% less than men. They are more likely to abide by traffic laws too, and take extra care with safety measures like seatbelts.[4] A 2020 study by Injury Prevention looked at 14,425 road fatalities between 2005 to 2015 and they discovered that male car drivers had twice the rate of fatalities per mile driven compared to women during that period. Male motorcyclists had 12 times the rate of fatalities compared to women too.

I'm reminded of an old meme that helps demonstrate this point clearly. It involves a father throwing his child into the air:

**AS THE FATHER SEES** | **AS THE CHILD SEES** | **AS THE MOTHER SEES**

The father is not worried about something going wrong here, he doesn't anticipate it would be particularly catastrophic if it did, and he thinks the fun is worth it. He has very low levels of neuroticism.

The mother has an entirely different perception. Because of her higher neuroticism score, she worries more that something will go wrong here, anticipates more pain if it did, and doesn't consider the activity itself to be worth the risk. She has higher levels of neuroticism.

You may have experienced this in your own life–males urging risk and females urging caution. I still have vivid childhood memories of my dad playing wrestling games, or throwing us in the air at the swimming pool, or taking the stabilisers off my bike before I felt ready. I also remember being quite small and my great uncle kicking a football off my face and my nose bleeding. And by the same token, whenever I was doing anything remotely energetic as a child, I remember my grandma's typical warning, "Eee! Watch, or you'll break your neck!" Everything was a potential neck-breaker to my grandma.

    I remember when I was small, my best friend Brendan had a go-kart, so our first thought was to go to the top of the biggest hill we could find, get in it together, and see how fast it would go. We didn't worry something could go wrong, and didn't anticipate it would be catastrophic if it did. Furthermore, we considered the fun to be worth it. Our first instinct was simply to push the limits. As it happens, we ended up crashing on our first run and getting the go-kart stuck in a hedge.

    Similarly, I remember the day I first tried a pair of roller blades, aged fourteen. Instead of getting the basics mastered in a safe manner on a flat surface, I immediately went to the top of the same hill where we'd crashed the go-kart, and I launched myself down it. I didn't fear anything going wrong, didn't anticipate it would be catastrophic if it did, and considered the fun worth the risk. Only halfway down did I remember I hadn't learned how to stop yet. I ended up crashing, landing flat on my back and winding myself. My next outing with those roller blades, again before I'd learned how to stop, saw me skating down the main street in Aberdeen city centre.

    Now, in times gone by, this kind of behaviour was regarded as natural rough-and-tumble boyishness, and parents generally would have accepted that kids would do risky things as a part of growing up. However, in the feminine Postmodern Era, this kind of stuff has become horrifying. We are a far more neurotic society now, and we are much more weighted towards caution. Indeed, we tend to now prioritise safety above every other consideration and we have become obsessive about eliminating all forms of risk entirely. Have you ever heard people lamenting that "health and safety has gone mad"? The Trench Theory makes sense of why. In our Postmodern Age, things were always going to develop in this way.

## Safety Above All.

The growing emphasis on safety in the Postmodern Era brought many advantages to begin with. Car seatbelts were one of the first developments, being made compulsory in new cars from 1968. In 1983, it became illegal not to make use of them. The same decade brought the arrival of airbags. And then in 2006, child car seats became mandatory.[5] Childproofing in the home became commonplace over the years—safety caps were added to toxic cleaning products, and stair gates stopped kids from tumbling down them. In the workplace, health and safety rules were tightened, meaning dangerous products and practices were eliminated. And as a result, injuries and deaths on the road, in the home, and in the workplace, plummeted significantly through the latter half of the 20th Century. From 1960 to 1990, there was a 48% reduction in injuries, accidents and deaths amongst 5-14 year olds.[6]

As we moved deeper into the Left Trench in the 21st Century however, healthy caution gradually turned into neuroses, and society began adopting a zero-tolerance attitude towards risk. For example, you may notice in the aftermath of tragic accidents like someone drowning in a lake, it has become common to hear experts on the news saying things like, "we must make sure accidents like this can *never* happen again." Or, "We must make sure families *never* experience this kind of grief again." It makes a good soundbite but making sure *nobody* can *ever* drown in a lake *ever* again? It's not only unfeasible to eliminate all risk from life, but the effort usually translates into laws, regulations, monitoring, controls, restrictions or even complete bans on what people can do. This is why we have seen a rise of the "nanny state" in the Postmodern Age, whereby the government starts treating citizens as if they were toddlers. The neurotic sensibility that has zero-tolerance for risk has become a backdoor through which more authoritarianism has entered into our world. It's a tyranny exercised "for our own good." See how all the virtues on each side automatically invoke the others?

## Mental and Emotional Safety.

In our Postmodern Age, with its focus on feelings, we have even begun to expand the concept of safety beyond the physical to the emotional and mental too. We now believe people should be protected from not only physical pain, but from all emotional and mental distress too.

In 2014 then, Oberlin College in Ohio, USA, posted guidelines for the faculty staff at the beginning of the semester, urging them to start making use of *"trigger warnings...to show students you care about their safety."*[6] I guess everyone knows what trigger warnings are by now, but it simply means that if you're going to say something that some students may find mentally or emotionally distressing, you warn them ahead of time so they can leave the room or protect themselves in some other way.

In another part of the Oberlin memo, they encouraged staff to start using student's preferred pronouns (for example, "zhe" or "they" for students who didn't want to be referred to as "he" or "she") specifically because if a professor used an incorrect pronoun, they felt this would *"prevent or impair [student's] safety in a classroom."* The Postmodern Age is the first time in human history that the concept has emerged that saying something upsetting could be considered putting someone "in danger." In the past, we may have said a student would feel offended by our words, but that it makes them *unsafe?* That upsetting them emotionally puts them in *danger?* This is a brand new idea. But again, an almost inevitable development for our Age once you understand the Trench Theory.

Keeping students safe from challenging ideas and hurt feelings led to the invention of *"Safe Spaces"* too. These were first introduced at Brown University in Rhode Island, when a debate was due on campus around rape culture. Feminist author, Wendy McElroy made the case that she didn't think the United States had a rape culture. However, since many Brown students believed it did have a rape culture, this would challenge their feelings, and perhaps even their "Lived Experience." Because having their feelings challenged may cause discomfort, many at the university believed the debate would put the students in "danger." To provide an escape route from the trauma, and so that their emotional comfort might be preserved, Brown

University created a "Safe Space" for students to retreat to. The room was equipped with cookies, colouring books, bubbles, play-doh, calming music, blankets and pillows, and a video of frolicking puppies. One student who later used the Safe Space said, *"I was feeling bombarded by a lot of viewpoints that really go against my dearly held beliefs."*[6]

In "The Coddling of the American Mind" by Greg Lukianoff and Jonathan Haidt, they call this extreme neuroticism, "Safetyism."[6] It's simply the very Postmodern, and naturally feminine, idea that safety should be prioritised above all other concerns and that there should be a zero-tolerance approach to all forms of risk—whether that be physical, mental or emotional.

## The Problem With Safetyism.

So what's wrong with safetyism? What's the harm in being a little neurotic? Why shouldn't we protect people at all costs? Isn't it always better to be safe than sorry? Shouldn't we try to eliminate all risk from life? Well, the problem is that this attitude can stunt personal growth, promote anxiety, and sometimes even create the very problems people are trying to prevent.

Haidt and Lukianoff use the example of peanut allergies to make the point. You see, up until the 1990s, peanut allergies were very rare amongst American children. One study found that only four in a thousand kids under the age of eight had any such problem. By 2008 however, that number had more than tripled—fourteen out of a thousand children now had a peanut allergy.

Nobody knew why children were becoming more allergic but in response to some scare stories in the news, many parents and schools decided it would be best to ban peanuts altogether. Even if the chance of dying was miniscule, it's better not to take the risk at all. And what's the harm in playing safe? Better safe than sorry, right? All it means is that parents have to slightly adapt when preparing lunches.

However, a later study found that it was exactly *because* parents and teachers had started over-protecting children from exposure to peanuts back in the 1990s that the numbers of those who were allergic started rising. Learning About Peanut Allergy (LEAP) found in 2015 that if a child is exposed to peanuts from infancy, their body learns to recognise and adapt to it. However, if the child is kept away from peanuts throughout childhood, when they are inevitably exposed to them in later life, the body doesn't recognise them, perceives them as a threat, and triggers an over-exaggerated allergic response.

The researchers at LEAP studied 640 infants who they believed were at high risk of a peanut intolerance, due to the fact they already had eczema or some other allergy. They told half the parents of these babies to follow a safety-first approach, and to keep their child away from peanuts at all costs. The other half were given a supply of snacks made from peanut butter, and they were told to give their child some three times a week. The researchers followed all the families carefully and when the babies turned five years old, they were tested for an allergic reaction to peanuts.

The results were clear. Among the children who had been "kept safe" from peanuts, 17% had developed an allergy.

Among the children who had been exposed to peanuts, only 3% had developed an allergy. One researcher said, *"For decades, allergists have been recommending that young infants avoid consuming allergenic foods such as peanuts to prevent food allergies. Our findings suggest this advice was incorrect and may have contributed to the rise in peanut and other food allergies."*[6]

Our immune system learns from experiences and if it doesn't have those experiences, it can't adapt. Indeed, our immune system actively *requires* exposure to a range of foods, bacteria, viruses, and even parasitic worms because that's how it learns what these things are, and develops a strong response. Vaccines typically work by this logic as well. Instead of trying to keep children away from viruses altogether, scientists discovered if you inject a little bit of the virus into the body in a controlled manner, it will learn what it is and learn how to destroy it. Meaning that in the future, that virus will cease to pose a serious threat.

There's a whole hypothesis around this called the "hygiene hypothesis." It basically notes how the more wealthy and clean a country gets, the more allergy rates tend to rise. Developmental psychologist, Alison Gopnik explains that there's a lesson to be learned here in how we raise our children. She says, *"Thanks to hygiene, antibiotics and too little outdoor play, children don't get exposed to microbes as they once did. This may lead them to develop immune systems that overreact to substances that aren't actually threatening—causing allergies."* She continues, *"In the same way, by shielding children from every possible risk, we may lead them to overreact with exaggerated fear to situations that aren't risky at all and isolate them from the adult skills that they will one day have to master."*[6]

Now we're getting to the nub of the problem of safetyism. In the same way our immune system need exposure to stressors to adapt, learn and grow strong, human beings as a whole need physical, emotional and mental stressors to adapt, learn and grow strong. If we are overprotected from those stressors as children, we become weaker, and we then tend to overreact with exaggerated fear to situations that aren't risky at all. In short, overprotection leads to anxiety and even more neuroticism.

Do you want to develop strong physical muscles? Then don't protect the muscles from stress; actively go looking for stress. Lift weights, run, swim, and go to the gym. It's stressful, but it's by that pain that your body grows strong and becomes capable of tackling inevitable future daily physical challenges. There will come a time when you need to climb stairs or run to catch a bus and it'll be easy. If you protect your body from stressors however, your muscles weaken and your joints lose range of motion; your cardio function declines; you perhaps develop chronic health problems; which means you will find it harder to tackle real life.

That's a picture of what we're doing when we try to overprotect people emotionally and mentally. If you want to be mentally robust, and develop critical thinking skills, and an ability to solve problems, and tackle real life, you don't hide from mental stressors but instead you embrace them. Schools and universities are supposed to be mental gyms where you are exposed to a wide range of ideas that challenge and confront and make you uncomfortable. This is how you learn, adapt and grow strong. If students don't get this at school and if they are overprotected from challenging ideas through trigger warnings and safe spaces, then as Gopnik says, they will later tend to *"overreact with exaggerated fear to situations that aren't risky at all"* and will be *"isolated from the adult skills that they will one day have to master."* Very clearly, by prioritising safety above everything, we are creating an overly neurotic generation that is incapable of handling real life, and that overreacts to perceived danger where there is none. That in turn, is causing a rise in anxiety and depression, because people begin to see the whole world as an overwhelming danger against which they have no agency.

## Antifragility.

In 2012, Professor of Risk Engineering at New York University, Nassim Nicholas Taleb, coined the term "Antifragile" to describe human beings. He said the world is composed broadly of three things—The Fragile, The Resilient and the Antifragile.

Fragile things are those that break easily and cannot heal themselves, like china teacups. If you drop one, it smashes into bits and it can't be put back together. It's fragile.

Resilient things are those that can withstand a beating but still deteriorate over time. Think of a toddler's juice cup. It's made of thick plastic so it can handle being bashed around and dropped on the floor. However, they don't benefit from them either. They will start looking the worse for wear eventually. But they're resilient.

And then finally, you've got antifragile things. These are things that *require* stressors and challenges to grow strong. Our immune systems are antifragile. Our muscles are antifragile. And *we* are antifragile. Taleb says, *"Just as spending a month in bed...leads to muscle atrophy, complex systems are weakened, even killed, when deprived of stressors. Much of our modern, structured, world has been harming us with top-down policies and contraptions...which do precisely this: an insult to the antifragility of systems. This is the tragedy of modernity: as with neurotically overprotective parents, those trying to help are often hurting us the most."*[6]

It's the repeating message of this book—that which starts as a virtue, if taken to extremes becomes a vice. A little bit of healthy caution is good but at the extreme end, neurotic safetyism creates a generation of weak, fearful, incapable, anxious, stressed, depressed, and overwhelmed people. And since the government has adopted this approach towards society in general, and since parents have adopted this approach towards their children, that is indeed the kind of generation we are creating.

A major contributor to this problem is that fathers are increasingly not present in their kid's lives. Indeed, it's reckoned that more than 1 in 4 are growing up without a father in the home.[7] Without that male influence that naturally encourages risk; that throws kids in the air; that takes stabilisers off their bikes at a too young age; that plays football with them a little too hard; children are not learning that sense of personal empowerment that they will need to overcome challenges of life in future. And from this we again see that the problems of our Age are not stemming from too much masculinity, but not enough. Indeed, this is the third negative outcome of what could be called, "toxic femininity." An over-emphasis on caution.

The best thing we can do at this juncture is start valuing what fathers, and what men in general, naturally bring to the table. Stop calling it "toxic" because we need it. We need the kind of masculinity that encourages kids to engage in unstructured play again; that provokes them to embrace risk and do challenging things; that gets them into activities where they might scrape their knees, get stuck in hedges with go-karts, and bloody their nose with a football or a snowball. The masculinity that gets kids dirty and covered in mud. The kind that challenges their minds with ideas that make them uncomfortable and that doesn't shield them too much from life's problems. If we don't re-balance by bringing this kind of masculinity back into our lives, our whole civilisation will suffer.

# 18
# The Fear Economy.

The pervading neuroticism of the Postmodern Age became especially prominent during the outbreak of Covid-19. And as you'd expect it was Liberals who were particularly prone to overestimate the danger.

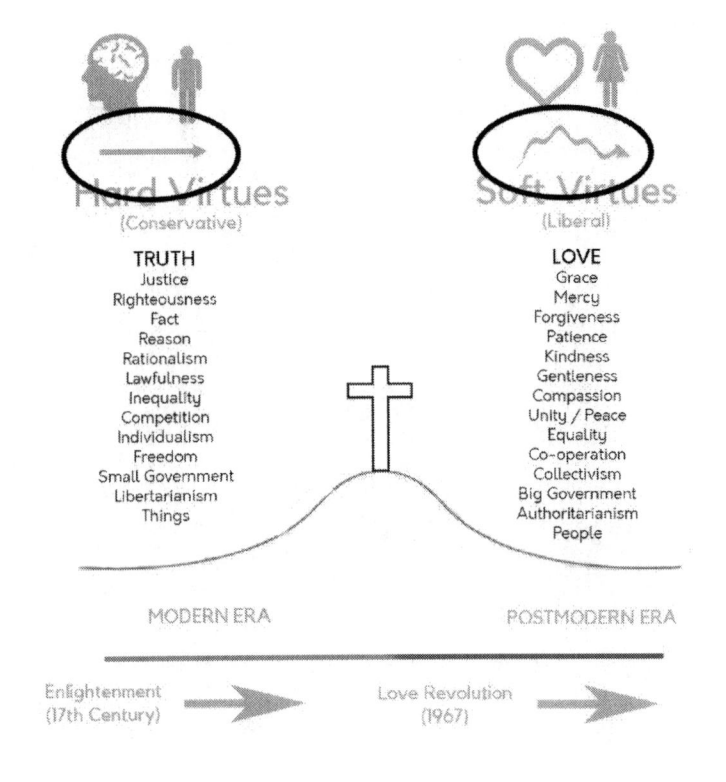

|  Hard Virtues  |  Soft Virtues  |
| :---: | :---: |
| (Conservative) | (Liberal) |
| **TRUTH** | **LOVE** |
| Justice | Grace |
| Righteousness | Mercy |
| Fact | Forgiveness |
| Reason | Patience |
| Rationalism | Kindness |
| Lawfulness | Gentleness |
| Inequality | Compassion |
| Competition | Unity / Peace |
| Individualism | Equality |
| Freedom | Co-operation |
| Small Government | Collectivism |
| Libertarianism | Big Government |
| Things | Authoritarianism |
|  | People |

MODERN ERA → POSTMODERN ERA

Enlightenment (17th Century) → Love Revolution (1967) →

Indeed, at times it seems many became completely overwhelmed by anxiety, calling for the government to do extraordinarily authoritarian things to mitigate against all possible risk and to keep us all safe. On the other hand, you may notice that Conservatives were much calmer and emotionally stable about the whole thing, being hardly worried about the virus at all, and primarily being concerned that the government leave their individual liberties alone. And of course, different priorities caused conflict between the two sides. One side prioritised safety and the other freedom.

Nevertheless, because we are in the Left Trench today, it's true to say that Liberals tended to win these arguments and governments generally pursued safetyism at all costs. This is why, even after it became clear the virus didn't pose a significant threat to most healthy people under seventy-years-old, and that the mortality risk was only around 1.64%, and even after the majority had been vaccinated, lockdowns, restrictions and punishments continued to prevail over civil liberty concerns.[1] It's why some governments chased nothing less than a Zero Covid strategy. It's why, when polls were conducted, significant numbers of people consistently called for the government wrap them in cotton wool until the threat had entirely disappeared. In one poll from November, 2021, even after most had been vaccinated twice and it was estimated around 95.3% of the adult population had acquired Covid antibodies to protect them from serious illness, the Independent discovered 40% of people still wanted the government to enforce another lockdown.[2]

As a Conservative-minded person, I find it astonishing really—people literally *demanding* to be imprisoned in their homes when the danger had become miniscule to non-existent. However, the Trench Theory helps us understand why. In the same way Brown University created a safe space for its students, filling with cookies and colouring books to feel like a nursery, many in this highly neurotic age would like the government to make the whole planet a completely safe space for them before they agree to come outside. This is where the term, "nanny state" comes from, of course. Liberals would like to depend on government like a toddler would on a parent or nanny, because they perceive the world to be overly dangerous and harrowing.

## Danger Overestimated.

Earlier I mentioned that in response to the murder of Sarah Everard, Baroness Jenny Jones called for a lockdown on all men after 6pm to eliminate the risk of this ever happening again to another woman. If you are unaware of the case, Everard was abducted and killed while walking home after dark by a man called Wayne Couzens. Couzens was a serving police officer who had used his badge to deceive her into thinking he was on official business.

Now after the news broke, The Guardian wrote a headline, "When Will Women Feel Safe on UK Streets?" It's a fair question, but of course, there are two elements at play here. There is the real danger, and the perceived danger. And the more neurotic an individual, or society at large becomes, the wider the gap becomes between those two things—the more they will overestimate the risks and become prone to worry unnecessarily. Therefore, "When Will Women Feel Safe On UK Streets?" There are two possible answers to this question. They'll feel safer either when we make the streets safer, or, if it transpires the streets are safe anyway and that neuroticism is at play, women will feel safer when they stop overestimating the dangers.

Now when you look at the basic figures, the real danger to women in the UK isn't very big. Indeed, if the truth be told, women are at far less risk on our city streets than men. Between 2010-2020, 4,493 men were victims of killings on the street, while 2,075 women were victims of killings—about half the amount.[7] Since the UK has a population of 67.2 million, the likelihood of women being killed on the street was therefore 0.003% during that period. It's not a high risk. Furthermore, while 43% of female killings were by people they didn't know, 61% of male killings were by people they didn't know. In other words, men are more susceptible to being killed by random strangers.

Now many people wrote newspaper articles after Everard's death saying, "Women feeling unsafe shouldn't be normal" and "every woman should feel safe to walk on our streets." And while that's completely true, I must repeat that there are two elements at play here—the real risk and the perceived risk. If women feel unsafe to walk on the streets and the hard data says they really shouldn't, the problem is not with the facts but how the facts are being presented and perceived.

After Everard's murder, there was a hashtag that began trending on Twitter, #reclaimthestreets. It gave the impression that women were having to stay inside because they weren't safe to step outside the front door in such a hostile environment. The reality is that in Western society, that's an unreasonable view and the streets don't need to be reclaimed at all.

Maybe I can put it like this. When I was very young, I had a vivid dream about a malevolent fox prowling around outside my house. When I woke up, I wasn't able to distinguish my dream from reality, so I was sure the fox was really there. It made me a bit afraid of going outside that day. But of course, the fox wasn't really there. Therefore, demanding that all foxes in the world be caged because I wanted a zero risk approach to the situation would clearly have been an overreaction. And likewise, when people demand that all men are locked up after 6pm, or that everyone must be locked inside their houses for a virus that's got a 98.36% survival rate, we are not thinking rationally but are instead overperceiving danger. We are being neurotic.

## Fear Makes Money.

Unfortunately, neuroticism makes us easy to manipulate and there are people who would like to keep us in a perpetual state of exaggerated fear, because they can prey upon it for money and control.

If I was to make a YouTube video for The Fuel Project that had the title, "The Gospel of Jesus Told in Five Minutes," it would draw a certain number of views. Because I am part of YouTube's ad revenue scheme, commercials would play before and after the video, and I would receive a certain amount of money for each view. Probably not very much if the truth be told.

However, if I was to make a video that specifically aimed to play on fear, I can guarantee that I'd get a lot more views. For example, if I gave the video the title, "Secret Satanic Altar Found In Bunker Underneath Disney Studios–Proves Existence of

Paedophile Ring Targeting YOUR kids." I guarantee that video would get hundreds of times more views than the first one about Jesus. I wouldn't need to substantiate the claims with any hard evidence either; I would simply need to make the video so shocking and salacious, and so scary, that people would fall over themselves to see and share it. The result would be that I would make a lot more money from the Satanic altar video than the Jesus one.

So if I were primarily motivated by money, what kind of content would I be encouraged to produce? That which is truthful and nourishing but that doesn't get many views? Or that which is fearmongering and false, but which generates the clicks? Clearly, the second option would be more attractive. And since the vast majority of the internet's economy is based upon this system of ad revenue for clicks and views, the whole thing encourages the proliferation of this kind of content.

It was long ago that the legacy media machine realised fear consistently drew the most eyeballs. The saying emerged on news channels that, *"If it bleeds, it leads."*[3] If you want that big viewership and the corresponding big ad revenue, you've got to lead with something shocking to hook people in. News channels therefore, gradually began to move away from merely reporting the news in accurate yet sometimes boring ways, towards sensationalism and alarmism. They began to use teasers like, *"What's in YOUR tap water that you need to know about? Tune in at 6 for the answer."* Because the news has provoked a sense of alarm that people might be drinking something that's killing them, they tune in. More views. More ad revenue.

Throughout the 1980s, this problem was compounded with the emergence of 24 hour rolling news. I sometimes think this was perhaps the worst thing to happen to Western society. It used to be the case that regular people would catch up on the daily events at some point in the evening for a half hour, and then they'd turn off the television set again and continue with their lives. With 24 hour rolling news however, the scare stories began to be pumped out around the clock. People can sit for hours having their heads filled with all kinds of nonsense designed to provoke negative emotion.

Many of the reports are not even about things that have happened or are happening, but only things that *may* happen. It's now common to hear, *"An expert today has warned that in ten years' time, the United Kingdom may run out of water entirely."* People then feel compelled to stay glued to the screen to discover what manner of thing could possibly cause such a catastrophe. In truth, most of these catastrophic predictions you hear about on the news today never come to pass.

I guess what I'm saying is that the growing Postmodern propensity for neuroticism has been very useful for governments because it's through scaring us that they acquire more authoritarian control. And it's also very useful for media companies who get wealthy through fearmongering. Because we are in a Left Trench Age, we're simply more susceptible to it. Our heightened fears are being gamed in a way that would have been much more difficult to do in previous generations.

During war-time, the British famously used to live by the mantra, "Keep Calm and Carry On." If the Nazi Luftwaffe were sending planes over your house every night and dropping bombs on your head...keep calm and carry on. If food shipments were being blown up in the Atlantic and there was an imminent risk of starvation...keep calm and carry on. There was a stiff-upper lip attitude that if anything, demanded that danger be underperceived. I remember watching "They Shall Not Grow Old," the documentary Peter Jackson made about World War I. It took old interviews and grainy footage from the trenches, and using modern technology and colourising techniques, brought that era to life. I remember the veterans saying they went to that war with a sense of excitement, not fully understanding the horrors that lay ahead for them. They underperceived the danger.

Today, it's the opposite. Our neurotic generation sees danger where it doesn't exist and panics at the merest hint of it. I was road tripping around England recently and a local news station reported that one petrol station had run dry. It was picked up by the 24 hour rolling news stations and within the day, a panic had swept around the whole country. Queues miles long were found everywhere and it actually became a self-fulfilling prophecy. Soon, petrol stations really were running dry because they hadn't anticipated the surge. Keep calm and carry on? Not in this generation. "Panic at the merest hint of trouble" is a more accurate motto for the Postmodernist. Of course, the same thing infamously happened at the beginning of the Covid-19 outbreak. As soon as a hint of danger came along, people started losing their minds with fear, stockpiling toilet rolls, emptying supermarket shelves, and getting into fights in the aisles.

It's been discovered that people who watch the news regularly end up feeling that their neighbourhoods are less safe than they really are; believe crime is rising when it's not; that problems are more serious than what they are; they overestimate their odds of becoming a victim of tragedy; and they consider the world to be a more dangerous place that it really is.[3] Yet it's all so very profitable to have people perpetually afraid, so the media continues to churn out the horrifying headlines that bear little relation to reality. Therefore, when newspapers like The Guardian run the headline, "When Will Women Feel Safe On Our Streets?" the real answer perhaps is, "when news organisations like yours stop fearmongering for profit."

## Don't Be Gamed.

I often look at my generation now with a sense of bemusement. I watch people getting into a flap about things in the same way David Attenborough might have looked at a recently discovered variety of armadillo in South America—with a kind of detached curiosity. While people are jumping from one foot to the other in abject terror at Covid-19, and screaming at one another on social media about how we're all going to die in a cloud of carbon, or running about in a blind panic to find petrol, or gluing themselves to the road to protest about imminent doom from climate change, I find myself increasingly shrugging and going about my business as I always would. I write this chapter a few weeks from Christmas and the most recent scare story has been that there will be a shortage of turkeys this year. People have predictably been panicked into rushing to clear the shelves of poultry. Why worry so much? Why allow ourselves to be manipulated like this? Are we not aware of what they're doing? Perhaps my problem is that I underperceive the dangers, but I think it's important we shake off the neuroticism that's such a feature of our age, and that is making us so susceptible to control. We are being played by people who stand to gain wealth and power if they can just convince us we're perpetually on the edge of disaster, when the reality is we're not.

There are clearly important things in the world worth knowing about and engaging with, but there's a great deal of noise in the media that has absolutely no positive impact on your life too, and which exists only to make you afraid. Know when to turn off and go live your life. Know when to focus on things that are really important. Your friends and family. Worship of God and fellowship. Know when it's time to do something more productive like enjoying God's creation, or making something, or learning a new skill. There are a lot more productive and life-enhancing things that can be done other than gluing your eyes to the media and allowing them to manipulate your fears all day long.

Perhaps with the advent of the internet it's just impossible to get away from the noise anymore. Earlier I said that 24 hour rolling news was perhaps the worst thing to happen to us, but the internet could trump it. Through our phones, we are constantly being fed information designed to make us scared, and often we simply shouldn't be. If we just switch off and go outside, we'll discover our fellow human beings are generally more friendly than the news is telling us. The world is less dangerous than they say it is. There are less monsters than we think, and more wonders than we've been told.

I'm not suggesting we ignore real problems or bury our heads in the sand. And there are real issues that we must confront. Especially in this Postmodern Age where tyranny is on the rise. But let's all at least be aware of what they're trying to do, and what they stand to gain by whipping us into such a frenzied chaos.

*"For God has not given us a spirit of fear and timidity, but of power, love, and self-discipline." (2 Timothy 1:7)*

*"That is why I tell you not to worry about everyday life— whether you have enough food and drink, or enough clothes to wear. Isn't life more than food, and your body more than clothing? Look at the birds. They don't plant or harvest or store food in barns, for your heavenly Father feeds them. And aren't you far more valuable to him than they are? Can all your worries add a single moment to your life? (Matthew 6:25-27)*

*"Keep Calm and Carry On."*

# 19
# Immorality.

I've spoken about nearly all the virtues on both sides of the divide now. However, there's one remaining *Hard Virtue* that we haven't dwelt upon, which will be shunned in the Postmodern Age too, and which deserves a chapter of its own. It's *Righteousness*.

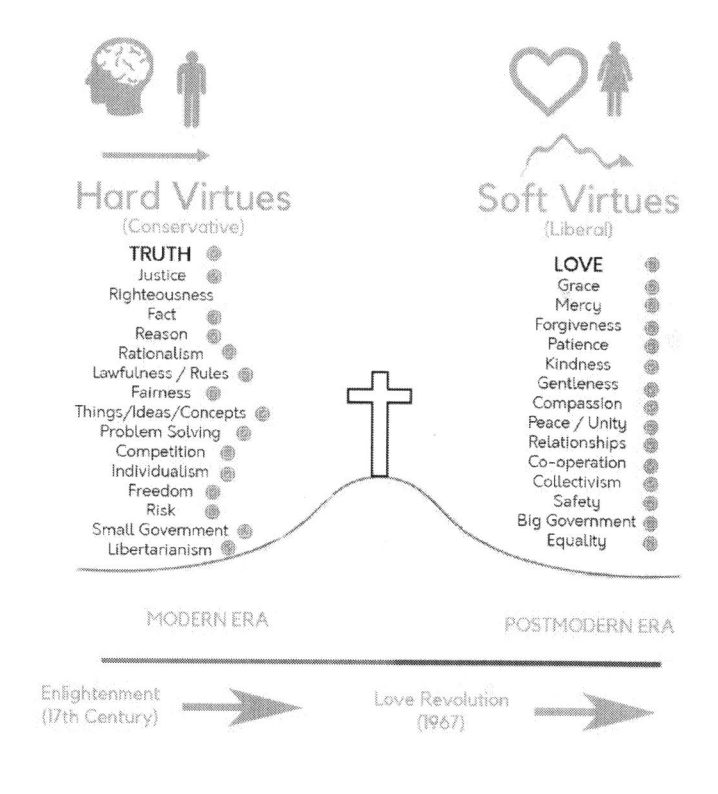

## Hard Virtues
(Conservative)

**TRUTH**
Justice
Righteousness
Fact
Reason
Rationalism
Lawfulness / Rules
Fairness
Things/Ideas/Concepts
Problem Solving
Competition
Individualism
Freedom
Risk
Small Government
Libertarianism

## Soft Virtues
(Liberal)

**LOVE**
Grace
Mercy
Forgiveness
Patience
Kindness
Gentleness
Compassion
Peace / Unity
Relationships
Co-operation
Collectivism
Safety
Big Government
Equality

MODERN ERA → POSTMODERN ERA

Enlightenment (17th Century) → Love Revolution (1967) →

Righteousness is a *Hard Virtue* because it's unyielding and exclusionary. *Righteousness* says, *"this thing is right and the other is wrong. This is black and that is white. Do this and you're a sinner; do that to be a saint. This path leads to heaven and that path leads to hell. This thing is moral and that thing is immoral."* Obviously dividing people unequally into righteous and unrighteous camps, calling them saint or sinner, is considered unacceptable to the Left Trench mentality, because it could be considered both inequitable and unkind, and so the very concept of morality is increasingly being downplayed or rejected in the Postmodern Age. Consequently, our society is becoming more immoral.

## Our Blind Spot.

Proving a moral decline to an immoral generation is quite difficult to do because the worse a society becomes, the less able we are to recognise it. CS Lewis once wrote, *"When a man is getting better he understands more and more clearly the evil that is still left in him. When a man is getting worse he understands his own badness less and less. A moderately bad man knows he is not very good: a thoroughly bad man thinks he is all right. This is common sense, really. You understand sleep when you are awake, not while you are sleeping. You can see mistakes in arithmetic when your mind is working properly: while you are making them you cannot see them. You can understand the nature of drunkenness when you are sober, not when you are drunk. Good people know about both good and evil: bad people do not know about either."* **The outcome of** this paradox is that many of the things I would highlight to prove our moral deterioration would now no longer be recognised by this generation as being immoral at all. In the same way our eyes get accustomed to the dark so that it no longer seems very dark, we become accustomed to our sin so that it no longer seems like sin.

For that reason, I'm going to attempt to prove our Postmodern decline using a definition of immorality that I once heard attributed to the Scottish Enlightenment philosopher, David Hume. He was apparently asked to give a secular humanistic definition of it without reference to God, and Hume said sin was *"that which causes harm to oneself or to another."*

Now with that in mind, are we falling into sin? Let's think about how our attitudes towards sex have developed in the Postmodern Age. Before the 1960s, the *Righteous* view of sex was that it was something sacred to be enjoyed within the safe confines of a marriage between one man and one woman. There are all kinds of good reasons for this that I won't get into here, but that sex should be practiced righteously had a Christian foundation. The Bible says, *"Drink water from your own well— share your love only with your wife. Why spill the water of your springs in the streets, having sex with just anyone? You should reserve it for yourselves. Never share it with strangers. Let your wife be a fountain of blessing for you."* (Proverbs 15:15-19) It also says, *"Give honour to marriage, and remain faithful to one another in marriage. God will surely judge people who are immoral and those who commit adultery."* (Hebrews 13:4)

Now of course, there have always been people who have done the immoral thing in regard to sex, committing adultery and having pre-marital sex, and in the Modern Era this was frowned upon as a sin and transgressors were pronounced as sinners. After the Love Revolution of 1967 however, this way of thinking was deemed too unkind and exclusionary–imagine telling anyone they were a sinner! Instead, hippies began promoting the idea of "free love." Essentially, this meant knocking down the moral boundaries of sex and encouraging people to sleep with whoever they wished, including strangers. That was a feature of the Summer of Love at Haight-Ashbury, and it's increasingly become a feature of life in general. Today we have become so hateful of Biblical sexual righteousness that it's considered bizarre for anyone to even suggest two people might wait until marriage.

Yet what has been the result of this shift? Harm to ourselves and to others. Sexually transmitted infections (STIs) now plague human health. The Royal Commission on Venereal Diseases notes that gonorrhoea and syphilis cases began spiking in the UK in the 1960s after the Love Revolution, and although there was a dip in the 1980s as people placed limits on their promiscuity in response to HIV/AIDS fears, once that threat was considered to be under control, cases began rising steeply again.[1] Indeed, by 2019, the Centers for Disease Control and Prevention was reporting a 6th consecutive record-breaking year of STI cases. Between 2014 and 2019 alone, the numbers had risen from 1.9 million to 2.6 million.[2]

Far more than damaging out bodies, sexual promiscuity has done unfathomable injury to our mental and emotional state. Promiscuity has been proven to lead to rejection and trust issues, low self-esteem, anxiety, and depression. It's also meant a rise in broken family units and fatherlessness, which in turn, has inflicted incredible damage upon successive generations of children. Those children then carry wounds into adulthood and into their own relationships. Promiscuity has meant a rise in unwanted pregnancies and abortions too. And all these things have a financial impact too, draining the economy of billions of pounds. There's a whole domino effect that we don't have the space for in this chapter. But the point I merely want to make here is that although our sexual promiscuity is harming us physically, mentally, emotionally, socially and financially, and although that qualifies it as immoral by Hume's own atheistic definition, we are now so deep into the Postmodern Age that we don't see it as immoral at all.

Another example of our sexual moral decline is the gradual acceptance of homosexuality which eventually led to the legalisation of gay marriage in the early 21st Century. Back in 1987, the British Social Attitudes Survey (BSAS) asked the general public for their attitudes towards homosexuality. At that time, 64% said it was "always wrong," 11% said it was "mostly wrong," and 8% said it was "sometimes wrong."[3] Combined then, 83% of the British public had some misgivings about the morality of homosexuality at that time.

Fast forward to 2018 however, and we had advanced deep enough into the Left Trench for the situation to reverse almost entirely. By that point, only 10% said it was always wrong, 6% said mostly wrong and 6% said sometimes wrong. This meant that combined, only 22% now had misgivings about it. Indeed, in 2018, 66% said homosexuality was "not wrong at all." Such was the swing of opinion that by 2013, gay marriage had already been legalised in the United Kingdom. Many other Western countries did the same thing around those years.

Yet the homosexual lifestyle is inherently more damaging than the heterosexual one. A 2013 study across the United States concluded it was more disease prone saying, *"Men who have sex with men (MSM) have higher rates of HIV and other sexually transmitted infections (STI) than women and heterosexual men. This elevated risk persists across age groups and reflects biological and behavioural factors."*[4]

The higher prevalence of disease amongst gay men was once considered so dangerous, that a 1997 report in the International Journal of Epidemiology conducted by the British Columbia Centre for Excellence in HIV/AIDS, said that gay and bisexual men could expect to live 8-21 years less than the heterosexual average.[5] Now since that '97 report, medicine has improved to the point that HIV and other diseases can be treated more effectively and it's not as life threatening. However, just because we can mitigate against the damage today, it doesn't mean the damage ceases to happen. Indeed, although gay and bisexual men account for just 2% of the population, they continue to account for 61% of new infections.[5]

Part of the reason homosexual men are more disease prone is because they are even more promiscuous that their heterosexual counterparts, and are far less able to form stable, lifelong partnerships. The originally referenced report said, *"Among homosexual men, 86% of 18-24 year olds and 72% of 35-39 year olds formed a new partnership during the prior year, compare to 56% of heterosexual men and 34% of women at ages 18-24, and 21% and 10% respectively, at ages 35-39."*

In short, homosexual relationships amongst men are more unstable to begin with and remain relatively unstable throughout all of life. In the heterosexual population however, although there is some relationship instability in the late teens and early twenties while men and women date one another and choose their life partner, by the time they reach their mid to late 30s, there's a good chance for both sexes that they will have settled down and created a solid platform upon which to build a family.

Again, it's not my intention to go too deeply into these issues here, but I merely want to quickly highlight that even though homosexuality is producing negative outcomes that harm individuals and society, and which therefore qualifies it as immoral by Hume's secular definition, we're now so far into the Left Trench that we no longer see homosexuality as evidence of moral decline at all.

## Future Prediction.

To really speak to this generation then, and to prove the theory that we are declining morally, I really need to look ahead at boundaries that have not yet been broken down–ones that would still be shocking for this generation to consider–but that if the Trench Theory holds true, will indeed be dismantled as we proceed through the Age.

It's for that reason that I predict that on our current trajectory, paedophilia will one day be legalised in the West. Or at least, even if the efforts don't succeed and we at last draw a line in the sand, there will still be significant attempts to break down that barrier in the Postmodern Age.

The way the LGBTQ lobby gained acceptance for gay marriage in the West was by appealing to the *Soft Virtues* that the Postmodernist prizes. For example, they came up with the slogan "Love is Love," which essentially meant that since love is so wonderful, no expression of it could ever be considered wrong. Man for woman; woman for man; man for man; woman for woman. It doesn't matter. All expressions of *Love* are equal and *Love* is always good. The LGBTQ lobby then proceeded to cleverly frame the legalisation of gay marriage with the term "Marriage Equality." Mentioning "Equality" is another home-run in this generation. And when gay marriage was eventually legalised, they flooded social media with the hashtag, #lovewins.

Now in the Soft Left Trench, what would stop paedophile groups using the same tactics to have their own sexual proclivity legalised? After all, if "love is love" and no expression of it could ever be considered wrong, then why is love between adults and minors wrong? It's love, right? And what would stop paedophiles talking about their need for "Relationship Equality?" What would stop them from saying they are being marginalised just like gay and lesbians had once been, and deserve to be included? And just as people who opposed gay marriage are derided as homophobes, what's to stop anyone who opposes paedophilia from being tagged a paedophobe?

The only thing that stops that happening is if we retain a sense that *Truth*, and particularly *Righteousness* matters. If we don't keep *Righteousness* in our armoury, so to speak, our Left Trench Age really has no remaining defence against this line of attack. There's no virtue in the *Soft* set alone that stops this from happening. Indeed, if *Love* remains our only priority and overrides every other concern, there is no reason why a paedophile can't say, "well, this is a kind of love? So why not me too?"

Too far-fetched? Perhaps. Thankfully, from my current perspective it seems like our generation still has enough sense of *Righteousness* to feel revulsion at the idea. However, it was only a few years ago that I thought it too far-fetched to suggest academics may argue that two and two doesn't equal four...and yet here we are.

## Attempts to Push Paedophilia.

Indeed, it's true that academics are already attempting to push the boundaries with paedophilia. As far back as 2013, Cambridge University held a conference for a range of academics to discuss it. Philip Tromovitch of Doshisha University attempted to normalise paedophilia in his speech saying, *"Normal males are aroused by children...the majority of men are probably paedophiles and hebephiles."*[6] Another presentation at the same conference was titled, *"Liberating the paedophile: a discursive analysis."* Andrew Gilligan reported on the event for The Times and was left in no doubt that, *"...there are attempts, right now, in parts of the academic establishment to push the boundaries on the acceptability of child sex."*

Gilligan in fact traced the origin of the efforts back to the aftermath of the 1967 Love Revolution. He said, *"With the Pill, the legalisation of homosexuality and shrinking taboos against premarital sex, the Seventies was an era of quite sudden sexual emancipation. Many liberals, of course, saw through PIE's (Pro-paedophilia group Paedophile Information Exchange) cynical rhetoric of 'child lib'. But to others on the Left, sex by or with children was just another repressive boundary to be swept away—and some of the most important backing came from academia."*

Margo Kaplan, a Rutgers-Camden professor of law who graduated from Harvard University, argued around the time of this Cambridge conference that paedophiles should be looked upon with more sympathy. Afterwards, she was asked by Philadelphia Magazine what the response had been to her statements. She said, *"I have to be honest. I am getting more emails of support than I ever expected."*[7]

In 2018, Mirjam Heine gave a TedTalk at the University of Wurzburg in Germany, where she talked about a paedophile acquaintance called Jonas. She attempted to garner sympathy for Jonas by saying that he was too scared to reveal his secret to anyone—that he was only attracted to female children between the ages of six and twelve—for fear of rejection and marginalisation. Poor thing! Not marginalisation! Not exclusion! During the talk, Heine tried to normalise it as a sexual orientation like any other, deserving of sympathy and compassion. Indeed, she claimed that some 60 million people in the world are also paedophiles.[8]

In November, 2021, Allyn Walker, a "non-binary" professor at Old Dominion University, Virginia, released a video fielding questions about a recently released book called "A Long

Dark Shadow..." in which she had tried to destigmatise paedophilia. One person asked why Walker had replaced the term, "paedophile" with "Minor Attracted Person" in the book. Walker replied, *"I use the term Minor Attracted Person in the title and throughout the book for multiple reasons. First of all, because I think it's important to use terminology for groups that members of that group want others to use for them. And MAP advocacy groups like "Before You Act" have advocated for the use of the term MAP. They've advocated for it primarily because it's less stigmatising than other terms like paedophile. A lot of people, when they hear the term, "paedophile", they automatically assume that it means a sex offender. And that isn't true, and it leads to a lot of misconceptions about attractions towards minors."*[9]

As I said before, there is thankfully still a lot of revulsion to the idea of paedophilia within the general public today, and people pushing this agenda are not gaining much success. However, you can see Left Trench academics very clearly trying to peck away at this boundary now–trying to further demolish our sense of *Righteousness* when it comes to sexual behaviour. Indeed, in many ways, as Andrew Gilligan noted, having already broken down our sense of morality about sexual promiscuity in the 1960s, and then homosexuality, paedophilia has become the natural next frontier.

Many people who now oppose the normalisation of paedophilia were alive in 1987 when statistically, there's an 83% chance they once also opposed homosexuality. Since their mind has now been changed about that issue, what would stop their mind being changed about this one? Again, only retaining a sense of *Righteousness* and a willingness to call out sin and sinners. However, the point I'm trying to make is that we are in a Soft Era where it's increasingly unpopular to call *anything* a sin, or to exclude *anyone* as a sinner.

Remember when Conservatives spoke up against increasing sexual promiscuity in the 1960s? They were denounced by Liberals as repressed prudes and squares. And remember when Conservatives spoke up against gay marriage in the 2000s? They were denounced by Liberals as homophobes and bigots. Conservatives have been consistently denounced throughout the Postmodern years for trying to preserve a sense of *Hard Righteousness* around sexuality, and have ultimately had to stand helpless while the prevailing Liberalism of the Age smashed them all down. And with that in mind, nobody should be shocked that having systematically undermined our sexual morality for decades, we now find some people emboldened to suggest sex with children. We are at the far end of a continuum. It was always going to happen. And we can only stop the slide if we find some way to re-balance and reintroduce some respect for Hard Virtues.

## As In The Days of Noah and Lot.

We've focused specifically on a decline of sexual morality in this chapter but I believe our generation's growing general contempt for *Righteousness* is evidenced in a whole myriad of ways.

Paul wrote to Timothy saying, *"You should know this, Timothy, that in the last days there will be very difficult times. For people will love only themselves and their money. They will be boastful and proud, scoffing at God, disobedient to their parents, and ungrateful. They will consider nothing sacred. They will be unloving and unforgiving; they will slander others and have no self-control. They will be cruel and hate what is good. They will betray their friends, be reckless, be puffed up with pride, and love pleasure rather than God. They will act religious but they will reject the power that could make them godly."* (2 Timothy 3:1-5) I think we can see elements of this unrighteousness coming clearly into view in this Postmodern Age. Social media has amplified pride and vanity. Cancel culture has made people cruel and unforgiving. We are a generation that loves pleasure rather than God. And it's this Postmodern slide into unrighteousness, along with the formation of a One World Order and religious system, that compounds the possibility that this Age could be the last.

I would never predict that definitively because of course—
no man knows the day or the hour—but Jesus said, *"When the Son of Man returns, it will be like it was in Noah's day. In those days, the people enjoyed banquets and parties and weddings right up to the time Noah entered his boat and the flood came and destroyed them all."* (Luke 17:26-27) He continues, *"And the world will be as it was in the days of Lot. People went about their daily business—eating and drinking, buying and selling, farming and building—until the morning Lot left Sodom. Then fire and burning sulphur rained down from heaven and destroyed them all."* (Luke 17:28-29)

The most prominent feature of both Noah and Lot's days, of course, is that they had fallen into a state of moral disrepair—Sodom especially was renowned for its sexual sin. Now we saw in Section One that God gives a grace period to civilisations that are failing; he warns repeatedly and sends his prophets. However, if the civilisation refuses to change direction, it will pass a point of no return and that's when God eventually intervenes. That's what appears to be happening right now. God is being patient with a culture on a moral decline, but if it's not reversed, the whole planet will return to how it was in Noah's day and Lot's day, and that's when Jesus will make his return.

Indeed Jesus said, *"Now learn a lesson from the fig tree. When its branches bud and its leaves begin to sprout, you know that summer is near. In the same way, when you see all these things, you can know his return is very near, right at the door."* (Matthew 24:32-33)\*

---

*\*If you'd like to know more about how we are moving towards the end-time world described in the Bible, I did a series for The Fuel Project called "The Coming Summer." Even though I only released it in 2018, developments have already occurred that move us on from that time. However, you still may find it useful to consider.*

# 20

# The Paradox of Evil.

We're nearing the end of the book now, but there are just a couple more things I'd like to say. Firstly, I hope this book has helped us understand why Liberals today often advocate for evil while still believing themselves to be on the side of good.

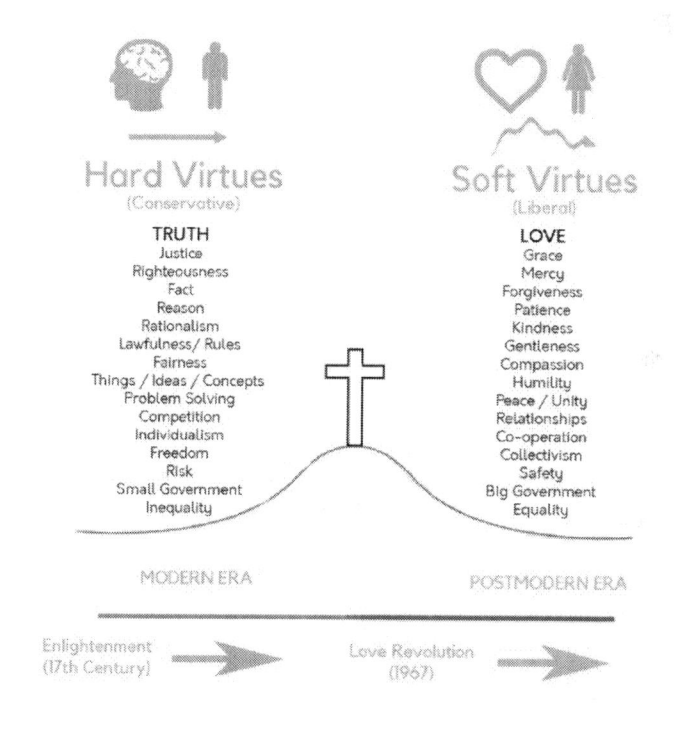

**Hard Virtues**
(Conservative)

TRUTH
Justice
Righteousness
Fact
Reason
Rationalism
Lawfulness/ Rules
Fairness
Things / Ideas / Concepts
Problem Solving
Competition
Individualism
Freedom
Risk
Small Government
Inequality

MODERN ERA

Enlightenment
(17th Century)

**Soft Virtues**
(Liberal)

LOVE
Grace
Mercy
Forgiveness
Patience
Kindness
Gentleness
Compassion
Humility
Peace / Unity
Relationships
Co-operation
Collectivism
Safety
Big Government
Equality

POSTMODERN ERA

Love Revolution
(1967)

After all, in this third section of the book, we have seen how Liberals now openly advocate against *Truth* and despise it, yet from their perspective they are only prioritising *Love*. We've seen how they advocate against *Justice* and often take the sides of deported criminals, yet from their perspective, they're only pursuing *Compassion*. We've seen how they want to banish *Knowledge* and *Reason*, even to the point of denying that only women have a cervix or that 2+2=4, and yet from their perspective they're only advocating for *Equality*. We've seen how they seek to quash freedom of speech and all expressions of individual thought, but in their eyes, they're only striving for *Unity*. We've seen how they want to impose a collectivist tyranny around the world, yet from their perspective they're merely pursuing *World Peace*. We've seen how they want to intimidate and ostracize dissenters, but in their eyes they're only trying to keep society *Harmonious*. We've seen how they promote authoritarianism, but in their eyes, they're just trying to prioritise *Safety*. We've seen how they want to destroy the Christian faith that has for centuries provided the moral foundation for Western civilisation, yet in their eyes they merely want to prioritise interfaith *Co-operation*. We've seen how they want to smash masculinity and male leadership, but in their eyes, they're only trying to make the world more *Gentle* and *Feminine*.

If you were to look at all these things through a Liberal lens, they would ask, "how can anyone argue against the pursuit of *Love, Compassion, Equality, Unity, World Peace, Harmony, Safety, Co-operation and Gentleness*. How can that be bad? This is how we will create Utopia on earth!" Yet in reality, virtues followed to their extremes and detached from the other side become vices. Therefore, the Postmodern Age is not headed towards Utopia but is rather becoming marked by all those things I just mentioned. Wilful ignorance, foolishness, anti-intellectualism, unjustness, tyranny, repression, intimidation, authoritarianism, hatred of men, cruelty, hatred of Christianity, and a misguided intention to destroying many of the things that make individuals happy and civilisations prosper.

## Lessons From History.

In truth, most of the world's worst historical evils have come from Utopians who believed themselves to be on the side of good.

Adolf Hitler was evil but he didn't see himself that way. In his own mind, Hitler was pursuing the *Unity* of Europe, and as a believer in racial *Purity*, he genuinely felt the continent was being polluted and held back by people with flawed genetic makeup—for example, the Jews, Slavics and the disabled. He felt if he could only purge Europe of these things, Utopia would lie on the other side. And how can anything bad come of pursuing such clear virtues as *Unity* and *Purity*?

Of course, he pursued *Purity* by establishing concentration camps to murder the Jews, Slavics and disabled. And to establish *Unity*, he went to war to eliminate ideological opponents, suppressed free speech, burned books, and silenced political opponents. Which are clear evils, of course. Yet Hitler genuinely thought the unified and purified end would justify the means. He imagined that once all was said and done and his paradise had finally been established, the people would thank and venerate him as a visionary hero. They would realise the tyranny had really been for their own good.

Trench

Which is extraordinary when you think about it, really. That someone could enact such evils while still regarding himself as being on the right side of history, and remaining utterly convinced of his own goodness.

Joseph Stalin was much the same—he was evil but he didn't regard himself as such. In his own mind, Stalin was pursuing the Marxist dream of social *Equality*, *Unity* and *Harmony*. He genuinely thought that in Communism, he had discovered the keys to an egalitarian paradise and that if he could just rid society of disruptive individualism, Utopia would lie on the other side. And how can anything bad come of pursuing such virtues as *Equality, Unity* and *Harmony*?

Because he believed so wholeheartedly in his Utopian ideology, he tried to establish *Equality* by stealing property and wealth. To establish *Unity*, he put dissidents in forced labour camps, suppressed ideological opposition and presided over the murder of 60 million people. Which are clear evils, of course. Yet Stalin genuinely thought the egalitarian end would justify the means. He imagined that once all was said and done and paradise had been established, the people would thank and venerate him as a visionary hero. They would realise the tyranny had really been for their own good.

Which again, is extraordinary when you think about it. That someone could enact such evils while still regarding himself as being on the right size of history, and remaining utterly convinced of his own goodness.

The same concept applies to the leaders of Islamic terrorist groups like ISIS. They are evil but they don't see themselves that way. In their own minds, the people who command and commit acts of terror are pursuing the *Holiness* and *Righteousness* of Allah, and creating a world of *Unity* under his rule. They genuinely think that if they can just rid society of the infidel, an Islamic Utopia lies on the other side. And how can anything bad come from pursuing such virtues as *Holiness*, *Righteousness* and *Unity*?

Because they believe so wholeheartedly in this Utopian ideology, they are prepared to subjugate non-Muslims, kill non-believers, fly planes into buildings, drive vehicles into crowds, ignite bombs in train stations and concert halls, chop off heads, burn people alive, suppress free speech, punish any critique of Muhammad, and eliminate ideological opponents. Which are clear evils, of course. Yet the terrorists genuinely believe the end justifies the means. They imagine that once all is said and done and Islamic paradise has been established, the people will thank and venerate them as visionary heroes. They will realise the tyranny has really been for their own good.

Which again, is extraordinary when you think about it–that people could oppress and murder innocent people while still regarding themselves as being on the right side of history, and remaining utterly convinced of their own goodness.

## The Emerging Pattern.

A clear pattern emerges when we consider the worst evils in world history then. An ideologue, or a group of ideologues, set up what they believe are virtuous goals which must be pursued at all costs. They convince themselves that if they pursue the virtues to their furthest end, there is a Utopia for all the world on the other side. In the process of pursuing the aims, they quickly find themselves detaching from opposing, balancing, virtues and they enact evils. Yet they believe in the Utopian vision so much that they convince themselves that the evils are necessary; that the end justifies the means. And so tyrants are created who, while bringing abject misery and death to the world, continue to be utterly convinced of their own goodness.

A similar pattern is threatening to emerge in the Postmodern Age with the Liberal elites, if it hasn't already. We are increasingly being dominated and ruled by collectivist authoritarians who attempt to enforce tyranny while remaining utterly convinced of their own goodness. They have a vision of a future Utopia and they believe that what they impose upon the world, they do for our own good. Indeed, they are even prepared to enact evils to make sure it's realised. This is why, with a clear conscience, Liberal elites attempt to eliminate free speech. It's why Big Tech will deplatform dissident views; why governments will legislate against individual thought; why police forces intimidate and harass; why rabbles cancel and destroy livelihoods. It's why they're prepared to enforce lockdowns, mandatory vaccines and covid passports. It's why they attack masculinity and Christianity. It's why they seek to destroy loyalty to God and family. It's why they seek to convince us that we should own nothing and be happy. It's why Liberal gangs have felt morally justified in roaming the streets in recent years, smashing the windows of innocents, burning buildings and destroying livelihoods.

These are clear evils. Yet they do these things truly convinced that they are on some moral crusade to build Utopia.

They truly believe that the end justifies all these destructive and hateful means. They believe that once all is said and done and a collectivist paradise of peace and love has been established, and once all the disruptive individualism has been eliminated, we will thank and venerate them as visionary heroes for all this. We will realise that the tyranny has been for our own good.

Which is extraordinary when you think about it. That people can advocate for totalitarian behaviour while still regarding themselves as being on the right side of history, and remaining utterly convinced of their own goodness. Yet they do.

CS Lewis wrote, *"Of all tyrannies, a tyranny sincerely exercised for the good of its victims may be the most oppressive. It would be better to live under robber barons than under omnipotent moral busybodies. The robber baron's cruelty may sometimes sleep, his cupidity may at some point be satiated; but those who torment us for our own good will torment us without end for they do so with the approval of their own conscience. They may be more likely to go to Heaven yet at the same time likelier to make a Hell of earth. This very kindness stings with intolerable insult. To be 'cured' against one's will and cured of states which we may not regard as a disease is to be put on a level of those who have not yet reached the age of reason or those who never will; to be classed with infants, imbeciles, and domestic animals."*[1]

The tyranny that the Liberal elite would like to impose upon the world is one they impose with the approval of their own conscience and that's what makes it so dangerous. In response to it, I would quote the Bible which says, *"There is a path before each person that seems right, but it ends in death."* (Proverbs 14:12)

The path that the Liberal elite have been following since 1967 may seem right to them, but its end is going to be death. To save ourselves from this error, we must always remember that no end justifies unrighteous means.

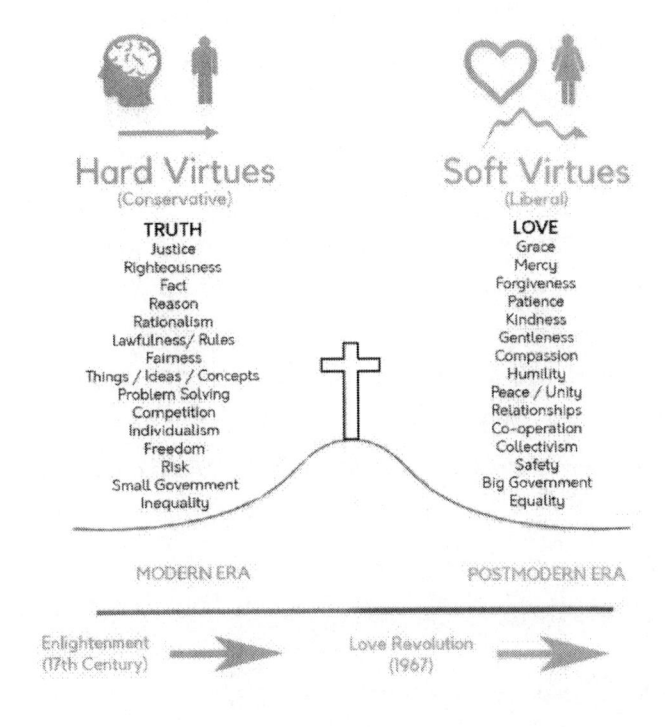

## Hard Virtues
(Conservative)

**TRUTH**
Justice
Righteousness
Fact
Reason
Rationalism
Lawfulness/ Rules
Fairness
Things / Ideas / Concepts
Problem Solving
Competition
Individualism
Freedom
Risk
Small Government
Inequality

## Soft Virtues
(Liberal)

**LOVE**
Grace
Mercy
Forgiveness
Patience
Kindness
Gentleness
Compassion
Humility
Peace / Unity
Relationships
Co-operation
Collectivism
Safety
Big Government
Equality

MODERN ERA — POSTMODERN ERA

Enlightenment (17th Century) → Love Revolution (1967) →

# 21

# Polarisation.

I think while writing this book, I've been asking myself, *"What is the ultimate purpose of this project?" "What would I like to achieve by it?"* There is, of course, the hope that I might speak to my generation so that I may reach people who are falling into the Left Trench, thereby saving them from being deceived by the pervading false wisdom of the Age. But I think I also find within myself a desire to help both sides of the culture war understand one another so that everyone might come back to the centre ground.

## The Case for Centrism.

Anyone who has lived through the years of Postmodernity can't help but notice how polarised our society is becoming. And there was a certain inevitability to that. Isaac Newton's Third Law says that "every action has an equal and opposite reaction." Therefore, as the majority of society has begun pursuing an extreme Leftist ideology, even to the extent of denying human anatomy and basic numeracy, it was always likely that natural conservatives would start moving further to the Right in an attempt to counter-balance the debate. From where now stand then, the gap between Left and Right looks positively chasmic.

As I've made clear repeatedly throughout this book, I believe extremism on both sides is unhelpful and even dangerous, and that a healthy society needs to retain a respect for the things that both sides naturally prefer. *Truth* and *Love*; *Justice* and *Unity*; *Righteousness* and *Compassion*. We need them all, even they seem to be contrary to one another and demand different outcomes to life's problems. And therefore, I'd like this book to play some part in facilitating dialogue between both sides so that even if we continue to disagree in the future, we at least understand what's motivating the other side. So that we stop villainising one another and instead argue in more productive ways.

As I've spent the majority of this book castigating the extremes of the Left, perhaps all I've done is push them further away. If I have, that wasn't my intention. My hope was just to reveal to the Left the flaws in their thinking so they might pull back from the path they're pursuing, in the knowledge that if they come back to the centre, the Right would respond in like manner. And as I hope I've made clear, the only reason I'm focusing on the dangers of Leftist extremism in this book is because that's the primary concern of the Postmodern Age. In truth, replacing it with extremism of the Right wouldn't be the answer and would create a whole litany of problems of its own. I say that as someone who naturally leans in that direction myself. I know that a civilisation with no *Soft Virtues* would be just as terrible as one with no *Hard*, and it's not one that I would call for.

For that reason, in spite of my natural tendencies, I'd like to think of myself as an ideological centrist. I believe it's the place where all Christians should aim to find themselves. In this polarised time, that probably isn't a very popular thing to say and it's probably not what many people reading this book would want to hear. But I refuse, although it's very difficult to restrain myself sometimes, to react to extreme Leftism with extreme Rightism. I refuse to fall in with the tribal mindset that says everything the Left have ever wanted is evil and everything the Right has ever wanted is good. As Alexander Solzhenitsyn warned, *"If only it were all so simple! If only there were evil people somewhere insidiously committing evil deeds, and it were necessary only to separate them from the rest of us and destroy them. But the line dividing good and evil cuts through the heart of every human being."*

If only it were true that all Liberals were evil from the start and all Conservatives were good. Or vice versa. It would be so easy to then fall in with the tribalism of our time. And tribalism is addictive for many reasons. There's a sense of belonging and camaraderie that comes with it. A sense of purpose. These are powerful motivations. And tribalism means not having to think about issues in deep and nuanced ways. But such tribalism is indeed too simplistic. In truth, the potential for evil really does lie within all of us, for we have all inherited a sinful nature. We must all therefore primarily make sure that we are not falling into a trench in our own hearts. That we're not becoming so focused on *Justice* that we're forgetting *Mercy*. Or that we're not becoming so focused on *Love* that we're forgetting *Truth* and *Righteousness*.

In considering this need for balance, I'm reminded of something Paul wrote to the Corinthians. He said that *"...when we preach that Christ was crucified, the Jews are offended and the Gentiles say it's all nonsense."* (1 Corinthians 1:23) In Paul's day, to be a true Christian meant not fitting neatly into either of the prevailing tribes, cultures or modes of thought. The same goes for us today, I think. When we conform to true Biblical Christianity, extreme Liberals should say we're too *Hard* and extreme Conservatives should say we're too *Soft*. The Far Left will complain we're speaking the *Truth* in the first place, and the Far Right will complain that we're speaking it in *Love*.

## Godlessness Polarises.

I think indeed, one of the main reasons Western civilisation has become so polarised is because it has lost touch with Biblical Christianity. As I highlighted in Section One, the God of the Bible embodies both virtue sets. And as we've also discussed, there was a time in Western civilisation when almost everyone read the Bible and went to church on a weekly basis to hear about this God. That's not to say that everyone was a genuine Christian, but the wisdom of the Bible nevertheless pervaded society and the vast majority had some conscious or subconscious knowledge and respect for what it said.

I believe it was through knowledge of this God that people kept a balanced perspective on life. After all, God is full of both *Truth* and *Love*. He is *Righteous* but full of *Grace*. He demands *Justice* but shows *Compassion* and *Mercy*. And sure, people in all ages have always had an individual leaning towards one side or the other, but it was by worshipping this God, that they stayed centred.

Maybe this image might help us understand what I'm driving at:

Hard Virtues ⟵ **God** ⟶ Soft Virtues

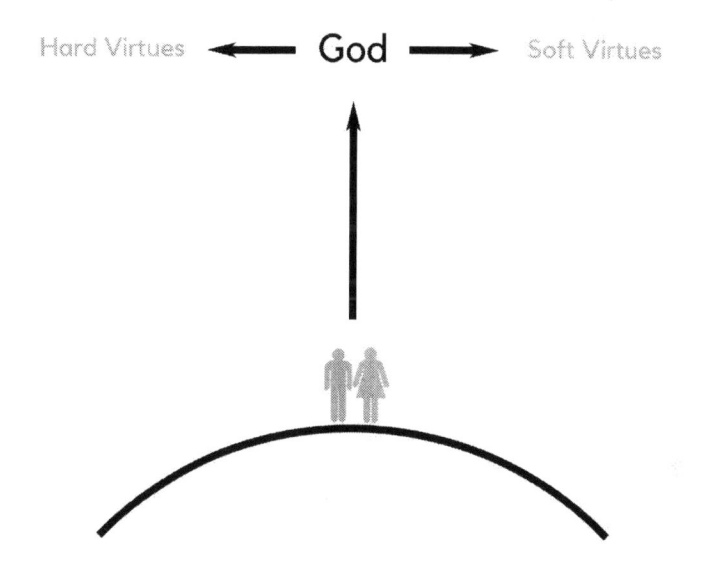

While people had God as their highest authority, they were told something about both sides and anchored by it. If someone had a natural leaning to the *Hard Virtues* and if that threatened to make them unloving, they would go to church and hear about Jesus associating with sinners and demanding that we love enemies. If someone had a natural affinity for the *Soft Virtues* and if that threatened to make them disdainful of *Truth* like we are seeing in this generation, they would read the Bible and hear about God's unyielding demands and Jesus' uncompromising claims about sin and hell, and it would curb their excesses and keep them centred too. The *Hard* crowd in following Jesus could not become too cold and the *Soft* crowd could not become too flimsy. And through mutual faith in the same God, each side would have a sense of connection and even brotherhood with the other. After all, wherever you stood politically, there was a shared faith that existed above political concerns that kept society bonded together.

From the middle of the 20<sup>th</sup> Century however, people began losing touch with that God and something like this happened.

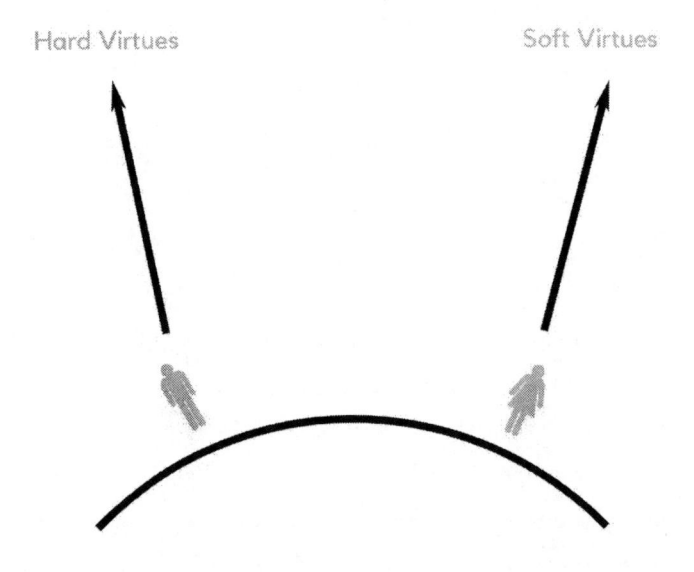

**Hard Virtues**             **Soft Virtues**

Without God to anchor people to the centre, people started slipping down into their respective trenches, driven by their natural leanings. I've used the male icon for the *Hard* and the female icon for the *Soft* but really sex is irrelevant here. You get men and women on both sides. There's now a chasm between them and no sense of a shared love of God to keep them in brotherhood.

Perhaps the fracturing of Western Civilisation; the dividing in two; the extreme polarisation, that has created the Culture War, was just a natural and inevitable consequence of turning away from God. And for it to be healed, we must all come back to him once more.

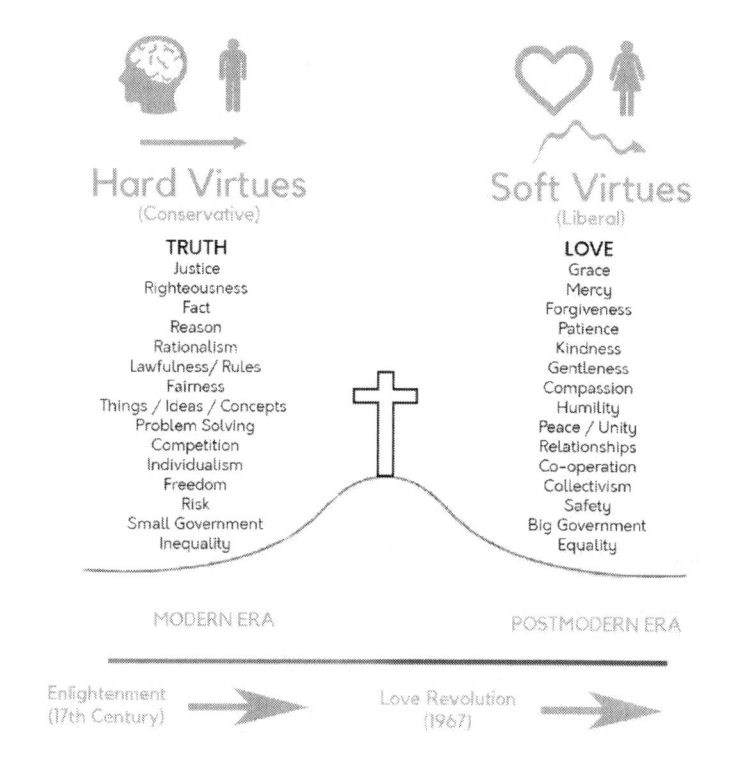

## Hard Virtues
(Conservative)

**TRUTH**
Justice
Righteousness
Fact
Reason
Rationalism
Lawfulness/ Rules
Fairness
Things / Ideas / Concepts
Problem Solving
Competition
Individualism
Freedom
Risk
Small Government
Inequality

MODERN ERA

Enlightenment
(17th Century)

## Soft Virtues
(Liberal)

**LOVE**
Grace
Mercy
Forgiveness
Patience
Kindness
Gentleness
Compassion
Humility
Peace / Unity
Relationships
Co-operation
Collectivism
Safety
Big Government
Equality

POSTMODERN ERA

Love Revolution
(1967)

# Conclusion.

When I originally conceived the idea for this book, my intention was to finish with a fourth section that would specifically deal with "Wokeism." However, having now reached this point, it feels like a complete work and the right place to stop. I've decided therefore, that what I was going to say about "Wokeism" will now be kept aside and used in a sequel at some point in the future.

In the meantime, I hope that what I've said here has made sense and provides a framework by which you can understand the Postmodern Age. I wrote in the introduction that I've been formulating this concept for years and trying to communicate it with varying degrees of success since at least 2014. I would like to think that this will become my final definitive attempt, superseding my previous attempt to commit it to paper in *"The War on Truth,"* and that once this book has been published and the accompanying video series concluded, there will not be a need to give it another pass.

I know I've made some very bold claims about the future of Western civilisation through this book. I've predicted the rise of authoritarian government and perhaps even a form of encroaching communism, driven by an increasingly powerful and confident China. I've also made predictions about a moral collapse that leads to possible legalisation of things like paedophilia. As I mentioned in the introduction, where I tended to hold back with making predictions using the *Trench Theory* in *"The War on Truth,"* perhaps not yet fully trusting its conclusions, I've been more bold this time around. Whether these things ever truly come to pass will become apparent in the passing of time. I've laid out the theory as to where I think we're heading and why. And I suppose whether we arrive at the destination predicted here will depend on whether our society can acknowledge the problems with our current direction of travel, and how quick we are to change course. Love is not all we need. We need some Truth and Righteousness too if our world is to prosper.

This is where the church needs to play an active role. During the Coronavirus pandemic between 2020 and 2021–the event that catapulted the West towards unprecedented levels of government authoritarianism–I was disturbed by how readily many church leaders accepted and bowed to it. How meekly they complied when the government told them the practicing of their faith was non-essential and how easily they agreed to stop worshipping or meeting. It made a mockery of the things they claim to believe. Indeed, many church leaders simply disappeared during those years–something that was noticed by secular commentators.

On 19th December, 2021, as unfounded fears about the Omicron variant of Coronavirus were rising, the vicar of an Anglican Church, William Pearson-Gee, gave a sermon saying, *"I spent two days last week batting off emails about whether we should close the church and cancel the services and I want to speak to you from my heart. We are not a cinema. We are not the O2 arena. We are not a football match. We're not going to play by those rules. We are a family of brothers and sisters in Christ who come together on a Sunday to worship the living*

*Jesus Christ. Not a football match. Not a film. I'm not going to close our services until I'm ordered by law to do so and even if that happens, it will be screaming and kicking. We are here to worship a God who is sovereign over all of this mess. Over all the ineptitude that the government can throw at us. And it is all the more important that we gather together to worship God."*

In response to this vicar finally showing some backbone in challenging rampant state authoritarianism, many secular commentators noted how absent this attitude had been for the previous two years. Bella Wallersteiner wrote, *"Throughout Covid there has been an absence of this spiritual leadership. Freedom of assembly and freedom of religion is fundamental to living in a free and fair society. The church needs to step it up."* Others spoke about it bringing tears to their eyes that someone from the church was finally challenging the illegal mandates.

Now although there were other leaders who were willing to take a stand during that period, there were far less than was needed. It served to amplify an idea that I raised in 2013's Restless Church, that we seem to largely be playing religion games on Sunday mornings. We say things in church that sound bold; we sing things that are hyperbolic; but when the time comes to put these words into action, we crumble. How many times have we stood in a worship event and sang to God that he's the most important thing in our lives; that worshipping him is more important to us than life or death; more important than the air we breathe; how if we didn't worship him the rocks would cry out? And yet the moment the government told us our faith was non-essential and to close the doors, many leaders complied instantly. It tells me that if we find ourselves being dragged into a leftist authoritarian dystopia in the future, many of the people who take to the pulpits on Sunday mornings around the land won't be worth following. They'll be hiding behind a sofa somewhere, preferring not to get into trouble with the authorities and desperately trying to retain their outward air of societal respectability instead of standing up for the free practice of Christian faith, and the right for us to do the same.

The church isn't a social club and our aim isn't to merely be outwardly respectable. These are dark times in which we are to be light. They are times where people have become hateful of truth and righteousness, but that only means we are to be all the more visible as standard-bearers for those things in the days ahead. Jesus *is* the truth. God *is* righteousness. We can't claim to be his and not take a stand for these things when the times require it. As Paul wrote, *"Instead, we will speak the Truth in Love, growing in every way more and more like Christ, who is the head of his body, the church."* (Ephesians 4:15) We will speak the truth in love but it is the truth we must speak nevertheless. I suppose we will say more about in the times ahead.

Indeed, although this books feels like a complete work, there's a lot more we could have spoken about. I wanted to discuss for example, how although both the *Hard* and *Soft Virtues* are of equal merit, it tends to be best to lead with the *Hard*. I wanted to discuss what that meant for male leadership and Conservative government. Indeed, what it meant for parenthood and family life. As we move beyond "Trench" and into future projects, I imagine we'll get into all that, and I'll be able to use what we've learned here to create a kind of short-hand way of talking. If you hear me referring to "left trench" concepts in the future, you'll now know exactly what I mean.

Now that I've presented the theory, you may also be able to mine your own truths from it. There may be consequences and outcomes that, if the theory holds true, are inevitable, but which I haven't yet spotted or mentioned here. If so, I look forward to hearing those theories and perhaps it can launch discussions that help us all navigate the times ahead.

Ultimately, I hope this book brings understanding during a confusing time and helps us form helpful attitudes and effective responses. Although I don't have the ego to believe this book could have any real impact on changing the course of Western civilisation, I guess some part of me wants to know I tried to stop the descending madness. And maybe in the process I can reach just one or two who would otherwise have fallen into the Left Trench along with the rest of society.

I'm reminded of the old story about the man who saw thousands of starfish who had washed up and become stranded on the beach. As he walked, he would bend down and throw the some back into the water. Another man approached him and said, *"Why are you doing that, you can't possibly hope to throw all these starfish back into the ocean by yourself?"* The man the man bent down, picked up another one, threw it into the water and replied, *"No, but I just made a difference to that one."* If I can make a difference to just some of the people who read this book, then the years it took to formulate and the months it took to write will have been worth the effort.

Thank you for reading.

Polarisation

# Bibliography.

## (And Notes.)

### Introduction

1. https://skeptics.stackexchange.com/questions/8742/did-einstein-say-if-you-cant-explain-it-simply-you-dont-understand-it-well-en

## SECTION ONE

### One - The Two Virtues

1. https://www.allaboutcareers.com/job-profile/police-officer/#:~:text=In%20a%20nutshell%2C%20police%20officers,crime%20prevention%2C%20prosecution%20and%20punishment.
2. https://www.dictionary.com/browse/just

### Three - Two Caricatures

1. From "The God Delusion" by Richard Dawkins
2. Cain, Jose Saramango
3. Hitchhiker's Guide To The Galaxy, Douglas Adams

### Three - The Violent Monster

1. https://en.wikipedia.org/wiki/Amalek
2. There's an interesting but highly speculative point here which I hesitate to mention and which certainly lies outside the remit of this book. The way in which the Amalekites formed alliances with neighbouring countries to destroy the Israelites because of generational hatred going back to Esau, is very reminiscent of more recent behaviour from Arab nations. I wondered, "could the generational hatred of Israel in Islam extend back much further to the Amalekites? Is there a link? According to some sources, the Arabs of the Middle East that became Muslim may indeed, at least in part, trace their heritage back to Esau. If so, it could

mean that the spirit of hatred that was found in the Amalekites towards Israel is the same unbroken spirit found in Arab Muslims today. Could it be that if Saul had carried out God's instructions with the Amalekites thousands of years ago, the Middle East problems of today simply wouldn't exist?

3. From "The Reason For God" by Timothy Keller

**Four – The Timid Softie**

1. From "The Lion, The Witch And The Wardrobe" by CS Lewis

**Six – Biases**

1. From "Mere Christianity" by CS Lewis
2. https://www.dw.com/en/two-years-since-germany-opened-its-borders-to-refugees-a-chronology/a-40327634
3. https://en.wikipedia.org/wiki/English_Channel_migrant_crossings_(2018%E2%80%93present)

**Seven – Head and Heart**

1. https://www.bbc.co.uk/news/uk-59412329
2. https://www.dailymail.co.uk/news/article-10186747/Deportation-flight-Jamaica-takes-just-FOUR-original-51-offenders-board.html
3. https://www.goodreads.com/quotes/450864-the-line-separating-good-and-evil-passes-not-through-states

**Eight – Inequality**

1. https://www.goodreads.com/quotes/180795-it-s-better-to-be-kind-than-to-be-right
2. People who hold this position tend not to realise that it's a self-defeating position. After all, saying "nothing is true" is itself an absolute truth statement. This idea can't support its own weight because it needs the help of the thing it wants to destroy in order to stand.

**Nine – Competition**

1. https://www.irishprimarype.com/wp-content/uploads/2019/09/Co-operative-Sports-day-handout-and-resource.pdf
2. https://everydaypower.com/pain-quotes/
3. https://www.forbes.com/quotes/91/

### Ten – Individual v Collective

1. http://www.differencebetween.net/miscellaneous/difference-between-collectivism-and-individualism/

### Anchors and Fires

1. As is so often the case, I'm reminded of a CS Lewis quote here: "Faith, in the sense in which I am here using the word, is the art of holding onto things your reason has once accepted, in spite of your changing moods."
2. https://www.nimblefins.co.uk/divorce-statistics-uk
3. https://rightlawyers.com/divorce-may-affect-health/
4. I'm painting with broad brush strokes here, and clearly there are many other factors to take into consideration when considering a person's psychological make-up and character. But hopefully you will see an essential truth in these words.

### Eleven – Men and Women

1. I'm sure it's not going to be the last!
2. https://www.stemwomen.com/blog/2021/01/women-in-stem-percentages-of-women-in-stem-statistics
3. https://www.newsecuritybeat.org/2020/04/state-worlds-nursing-report-unlocking-gender-dimensions/#:~:text=Nurses%20are%20the%20largest%20group,of%20primary%20health%20care%20worldwide.
4. https://nces.ed.gov/programs/coe/indicator/clr#:~:text=About%2076%20percent%20of%20public,school%20level%20(36%20percent).
5. If you're unfamiliar with Costco, the front-end department is the area around the checkouts. It's where the cashiers are and it also encompasses the assistants who help unload, pack and collect the carts in the car park outside. Overseeing the whole front-end operation are a small team of supervisors that are known in short-hand as "sups." Pronounced, "soops".

### Twelve – Disconnected

1. https://commonslibrary.parliament.uk/research-briefings/sn03336/#:~:text=Adult%20obesity%20in%20England,is%20classified%20as%20'overweight'.

## SECTION TWO

### One – Three Ages

1. In truth, you could sub-divide these eras further but for the purposes of this book, we can keep it simple.

### Two – From Darkness to Light

1. https://en.wikipedia.org/wiki/Talk%3AJohann_Tetzel#:~:text=Johann%20Tetzel%20(1465%20in%20Pirna,the%20soul%20from%20purgatory%20springs.%22
2. https://en.wikipedia.org/wiki/Life_expectancy

### Three – Faltering Modernity

1. https://phrontistery.info/isms.html
2. https://en.wikipedia.org/wiki/List_of_military_inventions
3. https://en.wikipedia.org/wiki/World_War_I_casualties
4. https://en.wikipedia.org/wiki/World_War_II_casualties
5. https://www.quora.com/It-has-been-reported-that-the-USA-has-been-at-war-for-222-of-its-239-years-Where-can-one-find-the-explanation

### Four - Heartless

1. https://en.wikipedia.org/wiki/Middle_Passage#:~:text=An%20estimated%2015%25%20of%20the,enslaved%20Africans%20to%20the%20ships.
2. https://www.youtube.com/watch?v=d-OKfcljAok
3. https://www.thenews.com.pk/print/595752-the-us-has-been-at-war-225-out-of-243-years-since-1776

### Five - The Love Revolution

1. https://en.wikipedia.org/wiki/Aquarius/Let_the_Sunshine_In
2. https://en.wikipedia.org/wiki/Summer_of_Love
3. https://www.azlyrics.com/lyrics/scottmckenzie/sanfranciscobesuretowearflowersinyourhair.html
4. https://en.wikipedia.org/wiki/Hippie
5. https://en.wikipedia.org/wiki/Our_World_(1967_TV_program)
6. The Times They Are A-Changin' by Bob Dylan (1964)

### Six – Warning Signs

1. http://www.beatlesradio.com/the-beatles-50-years-ago-today-august-7-1967

Trench

2. https://www.bbc.co.uk/news/uk-politics-58698406
3. https://www.cnet.com/health/parenting/women-arent-the-only-people-who-can-get-pregnant/
4. https://mercatornet.com/is-it-racist-to-say-that-224/65717/
5. https://www.glamourmagazine.co.uk/article/caitlyn-jenner-glamour-women-of-the-year-awards-america
6. https://www.orwellfoundation.com/the-orwell-youth-prize/2018-youth-prize/previous-winners-youth/2016-winners/if-liberty-means-anything-at-all-it-means-the-right-to-tell-people-what-they-do-not-want-to-hear-alexander-butcher/

**SECTION THREE**

### Two - Brainless

1. https://www.articlesvally.com/worldwide/unique-identification
2. Otherwise known as a "pacifier" in some parts of the world.
3. As reported in The Sun, 31st March, 2017. (https://www.thesun.co.uk/living/3221172/man-who-pretends-to-be-an-amputee-wants-his-leg-cut-off-even-though-theres-nothing-wrong-with-it/)
4. https://www.jkrowling.com/opinions/j-k-rowling-writes-about-her-reasons-for-speaking-out-on-sex-and-gender-issues/
5. UK Sports Council Report, September 2021, as reported in the Daily Mail (https://www.dailymail.co.uk/sport/sportsnews/article-10044995/Trans-athletes-retain-advantage-sport-say-UK-sports-councils.html)
6. https://www.sportskeeda.com/mma/news-when-transgender-fighter-fallon-fox-broke-opponent-s-skull-mma-fight
7. https://www.news-medical.net/news/20191007/Hundreds-of-trans-people-regret-changing-their-gender-says-trans-activist.aspx

### Three – Post-Truth

1. https://mindmatters.ai/2021/02/yes-there-really-is-a-war-on-math-in-our-schools/

### Four – Tyranny

1. https://www.goodreads.com/quotes/8204871-the-further-a-society-drifts-from-the-truth-the-more

2. https://www.goodreads.com/quotes/10542315-we-shall-soon-be-in-a-world-in-which-a
3. https://www.forbes.com/sites/evangerstmann/2019/10/03/virginia-school-district-fires-teacher-who-wouldnt-refer-to-transgender-student-using-male-pronouns/?sh=2c31f9836ed5
4. https://www.independent.co.uk/news/uk/home-news/christian-doctor-trans-woman-sacked-gender-pronouns-universal-credit-a8999176.html
5. https://www.theguardian.com/education/2021/oct/07/university-defends-academic-freedoms-after-calls-to-sack-professor
6. BBC Question Time, 14 October, 2021 (https://www.youtube.com/watch?v=sJFkibGI4kY)
7. https://www.bbc.co.uk/news/uk-politics-58698406
8. https://www.politics.co.uk/news-in-brief/pm-criticised-for-dodging-cervix-question/
9. https://www.bbc.co.uk/news/uk-england-humber-47005937
10. https://www.goodreads.com/quotes/78414-whoever-would-overthrow-the-liberty-of-a-nation-must-begin
11. https://www.orwellfoundation.com/the-orwell-youth-prize/2018-youth-prize/previous-winners-youth/2016-winners/if-liberty-means-anything-at-all-it-means-the-right-to-tell-people-what-they-do-not-want-to-hear-alexander-butcher/

## Five – Authoritarianism

1. https://www.dictionary.com/browse/communism
2. https://unherd.com/thepost/neil-ferguson-interview-china-changed-what-was-possible/

## Six - Globalism.

1. https://skeptics.stackexchange.com/questions/39398/did-brock-chisolm-the-first-director-of-the-united-nations-who-say-this-anti-i
2. http://www.noborders.org.uk/
3. https://www.dailymail.co.uk/news/article-10199165/Outgoing-UK-Border-Force-boss-triggers-political-row-saying-borders-just-pain-a.html
4. https://www.omfif.org/2021/07/cbdc-systems-should-focus-on-programmable-payments/
5. https://www.youtube.com/watch?v=4zUjsEaKbkM&t=2s
6. Back to the Future (https://www.youtube.com/watch?v=S1i5coU-0_Q)

## Seven – Inevitable Globalism

1. https://www.goodreads.com/quotes/293641-men-are-qualified-for-civil-liberty-in-exact-proportion-to

### Seven - No Religion

1. Wikipedia – Religion in the Soviet Union
2. www.icr.org/article/stalins-brutal-faith
3. https://www.youtube.com/watch?v=-6FfTxwTX34

### Eight – Ice-Cream

1. From Axelrod and Phillip's Encyclopaedia of Wars, as reported at: https://apholt.com/2018/12/26/counting-religious-wars-in-the-encyclopedia-of-wars/
2. https://www.nationmaster.com/country-info/stats/Religion/Religions

### Ten – No Possessions

1. https://www.merriam-webster.com/dictionary/communism
2. https://en.wikipedia.org/wiki/Ideology_of_the_Communist_Party_of_the_Soviet_Union
3. It's A Wonderful Life

### Eleven – Hypocrats

1. The suffix "-crat" comes from the Greek, where it has the meaning "ruler"; person having power, and is attached to roots to form nouns that mean "ruler". For example, autocrat, technocrat, bureaucrat etc. (definition from wordreference.com) Therefore, "hypocrat" is being used here to mean hypocritical rulers.
2. https://www.globaltimes.cn/content/1188064.shtml
3. https://www.globaltimes.cn/content/1182661.shtml
4. https://www.globaltimes.cn/content/1183364.shtml
5. https://www.bbc.co.uk/news/uk-politics-55620138
6. https://www.independent.co.uk/news/uk/politics/downing-street-christmas-parties-met-b1969855.html
7. https://www.theguardian.com/politics/2021/dec/01/boris-johnson-accused-of-flouting-covid-rules-with-no-10-parties-last-christmas
8. https://www.theguardian.com/politics/2021/jul/18/who-else-has-fallen-foul-of-covid-rules-boris-johnson-rishi-sunak
9. https://en.wikipedia.org/wiki/Dominic_Cummings_scandal
10. https://www.thetimes.co.uk/article/neil-ferguson-coronavirus-adviser-quits-after-breaking-lockdown-with-mistress-0d3jbjlz7
11. https://www.thesun.co.uk/news/15388014/matt-hancock-secret-affair-with-aide/
12. https://www.bbc.co.uk/news/uk-scotland-55419564
13. https://www.scotsman.com/news/politics/catherine-calderwood-admits-visiting-second-home-twice-during-lockdown-nicola-sturgeon-responds-2529881

14. https://www.theguardian.com/politics/2021/jul/18/who-else-has-fallen-foul-of-covid-rules-boris-johnson-rishi-sunak
15. https://www.dailymail.co.uk/news/article-10207819/Welsh-Minister-Mark-Drakeford-slammed-not-wearing-mask-Diwali-celebration.html
16. https://twitter.com/bigbrotherwatch/status/1369272255897812992

## Eleven – China

1. https://www.cfr.org/china-global-governance/
2. https://www.globaltimes.cn/page/202111/1238849.shtml
3. https://www.whitehouse.gov/briefing-room/speeches-remarks/2021/10/06/remarks-by-president-biden-on-the-need-to-raise-the-debt-ceiling-2/
4. https://www.goodreads.com/quotes/378690-the-real-division-is-not-between-conservatives-and-revolutionaries-but
5. https://www.independent.co.uk/news/uk/home-news/sarah-everard-men-curfew-green-party-peer-b1816267.html
6. https://www.rmg.co.uk/stories/topics/why-was-king-charles-i-executed

## Twelve - The Present Is Female

1. https://www.thesaurus.com/browse/toxic
2. https://www.rt.com/sport/539855-calvert-lewin-school-girl-cover/
3. https://www.goodhousekeeping.com/uk/news/a559625/headteacher-jo-heywood-heathfield-boarding-school-boys-wear-dresses/
4. https://www.thetimes.co.uk/article/let-boys-wear-dresses-head-tells-parents-head-let-boys-wear-dresses-and-make-up-says-pink-for-our-boys-footie-for-our-girls-q6vj932b9
5. https://www.thesun.co.uk/news/8103957/boys-encouraged-explore-gender-dresses-australia-schools/
6. https://www.manchestereveningnews.co.uk/news/parenting/boys-wear-skirts-primary-school-16461894
7. https://www.gbnews.uk/news/boys-and-teachers-asked-to-wear-skirts-in-scottish-school-to-break-down-gender-stereotypes/153854
8. War on Boys – Christina Hoff Sommers (https://www.youtube.com/watch?v=OFpYj0E-yb4)
9. https://www.ncbi.nlm.nih.gov/pmc/articles/PMC4327943/
10. https://eu.usatoday.com/story/opinion/2021/10/09/boys-falling-behind-how-schools-must-change-help-young-males/5913463001/
11. Media's Portrayal of Fathers (https://www.youtube.com/watch?v=GuZLAdacM1M)
12. https://titanicfacts.net/titanic-survivors/

## Thirteen – Toxic Femininity

1. https://www.politico.com/news/magazine/2020/11/19/masculinity-coronavirus-masks-pandemic-2020-trump-biden-438413

2. https://www.independent.co.uk/climate-change/sustainable-living/climate-crisis-emissions-men-women-study-b1887861.html
3. https://www.theguardian.com/environment/2021/jul/21/men-cause-more-climate-emissions-than-women-study-finds
4. https://www.unwomen.org/en/digitallibrary/multimedia/2020/2/illustration-equiterra-gender-equality-utopia
5. https://twitter.com/UN_Women/status/1343203747418296321
6. https://www.huffingtonpost.co.uk/entry/why-men-are-really-trash_uk_5ae97b12e4b081860d8ca14d
7. https://www.ncbi.nlm.nih.gov/pmc/articles/PMC3826202/
8. https://en.wikipedia.org/wiki/Cancel_culture

## Fourteen – Safetyism

1. https://www.britannica.com/science/neuroticism
2. https://journals.sagepub.com/doi/pdf/10.1177/147470490800600104#:~:text=We%20have%20shown%20that%20males,feature%20of%20human%20male%20psychology.
3. https://www.bankbazaar.com/driving-licence/women-are-more-safe-drivers.html
4. http://journal.sjdm.org/jdm06016.pdf
5. These dates are all based upon the United Kingdom.
6. From "The Coddling of the American Mind" by Jonathan Haidt and Greg Lukianoff
7. https://www.bbc.co.uk/news/explainers-56365412
8. https://www.fatherhood.org/father-absence-statistic#:~:text=According%20to%20the%20U.S.%20Census%20Bureau%2C%2019.5%20million%20children%2C%20more,a%20father%20in%20the%20home.&text=Father%20Facts%208%20%3E-,Source%3A%20U.S.%20Census%20Bureau,(2018).

## Fifteen – The Fear Economy

1. https://www.bmj.com/content/372/bmj.n579
2. https://www.independent.co.uk/news/uk/home-news/government-enforce-another-lockdown-poll-b1949215.html
3. https://www.psychologytoday.com/gb/blog/two-takes-depression/201106/if-it-bleeds-it-leads-understanding-fear-based-media
4. https://www.goodreads.com/quotes/559948-when-i-look-back-on-all-these-worries-i-remember

## Sixteen – The Paradox of Evil

1. https://www.goodreads.com/quotes/7588289-one-last-point-remember-that-as-i-said-the-right#:~:text=You%20can%20understand%20the%20nature,do%20not%20know%20about%20either.%E2%80%9D
2. https://www.goodreads.com/quotes/526469-of-all-tyrannies-a-tyranny-sincerely-exercised-for-the-good

## Eighteen – Immorality

1. https://pubmed.ncbi.nlm.nih.gov/29654061/
2. https://www.cdc.gov/nchhstp/newsroom/2021/2019-STD-surveillance-report.html
3. https://www.natcen.ac.uk/blog/over-the-rainbow
4. https://www.ncbi.nlm.nih.gov/pmc/articles/PMC3334840/
5. https://www.politifact.com/factchecks/2012/jun/07/bob-marshall/bob-marshall-says-homosexual-behavior-cuts-life-ex/
6. http://www.telegraph.co.uk/comment/10948796/Paedophilia-is-natural-and-normal-for-males.html
7. http://www.phillymag.com/news/2014/10/06/pedophilia-not-a-crime-rutgers-margo-kaplan/
8. https://www.youtube.com/watch?v=knaxQPjHn2k
5. https://twitter.com/libsoftiktok/status/1458985538334068740
6. https://singlemotherguide.com/single-mother-statistics/
7. https://www.ons.gov.uk/peoplepopulationandcommunity/birthsdeathsandmarriages/families/bulletins/familiesandhouseholds/2020#:~:text=There%20were%202.9%20million%20lone,over%20the%20last%2010%20years.

# About The Fuel Project.

The Fuel Project was established around 2011 with the sole purpose of informing, inspiring and igniting Christian faith. The aim has always been to do it by engaging with our world in Biblical and creative ways—whether that be through writing, video, film, photography, art, music, technology or animation. We want to reach people however we can.

Over the years, we have covered a wide range of subjects. Other topics include freedom, legalism, the church, Revelation and end-time prophecy, postmodernism, porn and masturbation, anxiety and depression, Biblical happiness, politics and current events. If you have enjoyed this book and would like to explore more about the other titles, please visit:

**thefuelproject.org**

If you would like to purchase any of the books relating to these subjects, they are all available in paperback and e-book format from **Amazon.** You can go to Amazon directly and search for Mark Fairley or The Fuel Project. Alternatively, there are relevant links on The Fuel Project website under the "Store" tab.

If you prefer to consume information by video, almost all the books have been converted into series on **YouTube.** In general, videos are released on a weekly basis. Our channel can be found at:

**youtube.com/thefuelproject**

Please subscribe to the channel and click the notification icon to be informed whenever a new video is released.

If you would like to download personal copies of any video series, you can also visit:

**thefuelproject.org/downloads**

It should be noted that only some of the series are currently available for download, but more will come online in future. You can also subscribe to our other social media channels:

**Twitter – twitter.com/thefuelproject**

**Facebook – facebook.com/thefuelproject**

**Instagram – instagram.com/thefuelproject**

All the ministry's latest activity can also be found at the "News" section of our website. If you'd like to find out what we've been up to, or would like to know what we're planning for the future, the address to visit is:

**thefuelproject.org/news**

Finally, The Fuel Project is made possible through financial support, primarily on Patreon. If you would like to contribute to this work, you can do so from as little as $2 a month. The page can be found at:

**patreon.com/thefuelproject**

PayPal donations can also be made using the email address, authenticfuel@gmail.com.

You can also donate using cards by going to our website and clicking the "Donate" button at the top-right corner. As a small ministry, all support is greatly appreciated and will help ensure that The Fuel Project can continue to exist, and hopefully even grow.

At the time of writing this book, 174 people have written to say they became a Christian as a direct result of this ministry. However, since most don't communicate their conversions and I only tend to find out in incidental ways, I believe that the real number is possibly much higher. I also hope that many more thousands come to Jesus through this ministry in the years ahead.

This book will now be turned into a video series with episodes being released on a weekly basis. If you'd like to follow along with the episodes, make sure to subscribe to the previously mentioned social media links. If you're reading this book more than a few months after this book's release, the project will likely already have been completed and will be available for download.

Thank you for supporting this ministry with your purchase and for reading. I hope the information within has proven helpful for your understanding of the times in which we live.

Mark Fairley
*The Fuel Project*

Printed in Great Britain
by Amazon